DISCLOSURELAND

The 2020 murder of George Floyd sparked mass protests that pushed many institutions, including corporations, to confront racial inequality. From 2020 to 2024, companies issued public statements to align with racial justice causes and protect their reputations from claims that their practices perpetuate inequality. In response to conservative backlash, many began to withdraw those commitments. *Disclosureland* argues that corporate rhetoric – whether omitting past involvement in racial inequality, presenting race-conscious disclosures as evidence of action, or retreating under pressure – limits meaningful racial progress. Even when companies pledged to hire and promote people of color or fund racial equity causes, those pledges often served to narrow the scope of corporate responsibility. Through detailed analysis, *Disclosureland* shows how these practices preserve corporate financial interests while appearing responsive. The book is critical, corrective, and hopeful, urging a functioning federal government and corporate stakeholders to hold companies accountable for their words to enable real progress.

Atinuke O. Adediran studies the relationship between business, law, and society. A legal scholar and sociologist, her research has won national awards, including recognition from the Ford School at the University of Michigan, the Ford Foundation, and the Russell Sage Foundation. She is currently a Professor of Law at Fordham University School of Law.

Disclosureland

HOW CORPORATE WORDS CONSTRAIN
RACIAL PROGRESS

ATINUKE O. ADEDIRAN
Fordham University

Shaftesbury Road, Cambridge CB2 8EA, United Kingdom

One Liberty Plaza, 20th Floor, New York, NY 10006, USA

477 Williamstown Road, Port Melbourne, VIC 3207, Australia

314–321, 3rd Floor, Plot 3, Splendor Forum, Jasola District Centre, New Delhi – 110025, India

103 Penang Road, #05–06/07, Visioncrest Commercial, Singapore 238467

Cambridge University Press is part of Cambridge University Press & Assessment, a department of the University of Cambridge.

We share the University's mission to contribute to society through the pursuit of education, learning and research at the highest international levels of excellence.

www.cambridge.org
Information on this title: www.cambridge.org/9781009442985

DOI: 10.1017/9781009443012

© Atinuke O. Adediran 2026

This publication is in copyright. Subject to statutory exception and to the provisions of relevant collective licensing agreements, no reproduction of any part may take place without the written permission of Cambridge University Press & Assessment.

When citing this work, please include a reference to the DOI 10.1017/9781009443012

First published 2026

A catalogue record for this publication is available from the British Library

Library of Congress Cataloging-in-Publication Data
NAMES: Adediran, Atinuke O. author
TITLE: Disclosureland : how corporate words constrain racial progress / Atinuke O. Adediran, Fordham University, New York.
DESCRIPTION: Cambridge [United Kingdom] ; New York : Cambridge University Press, 2026. | Includes bibliographical references and index.
IDENTIFIERS: LCCN 2025005485 | ISBN 9781009442985 hardback | ISBN 9781009443012 ebook
SUBJECTS: LCSH: Corporation law | Disclosure of information – Law and legislation | Race discrimination – Law and legislation | Corporate governance – Law and legislation | Social responsibility of business – Law and legislation
CLASSIFICATION: LCC K1315 .A37 2026 | DDC 346/.066–dc23/eng/20250208
LC record available at https://lccn.loc.gov/2025005485

ISBN 978-1-009-44298-5 Hardback

Cambridge University Press & Assessment has no responsibility for the persistence or accuracy of URLs for external or third-party internet websites referred to in this publication and does not guarantee that any content on such websites is, or will remain, accurate or appropriate.

For EU product safety concerns, contact us at Calle de José Abascal, 56, 1°, 28003 Madrid, Spain, or email eugpsr@cambridge.org

For Babatunde

Contents

List of Figures	page ix
List of Tables	xi
Preface and Acknowledgments	xiii
List of Abbreviations	xix
Introduction	1
1 Historical Case Study	20
2 Race-Conscious Disclosures, Image, and Reputation	48
3 Racial Targets	78
4 Corporate Racial Philanthropy	92
5 Race-Conscious Retraction	113
6 Regulating Race-Conscious Disclosures and Retraction	135
Conclusion	157
Methodology Appendix: Data and Methods	161
Bibliography	171
Index	191

Figures

1.1	Signing ceremony for Plans for Progress, program of President's Committee on Equal Employment Opportunity	page 30
2.1	Voluntary reports with general race-conscious disclosures	56
2.2	Mandatory reports with general race-conscious disclosures	56
2.3	Percentage of voluntary reports with statistics	57
2.4	Percentage of voluntary reports with statistics by racial or ethnic group	58
2.5	Voluntary reports with general race-conscious disclosures (private companies)	59
2.6	Percentage of voluntary reports with statistics by racial or ethnic group (private companies)	59
2.7	Shareholder proposal possible outcomes	61
2.8	Shareholder proposals and no-action letters	62
3.1	Racial targets in public companies by year	81
3.2	Racial targets in public companies by racial or ethnic group	81
3.3	Racial targets in private companies by year	82
4.1	Prevalence of CRP in corporate disclosures of giving to minority causes	99
5.1	*Wall Street Journal* use of terms in earnings calls, 2018–2023	117
5.2	AlphaSense chart: Axios Visuals mentions of DEI in earnings calls, 2020–2024	118
5.3	Percentage of voluntary disclosures with race-conscious disclosures	120
5.4	Percentage of companies making voluntary demographic disclosures with statistics	121
5.5	Average number of racial terms per voluntary report	122
5.6	Average use of five specific terms per voluntary report	123
5.7	Distribution of five specific terms per voluntary report	123
5.8	Evolution of race-conscious disclosures and retraction	126
A.1	Values of cosign similarity	166

Tables

2.1	Race-conscious disclosures	*page* 52
3.1	Racial targets in public companies by year	81
3.2	Racial targets in private companies by year	82
5.1	Average number of racial terms per voluntary report	121
A.1	Titles of voluntary reports	162
A.2	Dictionary of racial terms	165
A.3	List of interviewees	169

Preface and Acknowledgments

I became deeply interested in corporate relations and race when George Floyd was murdered. Prior to that, my research focused primarily on governance issues related to diversity and philanthropy in publicly traded and private firms. But Floyd's murder was a trigger. I still have not been able to bring myself to watch the video or look at pictures of Floyd as he begged for his life. Like so many police killings that came before it, Floyd's murder had disturbingly little impact on the criminal justice system. But other aspects of the aftermath seemed like they would be different at the time. Notably, institutions across sectors – private, government, and nonprofit – all wanted to do something, and, particularly, to say something, about the racial inequities in society. That was fascinating to me from a legal and sociological perspective. What were they saying, and why were they saying the things they were saying?

Given my previous background, I was first drawn to the philanthropic aspects of the phenomenon. I noticed that a multitude of large companies began to make commitments to fund minority-led and minority-serving nonprofit charities. I was fascinated by the legal implications of those commitments for corporate accountability. In my article, "Disclosures for Equity," I argued that to increase funding to nonprofit organizations that are led by minorities or serve communities of color and hold corporations and private foundations who make public commitments to fund these organizations accountable for their pledges, nonprofit organizations should disclose their donors and the race and ethnicity of managers, boards of directors, and the racial and ethnic compositions of the communities they serve. These disclosures will help to identify nonprofits that are minority led or that serve communities of color, as well as the institutional donors who donate to them annually.

That article was the beginning of my journey into the world of corporate voluntary disclosures. I began collecting data on corporate nonfinancial disclosures related to race, diversity, the environment, and other social issues. And I noticed a pattern. Many companies that had not made disclosures about diversity prior to 2020 were doing so. It was clear that Floyd's murder had activated public declarations. In another article titled, "Disclosing Corporate Diversity," I showed how this shift occurred over time and argued for the instrumental use of mandatory disclosures about race, ethnicity, gender, disabilities, and LGBTQIA+ status to increase corporate diversity.

With this book, however, I decided to write about race specifically, rather than a broadly defined notion of diversity. Having begun to examine the changed landscape of institutional disclosures after the murder of George Floyd and having argued for mandatory disclosures in the "diversity, equity, and inclusion" or DEI context, it became clear to me that an in-depth examination of how companies are actually using the systematic disclosures they are producing and what purposes they are serving was warranted. I began to map out race-conscious disclosures in 2021 and observed the political landscape and gradual shift after the United States Supreme Court decided *Students for Fair Admissions v. Harvard*, which invalidated the use of race in college and university admissions, but which conservative groups have used as support for any issue and context they deem related to diversity, equity, and inclusion. I observed the larger shift that began at the end of 2024 after Donald Trump was elected for a second term in office, and the even bigger shift that occurred in early 2025 after he began his second term.

I completed this book in April 2025 when the Trump administration's Department of Government Efficiency (DOGE), headed by the billionaire Elon Musk, was dismantling major federal government agencies. Most relevant for this book are Trump's executive orders, including the one that got rid of President Lyndon Johnson's executive order, which required companies doing business with the federal government to take affirmative steps toward hiring and promoting racial minorities. Trump has also dismantled programs, policies, standards, and even historical documents established to address racial inequality in the federal government, calling them "illegal DEI." Trump has targeted law firms for their diversity and inclusion programs. Federal agencies under his administration have also targeted companies for their DEI programs.

Needless to say, we are in a difficult moment in American history. But this book is not about the Trump administration. This book is written for a future – if we can conceive of it – when the United States again has a functioning executive branch whose goal is to ensure the wellbeing of its citizens and address inequalities that impact marginalized groups. I urge you to keep reading about how the past provides us with a blueprint for a future where corporations may not be able to use disclosures about race to advantage themselves.

* * *

Writing a book is unlike any other scholarly endeavor. It takes time and the support of many people and institutions. I first thought about being an author when I was about fourteen years old. I even had a title for the book I thought I would write (it has since changed). But it was not until 2020 that I began to seriously consider writing one. Even then, I thought that I would wait until I was a much more senior scholar to publish a book – it was my extraordinary mentor, sponsor, and friend,

Guy-Uriel Charles, who encouraged me to write a book now. Guy has supported me in charting my course as an interdisciplinary scholar with a deep interest in inequality. I am forever indebted to him for his support and for being a safe space. Guy was the first person with whom I shared the ideas for this book in the fall of 2021. I am grateful that he encouraged me to write it.

I began my academic career as the David and Pamela Donohue Assistant Professor of Business Law at Boston College Law School. I am grateful to the Donohues for their financial support of my research. It was the boost I needed to conduct bold empirical projects right away.

I joined the Fordham University School of Law Faculty in 2021. Matthew Diller, who was the dean at the time, was very supportive of my research. Matthew and then associate deans Joseph Landau (now dean) and Youngjae Lee supported my work then and have continued to do so. I also thank associate deans Pamela Bookman, Bennett Capers, and Benjamin Zipursky for their kindness and support. I am also exceedingly grateful to the Carlinsky Family Dean's Faculty Research Fund for providing some of the funding for this book.

I thank the incredible librarians at Fordham Law. My library liaison, Kathleen Thompson, went above and beyond to help me secure all kinds of sources. I also thank the director of the law library, Todd Melnick; the deputy director, Alissa Black-Dorward; the head of collection services, Angela Sinhart; and the head of interlibrary loans, Juan Fernandez, for their tireless assistance with finding and, when needed, acquiring sources.

I received many awards that were instrumental in writing this book. I acknowledge the incredible dedication of Fordham University's Office of Sponsored Research, particularly Marcy Funaro, grant writer extraordinaire, who guided me through the process of applying for fellowships and grants. Marcy went above and beyond, and for that, I am forever grateful.

The Russell Sage Foundation (RSF) believed in the book's contribution and awarded me both a Presidential Grant and a residential Visiting Scholar award. The Presidential Grant allowed me to purchase the text of disclosures for thousands of companies and to hire outstanding data scientists, especially Tatiana Chebonenko, an expert at using Python to turn text into data. Tatiana's rigor and expertise were so useful and much appreciated. In addition to the grant, the RSF Visiting Scholar award provided the space and time to complete the book. I am grateful to RSF leadership and staff and my fellow visiting scholars for the 2024–5 academic year.

I also received a nonresidential visiting faculty fellowship at the Center for Racial Justice at the University of Michigan's Gerald R. Ford School of Public Policy during the 2022–3 academic year. I thank Dean Celeste Watkins-Hayes for conceiving of the fellowship and for her support. I also thank the associate director of the Center, Dominique Adams-Santos, for her hard work in making the inaugural fellowship a success. The fellowship was key for moving the book forward: I wrote a chapter and significantly developed another during my time at the Ford

School. I had the great fortune of having Sherise McKinney as a PhD research assistant (RA) who provided excellent coding assistance, particularly for the chapter on racial philanthropy. I thank the Center's staff, especially Angela Nicoloff, for coordinating fellows' events and for making my time at the Ford School quite enjoyable.

The library staff at the University of Michigan and at the Ross School of Business, especially Corey Seeman, assisted me greatly with finding historical sources and additional data. I also had the privilege to join an enriching and memorable conversation on synergies at the intersection of business, sustainability, and justice at the Erb Institute for Global Sustainable Enterprise. I thank Thomas Lyon, the director of the institute, for inviting me to join the conversation, and Melissa Zaksek, the associate director for research who connected me with some of the corporate chief sustainability officers whom I interviewed for the book.

I convened an early-stage workshop for two chapters while at the University of Michigan. I am grateful to Ekow Yankah, Geeyoung Min, Vikramaditya Khanna, J. J. Prescott, and Megan Tompkins-Stange for their very helpful feedback and for providing a useful window into how my audiences might receive the book. Special thanks to Vikramaditya Khanna for serving as my discussant at the Ford School's fellows' showcase in March 2023. I thank attendees at the showcase for their feedback. I also thank Daniel Fryer for his support.

Other early conversations about the book's themes were extremely helpful. I am grateful to Douglas Baird, with whom I had many conversations during the very early stages of the book. I thank him and Scott Cummings for their feedback while I wrote the book's proposal. I also thank Nestor Davidson for his feedback during the early stages and for being a wonderful mentor.

I am also grateful to Randall Patton, author of *Lockheed, Atlanta, and the Struggle for Racial Integration*, for sharing sources with me and for his wisdom on how to obtain historical news articles on Lockheed Martin.

I had many conversations with sustainability and diversity officers in companies. To these individuals, I say thank you for your openness and candidness about the state of affairs in your companies. Outside of formal interviews, I had conversations with counsel who represent companies. I am grateful to David Curran, the co-chair of the Environmental, Social, and Governance (ESG) Advisory Practice and executive director of the ESG and Law Institute at Paul Weiss. I found David's insight as a lawyer who represents companies on rapidly changing ESG regulations helpful. I also thank the ESG team at Paul Weiss, including Lissette Duran and Madhuri Pavamani.

I am exceedingly grateful to my strong army of law student RAs at Fordham who worked tirelessly, each focused on a different portion of the book: Morgan Band, Emily Benevento, Michelle Buestan, Colbey Carpenter, Emily Chambers, Jade Crichlow, Tiara Edwards, Ashley Geisler, Serena Grewal, Teresa Huang, Catherine

Ingram, Simran Kashyap, Justin Lagera, Nancy Menagh, Aafke Pronk, Seamus Ronan, Emily Sadutto, Yumiko Shime, Samuel Sosa, and Evan Tart. I could not have met my publication deadline without these wonderful RAs.

I thank the many other colleagues who read and provided feedback on all or parts of the book: Molly Brady, John Coates, Kevin Davis, Jennifer Gordon, Jill Fisch, Sarah Haan, H. Timothy Lovelace Jr., Veronica Root Martinez, Ajay K. Mehrotra, Dana Brakman Reiser, Olivier Sylvain, and Shaun Ossei-Owusu. I am indebted to colleagues who read the entire manuscript and provided feedback during and after my manuscript workshop at Fordham: Monica Bell, Aziz Huq, and Bertrall Ross. I thank Bennett Capers for moderating the workshop. I cannot thank Aziz, Bennett, Bertrall, and Monica enough for their in-depth and thoughtful reading and feedback during the final writing stages. These incredible colleagues helped me shape and clarify my thinking as I finalized the book.

I also thank workshop and conference participants at the Association for Research on Nonprofit Organizations and Voluntary Action (ARNOVA); the Culp Colloquium at Harvard University; the Law and Inequality Colloquium at the University of Virginia School of Law; the Equality, Law and Social Justice Residency at King's College Dickson Poon School of Law, London, UK; the European Group for Organizational Studies Colloquium (EGOS) in Milan, Italy; the International Charity Law Network Conference in Toronto, Canada; the Interdisciplinary Workshop on Nonprofits at Columbia Law School; the workshop on Reckoning with Race in the Law at Princeton University Center for Human Values; the Inaugural Conference for the International Association on Regulation & Governance at the University of Pennsylvania Carey Law School; and the Law and Society Conference in Denver, Colorado.

Portions of Chapter 3 have previously appeared in the Northwestern Law Review. I thank the editorial staff there for editorial support.

I am grateful for the Manuscript and Book Publication Award from Fordham University that allowed me to hire my amazing developmental editor, Anna Skiba-Crafts, who provided invaluable feedback on the first draft of the manuscript. I also thank my copy editor, Kim Greenwell, for doing a phenomenal job. I am forever grateful to Laura Portwood-Stacer, the academic book proposal guru (and much more). I participated in her vitally important book proposal accelerator to write my book proposal.

A huge thanks to Matt Gallaway, my editor at Cambridge University Press, who believed in the book from the first time we communicated and supported it throughout the publishing process. I also thank my peer reviewers for Cambridge University Press: Lisa Fairfax, Tom C. W. Lin, Nancy Leong, and two anonymous reviewers, who provided feedback that has strengthened the book.

Finally, words cannot express my gratitude to my family and friends for their support and encouragement. My husband, my heart, Babatunde. I could not have written this book (or anything else) without your love, support, and listening ears.

I am also grateful to my son, Enioluwayan, who has kept me grounded since the day he was born. Finally, I acknowledge my late mother, Afolake Afolasade, a woman fueled by an unyielding work ethic and boundless resourcefulness. She believed in the power of determination and, without knowing it, instilled in me the strong belief that I could achieve anything I set my mind to. Her legacy lives on in the hearts of those she inspired.

Abbreviations

AAER	American Alliance for Equal Rights
ALEC	American Legislative Exchange Council
ARNOVA	Association for Research on Nonprofit Organizations and Voluntary Action
BILAP	Black, Indigenous, Latino(a) or Hispanic, Asian, Pacific Islander
BIPOC	Black, Indigenous, and people of color
BNY	Bank of New York
CDO	Chief diversity officer
CEO	Chief executive officer
CFO	Chief financial officer
COFEP	Committee on Fair Employment Practice
CRP	Corporate racial philanthropy
CSDDD	Corporate Sustainability Due Diligence Directive
CSO	Chief sustainability officer
CSR	Corporate social responsibility
DAN	Deep averaging network
DEI	Diversity, equity, and inclusion
EEOC	Equal Employment Opportunity Commission
EGOS	European Group for Organizational Studies Colloquium
EOA	Economic Opportunity Act
ESG	Environmental, social, and governance
EU	European Union
FDIC	Federal Deposit Insurance Corporation
FEPC	Fair Employment Practice Committee
FTC	Federal Trade Commission
HBCUs	Historically Black colleges and universities
ISS	Institutional Shareholder Services
JOBS	Job Opportunities in Business Sector
MDIs	Minority Depository Institutions
MOWM	March on Washington Movement

NAACP	National Association for the Advancement of Colored People
NAB	National Alliance of Businessmen
NLP	Natural language processing
NYSE	New York Stock Exchange
OEO	Office of Economic Opportunity
OFCC	Office of Federal Contract Compliance
P&G	Procter & Gamble
PFP	Plans for Progress
RSF	Russell Sage Foundation
SEC	Securities and Exchange Commission
STEM	Science, technology, engineering, and mathematics
VC	Venture capital
WSJ	*Wall Street Journal*

Introduction

In May 2020, Derek Chauvin, a white Minneapolis police officer murdered George Floyd, a Black man, by placing his knees on Floyd's neck even as Floyd begged for his life. Chauvin kept his knees on Floyd's neck even after Floyd had stopped moving and speaking, ensuring that life had left him.

There was immediate outcry and calls for accountability after the video of the murder was released to the public. Protests erupted in at least 140 cities across the United States.[1] By some estimates, about 15 to 26 million people in the United States participated in demonstrations.[2] Protests spread internationally to Africa, Asia, Europe, and the Middle East.[3] The protests and aftermath of Floyd's murder ignited responses from institutions within and outside of the criminal justice system, including corporations.

Corporations play an important role in shaping many people's lives through things like employment, environmental impacts, and philanthropy. It is therefore not surprising that corporations also attempted to be a part of the societal change for which Floyd's murder appeared to have served as a catalyst.

Like thousands of other corporations, Amazon.com (Amazon) and Walmart Inc. (Walmart), the two largest private, multinational corporations in the world with approximately 3.6 million employees combined, quickly responded to Floyd's murder with public statements on their websites, social media, and in voluntary sustainability reports made available to the public. Among other things, Amazon said, "Black lives matter and Amazon stands in solidarity with [its] Black employees, customers, and partners ... and [is] committed to helping build a country where everyone can live with dignity."[4] Walmart said it wanted "to help replace the structures of systemic racism and build in their place frameworks of equity and justice that solidify [its] commitment to the belief that, without question, Black Lives Matter."[5]

These corporate words seemed like they mattered. It seemed like corporations were beginning to reckon with racial injustice. A corporate chief diversity officer (CDO) I interviewed for this book told me that 2020 was a time of "awakening" in that it established an attentive audience "inside of the employee base from executives all the way on down."

However, in 2021, about a year after Amazon and Walmart expressed solidarity with their Black employees and communities, and declared aspirations toward addressing racial injustice, investors asked both companies to take active steps toward addressing racial inequality by conducting "racial equity audits." Among other concerns, investors pointed out apparent barriers to advancement for people of color in these corporations, even though both firms had declared their intent to dismantle such barriers. A racial equity audit is an independent analysis designed to identify whether a company's policies or practices have discriminatory effects on customers, suppliers, employees, and other stakeholders.[6]

At Amazon, for example, shareholders raised the issue of discrimination against the company's Black and Latino workers as evidenced by the low wages of both groups and their exposure to dangerous working conditions. The claims also emphasized that Amazon's low-wage Black employees received worse evaluations and were promoted at lower rates than others who were not Black.[7] There were also environmental justice concerns, including disproportionate air pollution from distribution facilities located in minority neighborhoods, and the disproportionate impact of Amazon's technology on people and communities of color.[8] Amazon's shareholders pointed out that these allegations were significant, posed serious risks, and raised questions regarding the company's actual commitment to, and alignment in practice with, its prior public statements.[9] To many, a racial equity audit seemed like a natural next step toward uncovering racial inequality and achieving racial progress.

Instead of taking this step, however, Amazon and Walmart took active steps to quelch their shareholders' respective audit requests by using the companies' previous statements about addressing racial inequality as evidence that they had indeed addressed the issue. The result was that both companies continued with business as usual, and the advancement concerns within both companies remained. While Amazon's workforce was majority minority in 2024 with only 30.2% white employees, 28.2% Black employees and 23.6% Latino employees, among its leadership ranks specifically, 66.6% were white, while only 5.5% were Black and 4.5% were Latino. Also, although Amazon continued to make public statements about race in 2024, in response to conservative backlash, the corporation eliminated its previous references to more specific terms like "racial justice" and "equity." Like Amazon, among other changes, Walmart chose to eliminate its Center for Racial Equity, a philanthropic program focused on creating equitable outcomes for Black communities and others in finance, health, education, and criminal justice.[10]

Disclosureland is about how corporate public statements constrain racial progress. Legal scholar Catharine MacKinnon wrote in her book *Only Words*, that "inequality is created and enforced through words and images."[11] This is true of corporate words too. Disclosure is the process of making facts or information known to the public. Disclosureland is a metaphor for a time and place where and when corporate shareholders and stakeholders – employees, customers, and others – expect companies to act and speak up and often about their values and their position on various social justice issues. In their efforts to meet this expectation on their own financial terms rather than in the interest of minority advancement, however, corporations make and use disclosures in ways that constrain the boundaries of racial progress. Indeed, the very parameters of how we define and think about racial progress is delimited by corporate communication.

Since 2020, large multinational companies have used voluntary disclosures – public statements about race and people of color – strategically for reputational and financial gain by indicating concern for addressing racial inequality, while at the same time constraining true racial progress. Corporations constrain racial progress through their words by not making disclosures about past racial inequality, using prior disclosures as evidence of racial progress, and engaging in what I refer to as "race-conscious retraction," which is the modification or elimination of language about race. The book proposes an innovative multi-institutional approach calling on a future federal government to assume the role of information enforcer and facilitator for stakeholders to hold corporations accountable for their use of disclosures about race.

Disclosureland does not argue that voluntary disclosures about race are bad, nor does it argue for mandatory disclosures. In my own work, I have been a proponent of using mandatory disclosures to achieve corporate diversity.[12] The book argues that corporations' voluntary disclosures, as currently used, largely benefit companies while constraining true racial progress, and this should be remedied. While there are varied definitions of racial progress, the book defines true racial progress as taking steps to facilitate advancement for the next generation of minority communities by breaking cycles of racial subordination. A multi-institutional approach to regulation, facilitated by the federal government, is a crucial part of the steps necessary to facilitate true racial progress.

The events of 2020 shifted public and institutional expectations about responding to racial inequality as corporate responses happened alongside the environmental, social and governance (ESG) movement.[13] Prior to 2020, the minimal focus on ESG centered climate change and the environment.[14] Afterward, ESG rose to the center of national and global dialogue on corporate governance, management, and investments.[15] Climate and the environment have become a central part of public discourse, and race took a considerable place in that dialogue as a large part of the "S" in ESG.[16]

In 2020, corporations began to use very particular types and combinations of words, which I refer to as "race-conscious disclosures," to shape their public images and create favorable reputations. This process involved the systematic disclosure of information that evokes attention to addressing institutional racism and racial inequality in response to pressure from shareholders, as well as stakeholders like employees, prospective employees, consumers, and the public. Image refers to how a company is perceived or viewed by shareholders, stakeholders and the public.[17] It is essentially what shareholders and stakeholders think about a company, based in large part on the messages the company itself disseminates. Broadly speaking, companies engaged in race-conscious disclosures to build their corporate reputation. Corporate reputation refers to judgements made about a firm,[18] often rooted in impressions of the firm's image.[19] A company can subsequently convert its reputation to reputational capital, or intangible assets based on value attributed to the perception of the firm as, in the case of companies between 2020 and 2024, a race-conscious domestic and global corporate citizen.[20] A good reputation enhances profitability because it attracts customers who purchase products, investors who invest in securities, and employees who supply labor.[21] It also attracts favorable media attention, which can further enhance a company's reputational capital.

Companies make race-conscious disclosures using a variety of methods, including via company websites, consumer communication through emails and other means, investor communication through earnings and conference calls, and through press releases. Companies also make disclosures through more formal methods, such as voluntary sustainability and diversity reports, and mandatory United States Securities and Exchange Commission (SEC) reports produced annually or a few times a year and made available to the public.

The book focuses on these formal means of disclosures through which corporations made: (1) general statements about the need to address institutional racial inequality; (2) statistics about past or current racial compositions of boards of directors, executives, managers, and employees; (3) "racial targets," or plans to hire, retain, or promote people of color by a certain time; and (4) statements regarding philanthropy, including "corporate racial philanthropy," or business-transaction-focused philanthropy with minority groups.

Many companies that prior to 2020 focused almost exclusively on making public statements about gender and LGBTQIA+ status, and only occasional vague statements about discrimination against racial minorities, changed course almost overnight after the murder of George Floyd, doubling down on race-conscious disclosures in large volumes. Disclosures about race before 2020 were often devoid of the language of racial inequality and injustice. Companies often lumped race with other identity factors and rarely specified what strategies they intended to take to address racial inequality. After 2020, disclosures became more frequent, more expansive in terms of detail, and more ambitious in terms of corporate goals.

Take Amazon again. Prior to 2020, the company made some general statements about diversity, often including cursory statements about race. In 2019, Amazon's diversity, equity, and inclusion (DEI) statement on its website noted that "its diverse perspectives come from many sources including gender, race, age, national origin, sexual orientation, culture … as well as professional and life experience."[22] In its 2020 sustainability report published after Floyd was murdered, the company changed course and began to make impassioned public race-conscious disclosures, particularly about Black communities.[23] The company also made race-conscious disclosures highlighting the percentages of racial and ethnic minorities among its employees and managers, and for the first time, pledged to donate a large sum to address racial inequality.[24] The company did not stop there. It also set a goal to increase the hiring of US Black employees by at least 30 percent from 2020 hiring.[25] Amazon's race-conscious disclosures continued into 2021, 2022, 2023, and 2024. But by 2025, Amazon had reverted back to what it used to disclose prior to 2020 by lumping disclosures about Black people into statements about a range of issues including diversity of geographies, cultures, genders, races, ethnicities, abilities, ages, religions, sexual orientations, military status, backgrounds, and political views.[26]

Thousands of other companies have made similar moves, including privately held companies that are not listed on stock exchanges and do not have shareholders, but are owned by wealthy individuals or families. A wide cross-section of companies – large, medium, and small – have joined in this phenomenon. The making and pulling back on race-conscious disclosures also defies sector boundaries. One might expect consumer-facing companies in banking and retail to engage in race-conscious disclosures and retraction, but private and public multinational companies in all sectors have made race-conscious disclosures and retractions. Only a tiny subset – fifty-six public companies or 3 percent of the over 2,000 companies I examined – did not made any race-conscious disclosures between 2020 and 2024. These companies are significantly more likely to be small – 95 percent of them have revenues ranging from about $1 million to $3 billion. Only one is a large company with revenues of about $12 billion, and only two are medium-sized companies with revenues of about $3 billion. With a few exceptions, most of these companies are headquartered in conservative states, like Arizona, Texas, and Virginia. These are some of the same states whose attorneys general have publicly opposed racial justice measures taken by corporations and the federal government.[27] It is no surprise then that these companies ignored reputational concerns from stakeholders and peer legitimacy even as many other companies in their industries made race-conscious disclosures and instead focused on their reputations as determined by political branches in those conservative states. There are some exceptions in the Northeast, including in Connecticut and New York. Despite being listed on Nasdaq or the New York Stock Exchange, these smaller companies with small workforces probably felt less pressure to create a race-conscious reputation. They have also not engaged in the retraction of race-conscious disclosures – a phenomenon I discuss in Chapter 5 – because they did not make disclosures in the first place. However, it is possible that they too will make race-conscious disclosures in a future cycle of disclosures as the book predicts.

The world of race-conscious corporate disclosures and retractions may not be something the average citizen thinks about, but it is a phenomenon that touches the lives of millions of individuals and businesses and has hugely significant implications for the economy. Corporate words impact employees, potential employees, consumers, shareholders, the government, and communities of color.

CORPORATE REPUTATION AND FINANCIAL INTERESTS

In her book, *Cannibal Capitalism: How Our System Is Devouring Democracy, Care, and the Planet – and What We Can Do about It*, political theorist Nancy Fraser presents capitalism as a system that devours the very foundations that she defines as life sustaining – care, democracy, and the environment.[28] Fraser views corporations as central actors in this capitalist system – using labor, nature, democracy, and care work – to sustain and expand corporate power and profits, while contributing to the broader crises of inequality, environmental degradation, and political corruption.

Disclosureland takes a much more granular approach by examining how corporations' dueling words and images impact racial progress. It takes as a premise that corporations would attempt to do or say something to advance racial equity, but only insofar as it aligns with their financial interests. The book documents a back-and-forth dialectic that shows that between 2020 and 2024, corporations were motivated to use race-conscious disclosures to construct race-conscious images primarily for their own financial gain and have been motivated since 2024 to engage in race-conscious retraction also for financial gain.

This back-and-forth dialectic functioned through the lens of corporate reputation. Corporate reputation – which manifests in various forms, including shareholder goodwill, positive evaluations, and appearance of relationship with advocacy groups – is largely effected through, and significantly impacted by, corporate image construction. Race-conscious image construction intensified among corporations in 2020, fueled by the desire for legitimacy, not only with investors, employees, and target consumers but also among peers. Corporate responses to George Floyd's murder proliferated, as no company wanted to be "left out," making the situation spread – a phenomenon sociologists refer to as "institutional isomorphism."[29] Race-conscious image construction was ultimately about corporate image and corporate reputation.

The driver of corporate financial gain operating primarily through corporate reputation diverges from previous potential motivations for engaging in race- or diversity-based activities. Before 2020, race and other forms of diversity measures were driven primarily by legal and compliance concerns as corporate responses tended to focus on conveying legality and compliance with antidiscrimination laws. For example, as documented by sociologist Ellen Berrey in *The Enigma of Diversity: The Language of Race and the Limits of Racial Justice*, a corporation managed its diversity programs and policies primarily in order to comply with law and industry standards, and to be perceived as a diverse firm.[30] In *Working Law: Courts, Corporations, and Symbolic Civil Rights*, legal scholar and sociologist Lauren Edelman documented the signaling effects of corporate diversity structures such as policies, grievance resolution mechanisms, and compliance positions, as evidence of compliance with antidiscrimination laws, and the role of courts in deferring to the presence of symbolic structures while companies continued to maintain practices that perpetuated racial and gender inequalities.[31] Similarly, in 2009, corporate diversity programs appeared to have been driven by legal pressures, as sociologist Frank Dobbin showed through his examination of the role of diversity managers in interpreting antidiscrimination laws in *Inventing Equal Opportunity*.[32]

Since 2020, corporations have responded to the social and political environments external to them by using race-conscious disclosures primarily to manage their litigation and reputational risks that emanate from shareholders, employees, prospective employees, customers, lawmakers, government agents, and the public. The motivations have therefore expanded beyond legal compliance to include building reputational capital and managing the risk of litigation that may arise from complying with the law, failing to comply with the law, responding to, and failing to respond to internal and external social and political pressures from stakeholders and the public to address racial inequality.

But while some of the changes since 2020 are unprecedented, others have at least historical parallels, for example, from the early 1960s to the late 1980s, when some companies used race-conscious disclosures motivated by similar concerns as companies making race-conscious disclosures today. President John F. Kennedy signed Executive Order 10925 in 1961. The Executive Order, which was affirmed by every president since Lyndon Johnson, was nullified by Trump in 2025. This mandated companies doing business with the United States government to take "affirmative action to ensure that applicants are employed, and that employees are treated … without regard to their race, creed, color, or national origin."[33] The government sought cooperation from large companies as the corporations came up with the "Plans for Progress" program, in which companies made public pledges to provide equal employment opportunity to Black people.[34]

In joining the Plans for Progress program, isomorphism was at work as companies followed a similar pattern.[35] In consultation with a representative of the President's Committee on Equal Employment Opportunity, a company would work out a plan with goals for desegregation, nondiscrimination, training, recruitment, and hiring Black individuals.[36] The vice president of the United States and the company's officer or representative would then sign that plan in the presence of the president of the United States in a public ceremony that was covered by national, state, local, and company press.[37] This high-profile signing and media dissemination in the pre-digital age allowed companies to establish a public image about their roles in ending racial segregation and racial discrimination and creating equal employment opportunity for people of color.[38] Many companies participated in the Plans for Progress program not because they were committed to advancing the racial and economic progress of Black people, but because the companies hoped that doing so would build goodwill in Black communities – an important customer base – and prevent boycotts and riots from impacting their businesses.[39]

RACIAL PROGRESS

Racial progress is material change in the lives of people of color that is likely to break cycles of subordination. In the employment context, racial progress is not only about hiring people of color to occupy mostly lower-level positions but should also incorporate pay equity, and opportunities to move up the proverbial corporate ladder, giving people agency and decision-making authority. In the philanthropic context, racial progress should not just be about financially supporting causes that involve racial and ethnic minorities but should also be about giving people of color the agency to define what those causes should be.

Corporations have used their words to constrain racial progress by defining what racial progress is instead of what it could be when it centers the experiences of people of color. Corporations set racial targets for racial minority employment based on the broad definition of hiring and promotions, rather than the categorical assessment of employment at various levels in the past to determine where they have fallen short regarding hiring and compensation, and prioritizing elevating minorities to positions with decision-making power. Corporations have delimited what racial progress means in terms of philanthropy by using business transactions as the basis for racial philanthropy, and prioritizing philanthropy that benefits corporations' financial standing.

Often, people think of corporate words as "cheap talk." But the two specific instances of making racial targets and disclosing corporate racial philanthropy could have helped the good faith corporate actor solve the credibility problem because both instances specify what corporations intended to do. However, even racial targets and racial philanthropy did not separate good faith corporate actors from others because virtually all corporations have used their words to shift societal understanding of what racial progress is and what it requires, away from what it should be and what it should require, which diminishes pressure on corporations to achieve true racial progress.

CONSTRAINING RACIAL PROGRESS

Corporations have constrained racial progress with their words in a number of ways. One way is by making disclosures that failed to or vaguely acknowledged past racial discrimination or inequality within a corporation. Another way is by actively deploying race-conscious disclosures to subvert racial equity concerns raised by stakeholders. A third way is through race-conscious retraction.

Only a tiny fraction of corporations have acknowledged past racial discrimination in their public statements. Some corporations have deployed disclosures to subvert racial equity concerns, hundreds of corporations have engaged in race-conscious retraction, and many more will likely do so in the future.

Lack of Acknowledgement of Past Racial Inequality

While there have been some high-profile public acknowledgements of brand names and images with racist pasts, like Aunt Jemima, Uncle Ben's, Mrs. Butterworth's, Cream of Wheat, and the NFL's Washington Redskins, most corporations have made race-conscious disclosures without acknowledging the racial inequalities that are the basis for those disclosures.[40] This constrains racial progress because race-conscious disclosures without a recognition of corporate contributions to racial inequality in the past are unlikely to fully address racial progress. If people are not aware of what companies have done in the distant and immediate past, they will not be able to evaluate whether the steps those companies now want to take toward achieving racial progress are likely to succeed, or, indeed, whether those companies are even genuinely interested in doing so. Without an acknowledgment of past racial inequality, race-conscious disclosures might also appear to favor people of color in corporations, because attention to racial minorities through corporate words would seem to have no basis in history or facts. Much conservative pushback on race-conscious disclosures could potentially be tapered by real acknowledgements of past racial inequality in individual corporations.

Deploying Disclosures to Challenge Racial Equity Concerns

Was the post-2020 boom in race-conscious disclosures good or bad for people of color and addressing societal racial inequality? At first glance, race-conscious disclosures seemed extremely positive. Companies that had been relatively silent on race for decades seemed to have finally reckoned with the problem and seemed willing to address it.

There are some potential benefits of race-conscious disclosures. Disclosures can reveal the lack of racial diversity in a company, can be used instrumentally to increase diversity,[41] can result in the hiring and promotion of people of color in companies,[42] and can arguably advance opportunities for communities of color through race-conscious philanthropy.[43] In *Challenging Boardroom Homogeneity*, legal scholar Aaron Dhir empirically demonstrated that corporate disclosures have helped to increase gender diversity in corporate boardrooms,[44] thus suggesting similar benefits could accrue from race-conscious disclosures.

However, race-conscious disclosures and race-conscious retraction are totally subject to corporate whim and do not seem to be designed to achieve true racial progress. Their use (or nonuse) by companies is completely determined by what will most benefit the company in a given moment, not the potential achievement of any positive external results. The problem of their being designed and employed to further corporations' own financial gain rather than actual societal benefit prevented disclosures from achieving racial progress.

Some corporations confronted with allegations of discrimination or other forms of racial injustice have used their words to evade accountability and limit corporate responsibility.

In 1962, during the civil rights movement, the Kansas Commission on Civil Rights requested a breakdown of General Motors's entire workforce in its Kansas operations to document and substantiate the National Association for the Advancement of Colored People (NAACP)'s claim of discrimination in its Kansas City plants.[45] General Motors was concerned about its reputation so it used its membership as a "Plans for Progress" company – that is, a company that participated in the Plans for Progress program – "as grounds for refusing to disclose information."[46] From the NAACP's perspective, General Motors only used its Plans for Progress participation as a coverup for egregious discrimination.[47]

Recall that in 2021, as Amazon declared its commitment to addressing racism within and outside of its firm, its shareholders requested it conduct a racial equity audit as an important first step. Instead of complying with this request, however, Amazon attempted to use its race-conscious disclosures as evidence that it was *already* addressing racial inequality and should therefore not have to comply with the request. Through what is called a "no-action letter" request Amazon first requested that the SEC excuse it from legal action if the company chose to exclude the shareholders' allegations from a shareholder meeting that would have allowed other shareholders to vote for or against the equity audit. A no-action letter request essentially asks that the SEC not act against the corporation if the corporation excludes a shareholder proposal from shareholder votes. When the SEC rejected Amazon's request, Amazon had to include the proposal in its proxy statement – a document that a corporation sends to all its shareholders with information on shareholder proposals that are up for votes. Shareholders can vote during shareholders' annual meetings or by proxy, which is like voting by absentee ballot. In its proxy statement, Amazon's board of directors asked shareholders to vote against Amazon conducting the racial equity audit. The statement read like any of Amazon's other race-conscious disclosures.

> We have initiated numerous programs to assess and address racial justice considerations across key aspects of our operations that we believe fully address the objectives of this proposal.
>
> In 2020, we set and achieved a goal to double the number of Black directors and vice presidents at the Company, and we are committed to doubling representation again in 2021. We also have a goal to increase the hiring of Black mid-level employees by 30% in 2021.

Amazon publicly declared that its race-conscious disclosures – including those quoted above as well as its "funding historically Black colleges and universities, running leadership programs for underrepresented minorities and channeling tens of millions of dollars to help close the racial wealth divide" – should excuse it from completing a racial equity audit to discover whether its products and policies discriminate against people of color.[48] As discussed further in Chapter 2, Amazon ended up agreeing to conduct only a limited audit of its low-wage workers.

Amazon is by no means unique. At least fifty companies have used their constructed race-conscious images to suppress concerns raised in hundreds of shareholder proposals and other informal settings requesting steps to address racial inequality by submitting no-action letter requests to the SEC, asking shareholders to vote against proposals, or using other means to state that their race-conscious disclosures should excuse them from completing racial equity audits.[49] And because of the systematic way in which race-conscious disclosures were deployed between 2020 and 2024, many more companies were poised to use their own constructed public images in this way.[50] This specious application of race-conscious disclosures is another mechanism by which companies use disclosures to constrain racial progress.

Race-Conscious Retraction

In 2022, conservative groups began to respond to race-conscious disclosures by bringing litigation or threatening to sue companies that engage in DEI efforts, which is often used synonymously with efforts related to addressing racial inequality. DEI-related programs and policies, conservative groups argued, violate the equal protection clause of the Fourteenth Amendment, Section 1981 of the Civil Rights Act of 1866, and/or Title VII of the Civil Rights Act of 1964. Their citation of the former clause, in particular, is noteworthy, as it has been used primarily by minorities alleging racial discrimination in employment contracts for more than a century.[51] The 2023 United States Supreme Court's decision in *Students for Fair Admissions v. Harvard*, which invalidated the use of race in the different context of college and university admissions, further fueled conservative efforts and media attention to race. In the years since the decision, the media has raised public awareness of conservative attempts to push back on corporate efforts to address racial inequality in disclosures and corporate programs and policies.

In response, companies have embraced two forms of race-conscious retraction. The first is "partial race-conscious retraction," which involves the replacement of the language of racial inequality and racial injustice with mundane language like inclusion and belonging, and making disclosures about people of color without noting how racial discrimination and injustices have impacted them. The second form is "complete race-conscious retraction," which involves the total erasure of previously made race-conscious disclosures. Complete race-conscious retraction would revert some companies to their pre-2020 disclosure regime, when companies tended to lump race with other forms of "diversity," or did not mention anything related to race in their disclosures. Corporate counsel have been the major proponents of race-conscious retraction in an attempt to shield companies from litigation, or the possibility of being targeted by the Trump administration.

The obvious problem is that it is unlikely that a company would address a social problem it does not name, because the incentives to address it would be limited, and the actors who would need to address it would lack important guidance. This applies also to corporations who engage in race-conscious retraction but claim to continue to engage in racial equity work stealthily within their firms.

But should companies be allowed to manipulate race-conscious disclosures for their own reputational and financial benefits without consequence?

This social or moral question aside, it is also worth asking whether or for how long companies can cater to two opposing constituencies at the same time – that is, by continuing racial equity work to appease the shareholders and stakeholders who still expect it, while simultaneously hiding any language referring to racial injustice or inequity, or completely getting rid of any mention of race or racial minorities in disclosures to appease conservative groups. Shareholders and stakeholders expecting corporations to address racial inequality tend to want clarity on what the corporations propose to do, while conservative groups balk at the idea of even naming racial inequality as a problem. Corporations have sought to keep both "sides" happy by cycling between race-conscious image construction and race-conscious retraction. This book questions not only whether that strategy is ultimately sustainable but also whether it is socially acceptable.

DISCLOSURELAND'S UNIQUE CONTRIBUTION

There are four features of *Disclosureland* that make it distinct from other works. First, and most importantly, it *centers* race and ethnicity rather than addressing broad notions of diversity – a rarity in academic and other writings on companies. This is important because race has often been deemphasized under the broad umbrella of diversity and inclusion but deserves its own examination, especially because the pattern of corporate disclosures that emerged in 2020 is uniquely centered on race. Indeed, since 2023, conservatives have used DEI synonymously with race and have targeted racial minorities in other areas of society, including in higher education, politics, and government.[52] Second, while acknowledging the importance of reputation and litigation risks to companies, it also documents corporate responses to societal, shareholder, and stakeholder pressure. Third, it incorporates the role of law in regulating the business of race-conscious disclosures and retraction. In this way, it follows other scholars who have addressed legal and market initiatives to improve things like corporate diversity, including the effectiveness and limitations of certain strategies, but brings the analysis to a different and entirely new context.[53] Fourth, *Disclosureland*'s philanthropy chapter establishes the concept of "corporate racial philanthropy," which shows how corporations use words to strategically expand philanthropy to include business transactions and the implications of a business-focused philanthropic strategy for racial progress.

Disclosureland makes significant contributions to the fields of corporate governance and race and private law. Corporate governance is the field primarily concerned with practices and processes used to direct and control a firm. The traditional view of corporate governance is that directors and officers should focus exclusively on the interests of shareholders.[54] However, the view that corporate decision-makers should also consider the interests of stakeholders such as employees, consumers, and the communities in which companies are embedded has become almost as prevalent as the traditional view.[55] But even among the many scholars who share the view that stakeholder interests have an important place in corporate governance, the ways in which racial inequality pervades shareholder and stakeholder concerns has not been a major focus in the field. This book reveals the embedded nature of racial inequality in corporate governance and shareholder and stakeholder interests. Through case studies and empirical research, it demonstrates how corporations have used disclosures about race to appear to address racial inequality, while simultaneously and in actuality constraining racial progress. The book shows the mechanisms by which boards of directors, managers, executives, shareholders, and stakeholders are involved in the cycle of race-conscious disclosures and retraction. It reveals how corporate governance structures may inadvertently perpetuate racial biases and disparities, even when companies claim to prioritize stakeholder interests.

Disclosureland also offers a groundbreaking exploration into the intersection of race and corporations, a key area of private law. The burgeoning field of race and private law asks how private entities and actors maintain and reproduce racial and socioeconomic hierarchies. In this book, I delve into how companies strategically utilize and manipulate disclosures about race to shape their public images while simultaneously constraining racial progress – and I analyze the legal frameworks that variously enable, regulate, or challenge these corporate behaviors. The book also underscores the need for new regulatory approaches that address the intersection of race, corporate governance, and accountability.

Finally, *Disclosureland* contributes to the Law and Political Economy framework by articulating the relationship between capitalism and racial inequality in corporations. The book offers reform strategies that bring together government and other groups, including customers, employees, and advocacy groups, to build coalition and transform how corporations use the power of words to shape how society understands racial progress.

DATA AND METHODOLOGY

Disclosureland draws on a wide range of original data spanning an eight-year period between 2018 and 2025. I collected data – particularly, texts of corporate disclosures – from a variety of sources, including voluntary sustainability and diversity reports, mandatory SEC reports, shareholder proposals, SEC no-action letter requests and responses, proxy statements, and news articles. I also conducted twenty-two in-depth interviews with CDOs and chief sustainability officers (CSOs) of publicly traded and privately held companies. The data used in the book cover 2,292 (2,093 public and 199 private) multinational companies headquartered in the United States.

I use natural language processing and qualitative content analysis to analyze hundreds of thousands of pages of disclosures to define the boundaries of race-conscious disclosures and empirically show their prevalence and trajectory over time. Interviews offer perspective on why companies made race-conscious disclosures and engage in race-conscious retraction and how companies have sought to respond to shareholders, customers, employees, and prospective employees with transparency and other strategies. A few interviews shed light on the growing impact of conservative groups and the Trump administration on race-conscious disclosures and retraction. I use historical documents, cases, statutes, and SEC rules to help connect the history of disclosures about race to current corporate governance concerns around employees, sustainability, and diversity, equity, and inclusion ("DEI"), and establish the role of regulation in responding to the use of race-conscious disclosures. Further discussions about the data and methods are included in the Appendix.

ORGANIZATION OF THE BOOK

Disclosureland is about how multinational corporations use words about race voluntarily and strategically in response to societal pressure and for financial gain. It is about how they use those words to stymie inquiries about business impacts on racial minorities and engage in race-conscious retraction in response to conservative pushback threatening litigation or targeting and accusing corporations of discrimination against white individuals. The book is also about how these strategies negatively impact true racial progress.

Chapters 1 and 2 offer historical and empirical analyses of how corporate words have shaped corporate reputation on race. Chapter 1 focuses on the 1940s to the 1970s. Chapter 2 focuses on 2020 to 2024. Chapters 3 and 4 then provide examples of race-conscious disclosures made between 2020 and 2023 in the employment and philanthropy contexts, respectively, and discusses how these disclosures offered some benefits to people of color but stopped short of yielding true racial progress. Chapter 5 delves into the mechanisms and dangers of race-conscious retraction starting from the end of 2024 to the present. Chapter 6 on regulation looks into the future and seeks to hold corporations accountable to at least the standards they have explicitly set for themselves under a functioning future federal government. Even if we assume corporations are, ultimately, driven by financial interests more than anything else, corporations' words nonetheless invoke and engage with notions of social justice, and racial progress, and those words should be used to evaluate corporate actions.

Chapter 1, "Historical Case Study," examines the Plans for Progress program of the 1960s. Building upon the work of historians like Randall Patton and Susan Reed,

Organization of the Book

the chapter explores how companies engaged in forms of race-conscious image construction in an earlier context. The chapter first describes early federal government efforts in the 1940s that, while mostly unsuccessful, laid the groundwork nonetheless for the version of race-conscious image construction that companies undertook in the 1960s, including the systematic disclosure of information demonstrating attention to addressing racial segregation and discrimination before the advent of digital print and online disclosures. It explores partnerships between the federal government and companies during John F. Kennedy's presidency, showing how the processes employed through this program helped corporations to establish their public images on race at the time. The chapter establishes that there was already a pattern, before 2020, for companies to use disclosures about race in ways that serve their own financial and reputational interests.

Chapter 2, "Disclosures, Image, and Reputation," defines the concept of race-conscious image construction, presents empirical evidence of it in action, and charts how corporations used race-conscious images to bolster their reputation between 2020 and 2024. It also demonstrates how the language and prevalence of disclosures about race changed during that time. The chapter discusses Amazon and Chevron Corporation (Chevron) as representative case studies that illustrate the image construction process undertaken by thousands of companies. It also explores the role of risk management in corporations' use of race-conscious disclosures, demonstrating that image construction is often employed as a shield from legal and reputational scrutiny.

Chapter 3, "Racial Targets," is the first of two chapters that zoom in to examine specific types of race-conscious disclosures that corporations have made. Racial targets are nonbinding, voluntary statements about goals to hire, retain, or promote people of color in the future. The chapter examines how companies have used racial targets and assesses the role of racial targets as part of the broader project of using race-conscious disclosures to show concern for and action toward addressing racial inequality. The chapter also discusses how companies attempted to meet their racial targets and argues that some corporate strategies to do so may have further entrenched racial inequality. The chapter illustrates the potential tensions between the positive aims of disclosures and their potential challenges for racial progress.

Chapter 4, "Corporate Racial Philanthropy," similarly explores one specific type of race-conscious disclosure in-depth – in this case, the role of philanthropy in race-conscious image construction. The chapter theoretically develops and then empirically demonstrates the concept of corporate racial philanthropy, hereafter CRP. CRP is the use of corporate words to define the parameters of philanthropy to focus on business transactions and the strategic pursuit of financial gain by targeting race and minority groups. It is within the framework of business development initiatives that use philanthropy to tap new markets and generate profit. The chapter not only examines the limits of CRP but also considers how companies might best implement CRP to achieve racial progress.

Chapter 5, "Race-Conscious Retraction," argues that race-conscious retraction constrains racial progress because it communicates that the issues of racial inequality companies identified previously were either not important or have become largely irrelevant. The chapter examines how conservative pushback has compelled companies to engage in either "partial race-conscious retraction" or "complete race-conscious retraction." The partial form involves the replacement of language about racial injustice with mundane terms. The complete form is about the erasure of race-conscious disclosures and subsuming race into other issues as companies did prior to 2020. The chapter argues that, left unregulated (as I discuss further in Chapter 6), race-conscious disclosures are likely to become cyclical, swinging back and forth between construction and retraction. During the construction phase, corporations will respond to future societal occurrences and social and political pressures to address racial inequality, with the result that race-conscious disclosures will be accommodated broadly, as was the case after 2020. During the retraction phase, race-conscious disclosures will become more infrequent or hollowed-out in their language and content.

Chapter 6, "Regulating Race-Conscious Disclosures and Retraction," argues that a future functioning federal government should assume an information-enforcing role to regulate race-conscious disclosures and retraction, and facilitate regulation by shareholders and stakeholders, including employees and consumers, who can use the information provided by the federal government to establish accountability structures. The chapter makes normative suggestions for what it calls a "multi-institutional approach" to regulating business.

NOTES

1. Derrick Bryson Taylor, "George Floyd Protests: A Timeline," *The New York Times*, November 5, 2021, www.nytimes.com/article/george-floyd-protests-timeline.html.
2. Ibid.
3. Jason Silverstein, "The Global Impact of George Floyd: How Black Lives Matter Protests Shaped Movements around the World," *CBS News*, June 4, 2021, www.cbsnews.com/news/george-floyd-black-lives-matter-impact/; Javier C. Hernández and Benjamin Mueller, "Global Anger Grows over George Floyd Death, and Becomes an Anti-Trump Cudgel," *New York Times*, September 7, 2021, www.nytimes.com/2020/06/01/world/asia/george-floyd-protest-global.html.
4. For example, @Amazon (May 31, 2020). The inequitable and brutal treatment of Black people in our country must stop. Together we stand in solidarity with the Black community – our employees, customers, and partners – in the fight against systemic racism and injustice. [X Post]. Retrieved from https://x.com/amazon/status/1267140211861073927.
5. For example, "Advancing Our Work on Racial Equity." Walmart website, June 12, 2020, https://corporate.walmart.com/news/2020/06/12/advancing-our-work-on-racial-equity.
6. Ron S. Berenblat and Elizabeth R. Gonzalez-Sussman, *Racial Equity Audits: A New ESG Initiative*, Harvard Law School Forum on Corporate Governance, October 30, 2021, https://corpgov.law.harvard.edu/2021/10/30/racial-equity-audits-a-new-esg-initiative/.
7. Jason Del Rey, "Bias, Disrespect, and Demotions: Black Employees Say Amazon Has a Race Problem," *Vox*, February 26, 2021.

8. SEC, *Schedule 14A: Proxy Statement Pursuant to Section 14(a) of the SEC Act of 1934*, 2021.
9. Amazon, *NYCRF Amazon Shareholder Proposal*, www.osc.state.ny.us/files/press/pdf/nycrf-amazon-shareholder-proposal.pdf.
10. Anne D'Innocenzio, "Walmart Becomes Latest – and Biggest – Company to Roll Back Its DEI Policies," *Associated Press*, November 25, 2024, https://apnews.com/article/walmart-dei-inclusion-diversity-34b06922e60e5116fe198696201ce4d9.
11. Catharine A. MacKinnon, *Only Words* (Cambridge, MA: Harvard University Press, 1993).
12. Atinuke O. Adediran, "Disclosing Corporate Diversity," Virginia *Law Review* 109, no. 2 (2023): 307–72. Like legal scholar Lisa Fairfax, I recognize the inextricable link between mandatory and voluntary disclosure and the corresponding need to value and embrace both forms of disclosures; see Lisa M. Fairfax, "Dynamic Disclosure: An Expose on the Mythical Divide between Voluntary and Mandatory ESG Disclosure," *Texas Law Review* 101, no. 2 (December 2022): 273–337.
13. A Google trend chart from January 2021 until December 2022 shows that use of the term "ESG" increased significantly starting from February 2020 to June 2020 and exploded in May 2021, "Explore – Google Trends," Google Trends, https://trends.google.com/trends/explore?date=2017-01-01%202022-12-23&geo=US&q=ESG (accessed May 26, 2024).
14. Nakita Cuttino, "Private Debt for Public Good," *Florida Law Review* (2024): 1, 17.
15. Elizabeth Pollman, "The Origins and Consequences of the ESG Moniker," *Institute of Law and Economics*, Research Paper No. 22–23, May 26, 2022.
16. Berenblat and Gonzalez-Sussman, "Racial Equity Audits"; Josh Mitchell, "Bank of America CEO Says ESG Movement Is Here to Stay," *Wall Street Journal*, January 18, 2023, www.wsj.com/livecoverage/davos2023/card/bank-of-america-ceo-says-esg-movement-is-here-to-stay-fF6faZMTISxTd3pYXgNx.
17. Charles J. Fombrun, *Reputation: Realizing Value from the Corporate Image* (Boston: Harvard Business School Press, 1996), 277; Kevin T. Jackson, *Building Reputational Capital: Strategies for Integrity and Fair Play That Improve the Bottom Line* (Oxford: Oxford University Press, 2004).
18. Michael L. Barnett, John M. Jermier, and Barbara A. Lafferty, "Corporate Reputation: The Definitional Landscape," *Corporate Reputation Review* 9, no. 1 (2006): 26–38.
19. Ibid.
20. See Joseph A. Petrick, Robert F. Scherer, James D. Brodzinski, John F. Quinn, and M. Fall Ainina, "Global Leadership Skills and Reputational Capital: Intangible Resources for Sustainable Competitive Advantage," *Academy of Management Perspectives* 13, no. 1 (1999): 58–69.
21. Fombrun, *Reputation*, 81.
22. "Diversity, Equity and Inclusion at Amazon," Amazon UK website, April 18, 2018, www.aboutamazon.co.uk/news/working-at-amazon/diversity-equity-and-inclusion-at-amazon. In 2018, Amazon US did not have a diversity and inclusion page. It's diversity and inclusion page was created in September 2020.
23. Amazon, *All In: Staying the Course on Our Commitment to Sustainability* 2020, https://perma.cc/63VH-X3K6.
24. Ibid.
25. Amazon Sustainability 2020 Report: *Further and Faster, Together*, https://perma.cc/2DLH-P8C8.
26. Amazon, "Our Positions," www.aboutamazon.com/about-us/our-positions.
27. Moody, Ashley. Attorney General Ashley Moody to EPA Administrator Michael S. Regan, Washington DC, April 16, 2024; Letter from 13 State Attorneys General to Fortune 100 Corporations, July 13, 2023, www.tn.gov/content/dam/tn/attorneygeneral/documents/pr/2023/pr23-27-letter.pdf.

28. Nancy Fraser, *Cannibal Capitalism: How Our System Is Devouring Democracy, Care, and the Planet, and What We Can Do about It* (London: Verso, 2023).
29. Paul J. DiMaggio and Walter W. Powell, "The Iron Cage Revisited: Institutional Isomorphism and Collective Rationality in Organizational Fields," *American Sociological Review* 48, no. 2 (1983): 147–60.
30. Ellen Berrey, *The Enigma of Diversity: The Language of Race and the Limits of Racial Justice* (Chicago: University of Chicago Press, 2015).
31. Lauren B. Edelman, *Working Law: Courts, Corporations, and Symbolic Civil Rights* (Chicago: University of Chicago Press, 2016).
32. Frank Dobbin, *Inventing Equal Opportunity* (Princeton: Princeton University Press, 2009).
33. "Executive Order 10925 of March 6, 1961, Establishing the President's Committee on Equal Employment Opportunity," *Code of Federal Regulations*, Title 3 (1961).
34. President's Committee on Equal Employment Opportunity, *Report to the President by the President's Committee on Equal Employment Opportunity* (Washington, DC: Government Printing Office, 1963), 2.
35. Michael I. Sovern, *Legal Restraints on Racial Discrimination in Employment* (New York: Twentieth Century Fund, 1966), 117.
36. Sovern, *Legal Restraints*, 117; Richard D. Alexander and Georges F. Doriot, *The Management of Racial Integration in Business: Special Report to Management* (New York: McGraw-Hill, 1964), 19.
37. Sovern, *Legal Restraints*, 117; "33 More Firms Pledge Equal Employment Plan," *Atlanta Daily World*, July 1, 1962.
38. Sovern, *Legal Restraints*, 117.
39. Alexander and Doriot, *Management of Racial Integration*, 6; Southern Regional Council, *Special Report, Plans for Progress: Atlanta Survey*, January 1963, 15; Milton Leon Barron, *Minorities in a Changing World* (New York: Alfred A. Knopf, 1967), 227.
40. Clare Duffy, "In the Face of a Cultural Reckoning, It Turns Out Massive Corporations Can Move Fast and Fix Things," *CNN*, June 21, 2020, www.cnn.com/2020/06/21/business/corporate-america-addresses-racism/index.html; Emma Bowman, "For Many Native Americans, the Washington Commanders' New Name offers some closure," *National Public Radio*, February 6, 2022, www.npr.org/2022/02/06/1078571919/washington-commanders-name-change-native-americans.
41. Adediran, "Disclosing Corporate Diversity."
42. My research shows that many large companies opened or expanded their offices in Atlanta, Georgia, after Floyd was murdered. Atlanta's population is about 50 percent Black. See also Lisa M. Fairfax's finding that Fortune 500 companies that made public statements about race were two times more likely to appoint a Black director as compared to companies that did not make public statements, in "Radical Rhetoric or Reality? Cautious Optimism on the Link between Corporate #BLM Speech and Behavior," *Columbia Business Law Review* 2022, no. 1 (2022): 118–205.
43. On the finding that large companies committed to fund large nonprofits that are led by people of color, see Atinuke O. Adediran, "Disclosures for Equity," *Columbia Law Review*, 122, no. 4 (2022): 865–922.
44. Aaron A. Dhir, *Challenging Boardroom Homogeneity: Corporate Law, Governance and Diversity* (New York: Cambridge University Press, 2016).
45. "Johnson Urged to Probe Job Bias in General Motors," *Atlanta Daily World*, December 2, 1962, 5.
46. Ibid.
47. Ibid.

48. Saijel Kishan, "Amazon to Undergo Racial Audit, Led by Former AG Lynch," *Bloomberg Law*, April 18, 2022, https://news.bloomberglaw.com/esg/amazon-to-undergo-racial-audit-led-by-former-ag-loretta-lynch.
49. Kishan, "Amazon to Undergo"; Andrew Ramonas, "ESG Investors Push More Racial Issues After Wins at Apple, J&J," *Bloomberg Law*, May 25, 2022, https://news.bloomberglaw.com/securities-law/esg-investors-push-more-racial-issues-after-wins-at-apple-j-j; Levi Sumagaysay, "Citigroup, Wells Fargo, Bank of America, Goldman Sachs, JP Morgan Urge Shareholders to Vote against Racial-equity Audits," *MarketWatch*, March 17, 2021, www.marketwatch.com/story/citigroup-wells-fargo-bank-of-america-urge-shareholders-to-vote-against-racial-equity-audits-11616026865; US Securities and Exchange Commission, *Schedule 14A, Proxy Statement*.
50. Stavros Gadinis and Amelia Miazad, "Corporate Law & Social Risk," *Vanderbilt Law Review* 73, no. 5 (2020), 1414. There is a notion that ESG activities are a form of risk management by companies, see Elizabeth Pollman, "The Making and Meaning of ESG," *Harvard Business Law Review* (2023), https://ssrn.com/abstract=4219857.
51. 42 U.S.C. § 1981 (1866).
52. See, for example, Sheryll Cashin, "First Conservatives Came for Affirmative Action. Now They're Gunning for DEI Programs," *Politico*, August 10, 2023, www.politico.com/news/magazine/2023/08/10/affirmative-action-gop-culture-war-00110558; Douglas Belkin, "Christopher Rufo Has Trump's Ear and Wants to End DEI for Good," *Wall Street Journal*, November 25, 2024, www.wsj.com/us-news/education/christopher-rufo-education-trump-dei-bb9e7178?mod=djem10point.
53. Dhir, *Challenging*; Akshaya Kamalnath, *The Corporate Diversity Jigsaw* (Cambridge, MA: Cambridge University Press, 2022); Frank Dobbin and Alexandra Kalev, *Getting to Diversity: What Works and What Doesn't* (Cambridge, MA: Harvard University Press, 2022); Iris Bohnet, *What Works: Gender Equality by Design* (Cambridge, MA: Harvard University Press, 2018).
54. Adolf A. Berle, Jr., "Corporate Powers as Powers in Trust," *Harvard Law Review* 44 (1931): 1049; Aneil Kovvali, "Countercyclical Corporate Governance," *North Carolina Law Review* 101, no. 1 (December 2022): 141–206.
55. E. Merrick Dodd, Jr., "For Whom Are Corporate Managers Trustees?," *Harvard Law Review* 45 (1932): 1145, 1158–61; Lisa M. Fairfax, "Stakeholderism, Corporate Purpose, and Credible Commitment," *Virginia Law Review* 108, no. 5 (September 2022): 1163–1242.

1

Historical Case Study

There is a large and complex history of how profit-seeking entities operate in a world characterized by profound racial injustice. This history goes as far back as the transatlantic slave trade when Africans were bought and sold for profit. As described by historian Eric Williams, the early to mid 1700s was marked by corporations profiting from and supporting the slave trade.[1] Williams and historian Padraic Scanlan have documented how corporations manufactured and sold iron, copper, brass, and lead, exported as brass pans and kettles, cutlery, and other goods; how banks financed slave traders and insured their cargoes; how insurance companies underwrote the risky and cyclical business of cotton cultivation; and how mining companies owned and purchased slaves whose labor the companies exploited.[2]

By the early to mid 1850s, when the buying and selling of human beings became costly because of laws abolishing the trade, government taxes, and monopolies held by corporations in the West Indies, American and British corporations became abolitionists arguing for and supporting the principle of free trade.[3] Cotton manufacturers, shipowners, sugar refineries, the Manchester Chamber of Commerce, and other businesses joined in the attack on West Indian slavery, not because of any moral duty to abolish slavery, but for self-interested economic reasons.[4]

From the slave trade to the American Civil War, to the Great Migration – when more than six million Black people moved from the rural Southern United States to cities in the North, Midwest, and West to take advantage of the need for industrial workers after World War I until the 1970s – to the civil rights movement and beyond, corporations have been involved in the exploitation of racial injustices for financial gain.[5]

To set the stage for the contemporary evaluation of corporate influence on racial progress, this chapter uses the Plans for Progress (PFP) program of the 1960s and subsequent similar measures as a historical case study of how corporations have attempted to address racial inequality while prioritizing financial gain. Corporations in the 1960s were responding to the social reality that they had to desegregate their businesses and take steps to address racial discrimination, and they did so by working with a national government that similarly lacked a genuine commitment to addressing racial segregation and discrimination.

The chapter begins by contextualizing corporate racial activities by documenting early federal government efforts in the 1940s that, even though mostly unsuccessful, were catalysts for later forms of race-conscious image construction in the 1960s, including the systematic disclosure of information that showed that corporations were taking steps toward addressing racial segregation and discrimination in the 1960s before the advent of digital print and online disclosures.

The chapter builds upon the work of historians like Randall Patton and Susan Reed on the history of Lockheed Aircraft Corporation's role as one of the earliest sites of desegregation in the American South during the civil rights movement of the 1960s and partnerships between the government and private firms through the establishment of the PFP program. President John F. Kennedy's administration established PFP in partnership with companies, starting with Lockheed Aircraft, in an attempt to persuade businesses to address racial segregation and discrimination.

After examining the PFP program, the chapter analyzes the relationship between PFP and contemporary race-conscious image construction, as well as various similarities and differences between the two, and draws lessons from the failures of the government in its involvement in PFP.

1940S–1950S: GOVERNMENT INTERVENTION

President Franklin Delano Roosevelt (FDR)'s wartime policies on employment discrimination changed the course of civil rights history as the first governmental intervention to positively address racial discrimination in employment since Reconstruction.[6] As America geared up for World War II, new defense industries were created and existing ones expanded.[7] White workers and business industries profited from increased economic activity, including the creation and retooling of factories and building of military planes to support the war.[8] White unemployment decreased significantly during this period, while the unemployment rate for Black people and other people of color remained high because of racial discrimination.[9] Manufacturing and defense jobs, in particular, were beyond the reach of most Black skilled workers.[10] In late 1940s, of the 11,000 skilled and semiskilled positions in the aircraft industry, less than 1 percent went to racial and ethnic minorities.[11] Defense companies refused to hire Black workers on the basis that white workers would strike if they did.[12]

Employment discrimination against Black people had become so severe by early 1941 that civil rights leaders believed that more drastic measures than traditional lobbying had to be taken to force companies and the government to hire Black people.[13] A. Philip Randolph, international president of the Brotherhood of Sleeping Car Porters, and a Black labor leader, proposed a massive protest on Washington, calling on the National Association for the Advancement of Colored People (NAACP) and all Black people to join in.[14] Randolph went on to establish an organization, called the March on Washington Movement (MOWM), formerly known as the Negro March on

Washington Committee, with regional offices in Harlem, Chicago, and other places, to build up support for the march. On June 5, 1941, Randolph informed the White House that MOWM had mobilized and assembled ten thousand Black people to march on Washington on July 1 to protest discrimination in the national defense effort.[15]

Although, at one point, the federal government, in a memorandum from the War Department, claimed it was "doing everything to prevent discrimination against [Black] workers in industry," under its defense contracts, companies were solely responsible for furnishing labor, and the government could only plead with them to eliminate discrimination against Black people.[16] These pleas were largely ignored.[17] In response, on June 23, 1941, Randolph reiterated the severity of the issue and demanded in a letter that the president act through an "executive order which is strong, definitive, and clear."[18] An executive order is a signed, written, and published directive from the President of the United States to manage or execute internal operations of federal agencies and federal programs and policies.[19] Executive orders are not legislation passed by Congress and cannot be overturned by Congress.[20] Congress's primary tool to oppose a president's executive order is to pass legislation that would make it challenging to carry it out, such as by removing funding from an administrative agency.[21] The president can revoke an executive order at any time, and only a sitting president can overturn an existing executive order by issuing another executive order to that effect.[22]

On June 25, 1941, FDR budged and issued Executive Order 8802 to prevent the march from going forward, and the event was subsequently canceled in response.[23] The order, the first to address racial inequality concerns, expressly prohibited discrimination on the basis of race in defense industries or government.[24] Executive Order 8802 was an extraordinary measure and the first time a sitting US president used an executive order to advance racial equity. To investigate complaints of discrimination in violation of the executive order, FDR established the President's Committee on Fair Employment Practice (COFEP), later known as the Fair Employment Practice Committee (FEPC), which historians and other commentators have characterized as a largely toothless agency given its severe lack of enforcement power and resources.[25] On August 20, 1942, Lawrence W. Cramer, the Executive Secretary of the FEPC sent the White House a report stating that "there has ... yet been little progress in modifying the employment practices of most government agencies, thus making it more difficult for the Committee to demand complete compliance with Executive Order 8802 on the part of private employers."[26] The FEPC processed about 12,000 complaints from the beginning of World War II until when it was dismantled.[27] Southern Democrats in Congress and the Southern states fiercely resisted the FEPC cases that challenged the Jim Crow South, and they thwarted efforts to turn the FEPC into a permanent government agency.[28] The FEPC expired when Congress terminated its funding in 1946.[29] Even before it expired, the FEPC had become a powerless feature of the executive order, until it completely folded in 1948.

Building on the momentum he and other civil rights activists gained during FDR's third term, Randolph and his allies continued to pressure the White House to take executive action during Harry S. Truman's presidency, which started in April 1945.[30] They threatened that Black people would boycott the military. Yielding to pressure, President Truman issued Executive Order 9981 in July 1948, banning segregation in the military.[31] The order established the President's Committee on Equality of Treatment and Opportunity in the Armed Forces, popularly known as the Fahy Committee, to oversee the process and examine the rules, practices, and procedures of the armed services and recommend ways to make desegregation a reality.[32] Notably, the Fahy Committee included two Black leaders.[33] Black activists criticized the executive order as not being explicit enough in terms of abolishing segregation in the military.[34] And while his efforts were not entirely successful because of Jim Crow segregation and deep racial animus – evidenced, for example, by the statement of General Omar Bradley, chief of staff of the army, that racial segregation would continue as long as the nation did – Truman's policies on discrimination on the military went further toward ending racial segregation and discrimination than those of most of his predecessors.[35] By 1950, all military jobs had opened up to Black people, the practice of *de jure* segregation in the military had been eliminated, and limits on Black enrollment in the military had reduced.[36] Truman's efforts became a crucial step toward advancing the civil rights movement during the presidency of John F. Kennedy in the 1960s.

1950S–1960S: MOSTLY SOCIETAL PRESSURES

Compared to Truman, Dwight D. Eisenhower (a.k.a. Ike) would prove to be less enthusiastic about using his executive authority to further the civil rights agenda. But there were several societal pressures in the decade leading up to the civil rights movement. In 1950, Black individuals earned wages at a level only 52 percent of that of white individuals.[37] By this time, twenty-one states had implemented fair employment laws, but much of these state legislations were deficient for the same reasons as the federal FEPC – inadequate enforcement mechanisms and lack of compliance, particularly in the South.[38]

In 1954, the US Supreme Court decided *Brown v. Board of Education*, which held that segregated schools were unconstitutional.[39] As soon as the Court decided *Brown*, white institutions and groups in the South organized to fight its implementation and racial progress for Black people in general.[40] Eisenhower would be forced to respond when segregationists in Little Rock, Arkansas, attempted to defy the Supreme Court when nine Black students sought entry into Central High School.[41] The groups used economic pressures, intimation, propaganda, violence, and terror to keep Black people in their place.[42]

In 1955, Emmett Till, a fourteen-year-old boy who was part of the Great Migration, traveled from Chicago to visit his relatives in Mississippi.[43] Shortly before Till arrived in Mississippi, two Black men who had registered to vote or cast their ballots had been lynched.[44] Two white men subsequently brutally lynched Till because he spoke to twenty-one-year-old Carolyn Bryant, the white, married proprietor of a local grocery store.[45] The lynching of Emmett Till in 1955 was one of the forces that galvanized the civil rights movement alongside Rosa Parks's refusal to move to the back of a bus in Alabama, despite the protestations of the bus driver who insisted that Rosa Parks remain in the "colored section" of the bus where Black people belonged.[46] Black people boycotted buses in Montgomery, Alabama, between 1955 and 1956, resulting in the desegregation of buses in Montgomery.[47]

These societal pressures pushed the federal government and corporations to desegregate and address racial discrimination in employment. While some racist executives intentionally wanted to prevent Black progress, most were simply complicit in racial injustice by being more concerned about the social and economic consequences of hiring Black people, including the cost of having separate bathroom facilities and white employee backlash, rather than addressing racial discrimination.[48] It was not until the federal government stepped in the early 1960s that large companies took steps toward desegregation and employment opportunities for Black people.

1960S: PRESIDENT KENNEDY AND LOCKHEED AIRCRAFT

On March 6, 1961, just two months into his presidency, President John F. Kennedy signed Executive Order 10925, which mandated companies doing business with the US government to take "affirmative action to ensure that applicants are employed, and that employees are treated … without regard to their race, creed, color, or national origin."[49] The affirmative action requirement covered hiring, promotion, demotion, transfer, recruitment, layoffs, termination, rates of pay, and training.[50] The President's executive order covered 35,000 companies and more than 15 million employees.[51] Companies that failed to comply risked losing their government contracts.[52] The executive order also established the President's Committee on Equal Employment Opportunity (hereafter, the Committee) to oversee compliance.[53]

Sixteen days later, on March 22, 1961, five Black employees at Lockheed Aircraft Corporation's facility in Marietta, Georgia, tried to eat breakfast in the designated white cafeteria.[54] In operation since 1951, Lockheed's Marietta plant had segregated facilities, segregated unions, an exclusionary apprenticeship program, and hiring patterns that confined Black people to unskilled and semiskilled job categories.[55] Lockheed's management had instructed the cafeteria workers to prevent integration, so the workers closed the line to block Black employees from eating there.[56] In response, the Black employees left the white cafeteria and informed other Black employees about their experience.[57] According to Eugene Mattison, Lockheed's head of labor relations, the anger over the segregated eating facilities resulted in "considerable unrest" at the facility.[58] Mattison and Lockheed's president, James Carmichael, met with the Black employees because "[a]ny incident of sufficient magnitude could cause the Government to switch [its] contract to Lockheed's competitors."[59]

Indeed, Lockheed had reason to be concerned because just three days before the president announced the executive order, the US government had issued a $1 billion contract to Lockheed to produce a new transport plane, the C-141.[60] Lockheed had been in competition for the contract with Boeing, Douglas, and Convair.[61] Because of major financial losses due in part to a crash of one of its commercial aircraft, and resulting workforce reductions, Lockheed desperately needed the contract.[62] With the new contract, Lockheed no longer had to shrink its workforce and instead decided to hire 5,000 additional employees,[63] including increasing its Marietta workforce to between 11,000 and 12,000 by mid 1963.[64] The year 1961 was one of Lockheed's most successful years because of its robust earnings totals and sales volume.[65] Not surprisingly, a large portion of its sales revenue from 1961 came from government airplanes and other services.[66]

In addition to being transformative to Lockheed itself, the contract was a boon to the local economy and was embraced by politicians with enthusiasm. Ivan Allen, Jr., president of the Atlanta Chamber of Commerce, called it "a catalyst that should produce a lot of related business activity in Metropolitan Atlanta."[67] Georgia Senators Richard Russell and Herman Talmadge and Representatives Carl Vinson and John W. Davis also applauded the contract as a major economic boost for Georgia.[68] The front-page news in the *Atlanta Constitution* on March 14, 1961, described how "[t]he recession-etched frown on Georgia's economy gave way to a broad smile Monday night after Lockheed Aircraft won [...] a billion dollar boost for the state's economy."[69]

The NAACP had been vocal that the segregation and employment discrimination that continued at Lockheed after the president's executive order made a "shameful mockery" of it.[70] In response to the March 22 events, Jerry R. J. Holleman, executive vice chairman of the President's Committee pledged that the Committee would seek contract cancelation if Lockheed or any other federal contractor refused to comply with the executive order.[71] On April 2, thirty days after Kennedy signed the executive order and a few days before it went into effect, Roy Wilkins, executive secretary of the NAACP, wrote to Vice President Lyndon B. Johnson, chair of the Committee, to protest continued discrimination and urged the government to reexamine the C-141 contract with Lockheed.[72] On April 12, Vice President Johnson reiterated the plan to enforce compliance and stated that "the federal government will act to eliminate segregation at [] Lockheed ... [w]hatever action is needed will be taken to insure [sic] compliance with the policy."[73] After this statement, Lockheed responded publicly that "[it was] willing as always to work with the President's Committee."[74]

And willing it was. The quest to retain its government contract motivated Lockheed to figure out how to take "affirmative action." So, while Lockheed Georgia's management thought that the NAACP's focus on Lockheed was unfair given that many other companies engaged in worse racial discrimination,[75] the company had to do something to keep its contract for political, and economic reasons.

Lockheed's management, in consultation with the Committee's executive director, John G. Field,[76] who became the point person from the federal government's PFP program assigned to work with the company on this issue, drafted the first PFP plan to increase minority hiring, promotion, and retention. As discussed below, Lockheed, a private enterprise, was handed the reigns to determine how to comply with the executive order.

PFP was not the first time that the government and companies had collaborated on issues of race. But PFP was the first time in the history of the United States that the federal government and private companies collaborated on a grand scale toward addressing racial segregation and discrimination. The Committee encouraged all companies – government contractors who were subject to the executive order and nongovernment contractors who were not – to join PFP.[77] Robert Troutman, a member of the Committee and the staunchest advocate for the PFP program, pointed out to President Kennedy that twenty years of FEPC approach under the federal government had yielded limited success because Black people "didn't have enough dignified work to count. All they were doing was sweeping floors and cleaning toilets."[78] According to Troutman, Kennedy examined the statistics and "couldn't believe it."[79]

As part of the PFP program, Lockheed was to submit statistical data on its personnel and respond to Committee questions confidentially regarding its employment policies and practices.[80] Lockheed stated that it would conduct a periodic and likely yearly review of its plan with the Committee to measure its progress.[81] In five pages, the company then enumerated its specific plan in categories, including recruitment, employment, placement, promotion, and training.[82] In the recruitment section, the plan expressed the intent to aggressively seek out qualified racial minorities:

> Lockheed will in its employment recruitment *aggressively* seek out more qualified minority group candidates in order to increase the number of employees in many job categories, including but not limited to: Professional Engineering positions, such as design engineers, mathematicians, associate engineers and draftsmen; Technical positions, such as computer technicians and tabulating analysts; Administrative positions, such as accountants and buyers.[83]

In the employment section, the plan stated that the company would ensure that eligible minority employees have been considered for hiring and promotion:

> Lockheed will re-analyze its openings for salaried jobs to be certain that all eligible minority group employees have been considered for placement and upgrading. Its industrial relations staff, working with other members of management, will re-examine personnel records of minority group employees to make certain that employee skill and potential beyond current job requirements have been properly identified therein for use in filling job openings.[84]

President Kennedy hailed Lockheed's plan as "a milestone in the history of civil rights in this country."[85] He further described it as a "long-range commitment by the Lockheed corporation and by the United States government to work together in improving and expanding the job opportunities available to members of minority groups," as "voluntary action" that would result in "real and measurable progress toward the goal of equal opportunity."[86] The president looked on with approval and smiled as Vice President Lyndon B. Johnson, chairman of the Committee, and Lockheed's president, Courtland Gross, signed the document in his office.[87] The occasion was then published in news media, including those frequently read by Black people at the time, such as the *Atlanta Daily World* and the *Atlanta Constitution*, as well as mainstream media like the *New York Times*.[88]

After Lockheed and the Committee established the first PFP program, most of the country's largest companies at the time, motivated by the financial benefits that could come from government contracts and avoiding racial riots and boycotts, joined the movement, emphasizing their willingness and approval because of the purported voluntary nature of the plan. In its plan, the General Electric Company emphasized "the opportunity to cooperate on a voluntary basis with [the] Committee."[89] The Douglas Aircraft Company expressed that it "welcomes and endorses the Committee's approach to these problems by its solicitation of the voluntary and constructive cooperation of the nation's leading employers."[90] Companies that were not government contractors, and therefore not directly subject to the executive order, particularly believed that they "voluntarily signed their plans as an expression of their support of the national program."[91]

Historians disagree about the voluntary nature of the PFP program.[92] On the one hand, PFP can be viewed as voluntary because Lockheed and other companies crafted and designed the meaning of affirmative action in the employment context. On the other hand, PFP was urged by the government, even though the government minimally monitored what companies did with their plans. Companies shared information through the Committee, which through conferences and meetings kept tabs on what companies were doing.[93]

I would argue that PFP was neither voluntary nor compelled, but somewhere in between. It can best be described as "a cooperative venture between business and government,"[94] as indeed it was described in the Federal Register, or as it was described in the words of North American Aviation, as "the voluntary efforts of industry in cooperation with government."[95] The government did very little to enforce the program, but the Committee was ever-present in promoting and publicly communicating its monitoring of companies under the program. There was also pressure from minority organizations and workers for corporations to do something. Ultimately, a range of enforcement problems frustrated the PFP program, and it was not very successful in mitigating racial and economic inequality and providing equal opportunity for people of color.

EXECUTIVE ORDER 10925 AND THE PRESIDENT'S COMMITTEE

The Committee, which was established by President Kennedy's Executive Order 10925, mandated government contractors to take affirmative action in hiring and non-discrimination in employment on the basis of race. The Committee began its work in April 1961 after the NAACP filed complaints against Lockheed for racial discrimination.[96] The executive order authorized the Committee to make rules, engage in recordkeeping, develop an education program, respond to complaints of discrimination, and impose penalties for noncompliance, such as canceling government contracts and barring future ones.[97] The executive order had three provisions designed to drive equal employment for people of color: (1) a provision authorizing the Committee to coordinate the activities of government agencies to promote equal employment opportunity; (2) a provision requiring government contractors to submit annual employment profiles to the Committee as proof of compliance with the executive order; and (3) a provision for sanctions in the form of authority to cancel contracts or bar from future contracts any employer who refused to adhere to the executive order.[98]

The executive order, though worded like a mandate, was meant to be enforced in a conciliatory manner. It expected contracting agencies to make reasonable effort to secure compliance through conference, conciliation, mediation, and persuasion before proceedings would be instituted to terminate a contract for failure to comply with the order.[99] This meant that the Committee's authority was much narrower than its language might have suggested. For instance, as soon as the Committee was established, and the NAACP filed allegations against Lockheed for discrimination, the Committee conducted an investigation and found that the NAACP's allegations were substantiated.[100] But instead of imposing penalties against Lockheed, as the Committee was authorized to do by perhaps canceling Lockheed's contract or barring it from future contracts, the Committee allowed Lockheed to come up with a "voluntary plan" to eliminate discrimination, which then evolved into the company's own PFP.[101] This was consistent with making "reasonable efforts ... to secure compliance ... by methods of ... conciliation."[102] This move set the stage for the Committee's future role in implementing the president's executive order as essentially strengthening the administration's PFP program, rather than acting as an enforcement agency.

Moving forward, the Committee's role became largely focused on efficiently processing and disposing of complaints about racial discrimination, using them largely to recruit companies into the PFP program, and assisting new companies to join the program.[103]

DIFFUSION AND PUBLICIZING

Lockheed's plan quickly diffused across other large companies because, like Lockheed, they had a lot to lose if they fell out of favor in Washington.[104] By

July 1961, eight of the nation's largest defense contractors – including Western Electric Co., General Electric Co., North American Aviation, Radio Corporation of America, and United Aircraft Corp. – which collectively employed a total of 760,000 people, had joined the PFP program.[105] A year later, in July 1962, eighty-five companies had joined the PFP program.[106] And by November 1963, 115 companies had joined the program, including companies that did not hold government contracts.[107]

PFP was established to be an "adjunct" to the Committee. There was considerable feeling at the time that buy-in from leading companies, particularly government contractors, was necessary to enforce the executive order.[108] The Committee sold the program as establishing "a basis for communication and cooperation with minority groups, other employers, training and recruitment sources, and government agencies."[109] The idea was that "the exchange of information by member firms ... will benefit all participants by providing an experience base from which to formulate their decision-making policies for implementing equal employment opportunity."[110] In June 1964, a selection of companies, headed by the Advisory Council on PFP, published a guide with "practical information about the techniques used by companies participating in PFP."[111] The goal of the guide was to get more companies to join.

In joining the program, companies followed a similar pattern.[112] In consultation with a Committee representative, a company would work out a PFP.[113] The vice president of the United States and the company's officer or representative would then sign the plan in the presence of the president of the United States in a public ceremony with press coverage in national, state, local, and company press (Figure 1.1).[114] In the pre-digital age, this high-profile signing and media dissemination allowed companies to establish a public image about their role in ending racial segregation, ending racial discrimination, and creating equal employment opportunity for people of color. Corporations benefitted by being rewarded with Certificates of Merit from the government, potential opportunities to enter into government contracts, and goodwill from Black workers and minority organizations such as the NAACP.[115]

Plans for Progress varied from company to company in terms of the details of the plans, but with few exceptions, most followed the basic template that Lockheed established.[116] In addition to concrete plans for recruitment and employment, common components included condemning discrimination in all phases of the company's personnel policies, particularly in training and education programs; stating the company's intention to take action to recruit minority applicants for employment, training, and promotion; promising to disseminate the company's equal opportunity policies to company personnel and recruitment sources; and providing some detail about how these commitments would be implemented, including by filing confidential progress reports with the Committee over time.[117]

FIGURE 1.1 Signing ceremony for Plans for Progress, program of President's Committee on Equal Employment Opportunity. Photograph by Abbie Rowe, 1962. National Park Service/John F. Kennedy Presidential Library and Museum

COMPLAINT PROCESSING FOR RECRUITMENT

The Committee used its complaints program to convince companies to join the PFP program, making the process a recruitment tool for the program rather than a regulatory mechanism for compliance. In the push to recruit companies to join PFP, the Committee made clear that it did not require companies to hire Black people and other people of color, but that its goal was to "create open conditions in which all qualified applicants will be fully and fairly considered."[118] The Committee's enforcement was therefore toothless against participating companies' strategies to create PFP without actually providing employment opportunities.

In April 1962, the vice president, who was also the chairman of the Committee, the secretary of labor, Authur Goldberg, and assistant secretary of labor, Jerry R. Holleman, presented a report to the president covering the first nine months of the Committee's operations from April 1961 to January 1962. Included with the report was a supplemental statement covering complaints the Committee handled between April 1961 and March 1962. The statement showed that the Committee received 1,850 complaints in its first year.[119] Of those complaints, it carried only 215 to completion and took corrective action with only about one in every ten complaints it received.[120] The report declared that:

> Although substantial progress has been made in the first year, we necessarily have devoted considerable effort to laying the groundwork for even more effective programs in the years ahead ... [we] are now prepared not only to process complaints more quickly but also to develop more effective affirmative action programs in the field of equal employment opportunity.[121]

The report then listed what it labeled as "significant developments" in the first nine months, including, "[a]ffirmative steps for insuring equal opportunity have been taken by a sizable number of business firms either through the PFP program or as a result of complaints filed with the Committee."[122] However, the report continued, "it is difficult if not impossible to measure progress in this field in terms of numbers of percentages ... real progress is shown, however, in minority employment trends, affirmative actions taken and significant 'breakthroughs' in some fields of work."[123]

The report suggested that having companies join PFP was a major goal for the Committee. Some companies joined without being recruited, while others signed up for PFP after employees complained about discrimination. Joining PFP was a signal of cooperation by a company. Indeed, in July 1961, Jerry Holleman, executive vice chairman of the Committee told the Industrial Relations Research Association that the Committee's goal was to quietly investigate complaints in order to get companies to sign up for PFP.[124] According to historian Nancy MacLean, the program "left it up to the discriminator to decide how much and what kind of compliance there will be with the law."[125]

By October 1963, which was about two and a half years into the Committee's existence, it had received 2,111 complaints about companies discriminating against people of color in violation of the executive order.[126] Most complaints were closed within ninety days. Committee staff dismissed some complaints for procedural reasons, such as whether the company complained of was a government contractor, and what agencies the company held contracts with.[127] Once the Committee confirmed the agencies involved, it required the contracting agencies to process the complaint within sixty days from receipt "or within such additional time as may be allowed by the executive Vice Chairman for good cause shown."[128] The Committee staff and the agency investigated and worked with the company to cooperate, which often meant producing a PFP.[129] For example, a complaint that a Virginia textile company racially discriminated in promotions led to an investigation by the Committee.[130] The company thereafter came up with a PFP to open its training programs to Black employees and establish contracts with historically Black colleges and universities (HBCUs) for referral.[131]

There were very few exceptions when the Committee took additional steps to address a complaint beyond working with a company to come up with its own PFP. Two exceptions worth noting, however, were complaints involving Comet Rice Mills, Inc. and Danly Machine Specialties, Inc. The Committee barred both companies from receiving new government contracts until they provided reports on their employment practices.[132] While the executive order also gave the Committee the power to take away existing contracts, it did not bar either company from future contracts.[133] However, both companies immediately complied by providing employment information and promising to provide information that was akin to a PFP. The Committee subsequently lifted the bar for Comet within two weeks and for Danly within a month.[134] Another exception was the case of an unnamed North Carolina contractor who did not comply with the executive order.[135] The Committee required the contractor to submit employment reports as it would have if it had signed up for PFP and, upon receiving those reports, subsequently lifted its ban on future government contracts.[136]

Outside of these exceptional cases, which generated minimal short-term inconveniences of submitting demographic information to the Committee, sanctions and penalties were rare. Some civil rights advocates at the time referred to the executive order as a "sleeping giant lying in the money it controls."[137]

PLANS FOR PROGRESS LACKING IN PROGRESS

General Motors provides an example of a PFP company that used the fact that it joined the PFP program as license to foreclose any inquiry into racial discrimination at the company. In December 1962, the NAACP's Leonard Carter pointed out that General Motors had used being a part of the PFP program "as grounds for refusing to disclose information that would document and substantiate [the NAACP's] claim of discrimination in its Kansas City plants."[138] The Kansas Commission on Civil Rights had requested a breakdown of the company's entire workforce in its Kansas offices to show a pattern of discrimination, and the company had refused to provide that information because it was part of PFP.[139] The NAACP was concerned that by withholding this information, General Motors was using its PFP participation as a coverup for egregious discrimination.[140]

Despite situations like this, the government continued to cheer companies on insofar as they joined the program. In December 1963, a year after General Motors refused to disclose information to the Kansas Commission on Civil Rights, it was clear that the fanfare around the PFP program exceeded actual improvement in employment opportunities for people of color.

When now-President Johnson made a statement at a meeting about the status of the program in December 1963, his comments were largely conclusory. He acknowledged that while "114 large firms already have ... PFP" and that "another signing session [was to] be held on January 22, probably at the White House ... reports from 90 companies indicate sizable increases in the number of non-white salaried employees ... but [there was] still ... a long way to go."[141] The president provided no specific numbers, nor did he quantify the meaning of "sizable increases."[142] After the meeting, Secretary of Labor W. Willard Wiriz told reporters that the president's talk was "low-keyed," but that his message was clear enough: "The job can be done."[143] By "low-keyed," Wiriz was probably acknowledging that the talk was vague and that the president's conclusion was far from clear in establishing that meaningful progress had been made.

An investigation of twenty-four companies in response to a report issued by the Southern Regional Council, a nonprofit organization established to promote racial equality in the Southern United States, found that "except for a handful of companies, Plans for Progress [was] largely meaningless."[144]

Most of the progress made toward the training and hiring of racial minorities was spearheaded by companies that had formal employee complaints of discrimination to which they had to respond. But even among those companies, progress was minimal.[145] While companies were apt to highlight and talk about their training programs, many did not hire minority trainees.[146] A report on Lockheed's four plants in Georgia, California, and New Jersey showed that while there was some increase in Black employment, "the numerical changes ... in particular job categories were small."[147] Still, Vice President Johnson hailed Lockheed as an exemplar, stating that "the changes [were] significant and extremely important as demonstrations of what [could] be done."[148]

The Committee tried to paint an optimistic picture. In its progress reports, it claimed that Lockheed's Plan for Progress had led to an increase in Black employment by "26 percent in six months."[149] Another Committee progress report for PFP companies in general claimed that jobs held by people of color increased from 3.4 percent to 6.7 percent between May and December 1961, and "more than 2,000 new jobs were filled by non-whites, twice the number that would have gone to them under the old hiring ratio."[150] However, statistics from other sources did not paint such a positive picture. A 1963 report in the *Negro Heritage* explained that Black people in metropolitan areas suffered most from unemployment and job discrimination, even in PFP companies.[151] In 1963, the percentage of employees in PFP companies who were people of color was 5.1 percent.[152] According to economist Bernard Anderson, "[d]espite their commitment to take strong measures to advance [Black] employment," the record of PFP members "was no better than that of other government contractors" given the difficulty of trying to change racial employment practices through weak compliance enforcement by the Committee.[153] This was even though PFP companies committed to providing training and educational programs to Black workers to gain necessary skills so that those skilled workers could then be hired and promoted.

It was not until after Congress passed Title VII, which made it unlawful to discriminate on the basis of race as discussed in Section "Plans for Progress Winds Down," that there were incremental increases in the percentage of employees in PFP companies who were people of color from 5.1 in 1963 to 6.3 percent in 1964, 7 percent in 1965, and 9.3 percent in 1966.[154] Despite Title VII, of these minority employees, those in white-collar positions comprised only 1.5 percent in 1963, 2.4 percent in 1964, 2.8 percent in 1965, and 4 percent in 1966. This means that, despite tiny amounts of progress, most people of color were still hired as low-wage workers in companies. And, in fact, the Equal Employment Opportunity Commission (EEOC), which Congress established to enforce Title VII,[155] found that in white-collar jobs such as in the banking industry, PFP companies had "substantially lower" racial minorities than companies that did not sign up for PFP.[156] In remarks at the 1967 PFP conference, former chairman of the EEOC, Steven N. Shulman, used data from EEO-1 forms that the government required companies to submit to the EEOC, to show that PFP companies were not ahead of the nation in their employment of Black people.[157] In 1967, 25 percent or one out of four PFP companies employed less than 3 percent Black people in their entire workforces.[158]

Despite the limited progress made, some scholars have credited the PFP program with creating real opportunities leading to the hiring of Black people in large companies.[159] For many companies, the hiring of Black people was unprecedented and perhaps it is worth celebrating the PFP's creation of opportunity for even minimal progress. The reality, however, is much more complicated. Legal scholar and former Columbia Law School Dean Michael Sovern has argued that there is no way to prove that miniscule gains attributed to the PFP program occurred as a result of it, given exogenous factors that likely had an effect on these changes, including the Committee's pressure on companies that had formal employment complaints as well as pressure from Black employees through boycotts and threats of boycotts.[160]

The civil rights movement was also in full swing at this time, which inevitably had an impact on institutions and the Black experience in American institutions.[161] Sociopolitical forces had an impact on the condition of people of color outside of the PFP program. Civil rights activists used demonstrations, protests, sit-ins, and boycotts to make demands of corporations to hire more Black people in nonmenial positions and to train them for promotion.[162] The movement had a major role in pressuring companies to widen the previously minimal job opportunities available to Black people and other racial minorities to "encompass every level, from apprentice to foreman to the executive suite."[163] The president of a boycotted bank reported that his competitors privately encouraged him to fight Black demonstrations but publicly supported the need for increased integration and, indeed, hired additional Black people to show their interest in equal employment.[164]

Aside from the lack of true racial progress, including placement in skilled and white-collar positions, some PFP companies also failed to comply with the actual terms of their own plans. For example, some companies failed to comply with the limited requirement to post job opportunities so that people of color would have access to them and establish broader sources of recruitment for Black people, as their plans had stated.[165] Without meaningful accountability, PFP plans were simply plans that were written and publicized – not necessarily adhered to.

Even when companies complied with their plans, they often did so in a perfunctory manner. For example, to comply with a plan in which a company stated that it would contact employment-oriented minority organizations to make connections to potentially hire people of color, the company would simply send a form letter informing the organization that the company was an equal opportunity employer, or request that the organization refer a "highly skilled applicant" within a day or week, which could be challenging or even impossible.[166] Companies also failed to provide the Committee with timely and detailed statistical data on their progress toward equal employment.[167] These forms of perfunctory compliance occurred even though some companies hired personnel to manage their PFP programs.[168]

The government did little to hold companies accountable for not complying with the executive order or their respective plans, partly due to a lack of desire on the government's part and partly due to its lack of manpower. The number of companies far exceeded the capacity of government equal employment opportunity specialists.[169] Visits to ensure compliance were infrequent and follow-ups were limited.[170] The specialists also lacked time and resources to connect their efforts with those of civil rights groups working on employment programs for the communities PFP was meant to benefit, even though many plans included components that required companies to partner with those groups.[171]

PLANS FOR PROGRESS WINDS DOWN

The PFP program ended gradually because of other programs, policies, and changes in law under the administrations of Presidents Johnson and Richard Nixon. In 1963, President Johnson, who took office after Kennedy was assassinated, passed Executive Order 11246, which superseded Kennedy's Executive Order 10925.[172] While the executive orders were similar and the requirements for government contractors remained unchanged, Johnson's order abolished the Committee and assigned its role to the Labor Department's new Office of Federal Contract Compliance (OFCC).[173] From its inception, the OFCC announced that its approach was different from the *laissez-faire* approach the Committee took with the PFP program because government credibility had been established under PFP and its job was to "enforce the equal employment clause in the same way that other contract clauses are enforced."[174]

The Economic Opportunity Act (EOA) of 1964 was designed in large part to address the problems of poverty and unemployment in Black communities.[175] President Johnson's political agenda, with its focus on the War on Poverty – particularly the Job Opportunities in Business Sector Program (JOBS) program described later in this section – also likely deprioritized PFP because it took attention away from racial inequality and focused on eradicating poverty in general.[176] When Johnson first launched his War on Poverty in January 1964, establishing the War on Poverty task force, which later became the basis for the Office of Economic Opportunity (OEO), his goals were aligned with addressing racial discrimination as OEO programs included the Neighborhood Youth Corps, the Job Corps, and the New Careers program. Most of the trainees in these programs were Black.[177] However, beginning in the fall of 1965, the OEO began to falter. In September 1965, the Johnson administration's budget director, Charles L. Schultze, sent President Johnson a memo criticizing the OEO for "organizing the poor politically" and "arousing fears among the mayors" of large cities.[178] In December 1965, Congress cut the OEO's funding from the expected $4 billion to $1.8 billion.[179]

In 1968, President Johnson made another move in his declared War on Poverty by creating the National Alliance of Businessmen (NAB), which was headed by Henry Ford, the president of Ford Motor Company, and a man known for being racist and antisemitic during his lifetime.[180]

The goal of NAB was to "encourage leading employers and businessmen to hire and train the most disadvantaged citizens, known as the hard-core unemployed," through the JOBS program.[181] JOBS focused on training and transportation from low-income neighborhoods to industrial sites. The government paid employers an average of $3,500 for each low-income man trained and hired.[182] The fifteen-member NAB board included top executives from Ford, Coca-Cola, ITT, Aluminum Company of America, McDonnell-Douglas, Levi-Straus and Company, and Mobil Oil.[183]

Within a year of creating the NAB-JOBS program, 12,000 companies had pledged to create a total of 172,153 jobs for the hard-core unemployed.[184] Most of these jobs were low-level jobs and, according to some Black people at the time, not the "kinds of jobs everyone else [had]."[185] And companies were largely not interested in employing Black people beyond low-level positions.[186] This was true even of the companies that were purported exemplars in providing opportunities for racial minorities. Management scholar and former president of Morehouse College, David Thomas, and his coauthor, management scholar John Gabarro, document that efforts were not focused on the upper echelons of the three exemplar firms they studied.[187] Instead, they aimed to recruit minorities in sales or manufacturing, that is, technical jobs with little customer contact.[188]

Changes in the law also had an impact on PFP. Congress enacted Title VII of the Civil Rights Act of 1964, which prohibits discrimination on the basis of race, color, sex, national origin, and religion.[189] In passing Title VII, Congress created the EEOC to enforce the Act.[190] The EEOC's enforcement power was weak at its inception because its role was confined to investigation and reconciliation until the passage of the Equal Employment Opportunity Act of 1972, which amended Title VII to permit the EEOC to sue private employers in federal court.[191]

The passage of Title VII and a 1968 OFCC regulation requiring federal contractors "with 50 or more employees and a prime contract or a subcontract for more than $50,000" to maintain "a written affirmative action compliance program" resulted in companies establishing structures to show that they were in compliance with the law – nondiscrimination policies, recruitment systems, and diversity programs – rather than intentionally addressing the lack of employment opportunities still largely disproportionately experienced by people of color.[192]

President Nixon also influenced the direction of the PFP program. In 1969, Nixon merged the PFP program with NAB. By then, there were 441 PFP companies encompassing 9.7 million employees, of which about 10 percent were racial and ethnic minorities.[193] To Nixon, "the purposes of the two organizations [had] been related if not identical."[194] Some scholars have disagreed with Nixon's approach—and I agree with those scholars—that the programs are different because the PFP program was established to create employment opportunities for Black people of all economic classes, while the NAB-JOBS program was founded to help "the disadvantaged," which included not only low-income Black people but also other racial and ethnic minorities, ex-convicts, Vietnam veterans, and people with mental and physical disabilities.[195] While some companies participated in both programs, this merger probably created an out for companies that were not entirely interested in hiring people of color but would hire low-income individuals.[196] Indeed, as economic historian Gavin Wright's research suggests, because Nixon's approach focused solely on poverty and many Black people migrated to the Midwest and northern states during the Great Migration, OEO's policy may not have been as beneficial to Black people who left the South.[197] Labor markets in northern cities were not welcoming to low-income Black southerners with limited education, so migration often transferred poverty from the rural South to the urban North.[198]

By 1971, companies were redefining their PFP efforts. Lockheed redefined its PFP efforts to be about conducting "special training programs for the hard-core unemployed ... [and hired] 140 hard-core workers."[199] Western Electric embraced the merger of PFP with the JOBS program and treated them as one.[200] Western Electric noted that because of its participation in PFP and the JOBS program, the company had hired 7,500 unemployed and underemployed people but provided no indication of the percentage of Black people and other people of color it had hired.[201]

COMPARING PFP WITH IMAGE CONSTRUCTION AFTER 2020

While the use of race-conscious disclosures for image construction is largely a post-2020 corporate strategy, the PFP program provides a similar example and notable precedent in history. Prior to PFP, most corporations were not supportive of Black integration and were not eager to make disclosures about their integration or hiring people of color. PFP was the first-time major companies used disclosures to create a public image for themselves in relation to race. With guidance and approval from the federal government, the PFP program created a structure that allowed companies to establish a public image centered on their role in ending racial segregation and discrimination and creating equal employment opportunity for people of color, through training, hiring, promotion, funding, and outreach to HBCUs to encourage Black youth to pursue business.[202]

The PFP program and its evolution share some interesting features with post-2020 image construction. The diffusion of PFP in the 1960s and race-conscious image construction after the murder of George Floyd include the systematic disclosure of public statements about the racial composition of employees, executives, and boards, plans to hire and promote more people of color, and commitments to fund racial equity causes. Instead of a high-profile signing at the White House, companies now publicly disseminate their plans through public disclosures leveraging technological advances to reach large groups quickly and effectively, allowing them to establish a public image about their role in mitigating racial inequities. PFP, like post-2020 modes of image construction, established a system in which companies could claim participation in solving a problem as complex and as far-reaching as racial inequities created by centuries of racism, and social, economic, and racial inequality – a problem in which they were not innocent bystanders.

Another similarity is that financial and reputational benefits seem to be a motivating factor in both cases. Companies heavily weighed the financial advantages that resulted from joining PFP. Similarly, companies today are driven by reputational and financial benefits to use race-conscious disclosures to construct a race-conscious image post-2020 and to engage in race-conscious retraction when conservatives began to pushback on those disclosures. There is also a similarity between the strategy some PFP companies used to disavow claims of racial discrimination in their businesses, and the strategies used by companies today for similar reasons, as I discuss further in Chapter 2. Post-2020, companies use their public image, constructed through race-conscious disclosures, to weaken suggestions that their businesses are sources of racial bias, discrimination, or disparate impact on communities of color.

Finally, by government design, PFP morphed into the JOBS program to focus on low-income individuals and groups, and by the late 1960s and early 1970s, was no longer explicitly focused on addressing racial inequality, although it would have continued to benefit low-income minorities. Similarly, partial race-conscious retraction, discussed in depth in Chapter 5, is a process whereby race-conscious disclosures morph into a focus on everything *but* addressing racial inequality.

Despite the similarities between the PFP program and post-2020 race-conscious image construction, there are two key differences with a caveat. First, the federal government was involved in PFP, albeit on a limited basis, while with post-2020 race-conscious disclosures, companies had complete freedom to function in an unregulated milieu until the second Trump administration commenced in 2025. This freedom allowed them to craft and implement their intervention into addressing racial inequities as they deemed fit. With PFP, the government promoted the content and process of diffusing the plans. With post-2020 image construction, companies themselves promoted and diffused their race-conscious disclosures. Companies were the drafters, designers, signers, and implementers of the plan with little to no government intervention. This distinction illustrates how disclosures about race were completely subject to corporate whim, without an overseer or process of accountability. The caveat is that the Trump administration created an unprecedented monitoring of race-conscious disclosures starting in 2025, including by the use of threats to force companies to retract their post-2020 race-conscious disclosures.

Second, technological advancements have changed how companies make race-conscious disclosures or engage in race-conscious retraction because companies can now strategically place race-conscious disclosures online, in voluntary and mandatory public disclosures, and in traditional and social media, reaching millions of people at the same time.

As discussed in this chapter, the PFP program was ultimately unsuccessful in stamping out racial discrimination and inequality in companies, in part because government intervention was limited to monitoring and publicity. The lack of enforcement by the government of its own executive order was directly related to the failure of the program. While Truman's previous Executive Order 9981, banning segregation in the military a decade and a half earlier, did not concern the private sector, unlike Kennedy and his executive order, Truman put structures in place to ensure some level of success in implementing its policies. This suggests that Kennedy's administration and the Committee could have done better by implementing and enforcing the executive order. Letting companies dictate the meaning of the order was the downfall of the executive order that was meant to improve economic and social conditions for racial minorities.

It is unclear whether companies were truly motivated to make real progress happen during the civil rights movement, but the *New York Times* reported that many companies claimed to have been ready for the government to provide guidance on how to achieve true equal employment opportunity, but the government failed to do.[203] The Southern Regional Council noted that in the Atlanta area, "interpretation of the voluntary and affirmative provisions of the program [was] left to the individual signers themselves."[204] The Committee's activities were limited to recruiting, guidance, facilitating information sharing among companies, minimally monitoring progress, and publicizing participation in the plans. The Committee did little to ensure that companies executed the plans which companies characterized as "voluntary."

Lack of implementation and accountability were therefore the major downfalls of the program. PFP was unsuccessful in large part because it was symbolic from inception.[205] The government helped companies create a public image of compliance with the program, with little focus on taking meaningful action. As sociologist and legal scholar Lauren Edelman has argued, the PFP program planted seeds for symbolic compliance strategies that allowed companies to continue business as usual, while looking like they were partners in stamping out racial discrimination in employment.[206] A regulatory scheme should require companies to fully embrace their roles in addressing racial inequality if they choose to make race-conscious disclosures, and enjoy the benefits that accrue from doing so, although the benefits may be smaller than if they are allowed to use race-conscious disclosures in completely unrestricted ways.

As I argue later in the book, a federal government that is interested in advancing racial progress, and other institutions and actors, have an important role to play in regulating the impact of corporate words. Despite the failures of PFP and the reality of a Trump administration, this book argues that the government should have a larger role in regulating contemporary race-conscious disclosures and retraction. Strong government regulation of image construction has the potential to be beneficial, but it must try to avoid the pitfalls of the PFP program by ensuring enforcement and accountability.

NOTES

1. Eric Eustace Williams, William A. Darity, Jr., and Colin A. Palmer, *Capitalism & Slavery*. 3rd ed. (Chapel Hill: University of North Carolina Press, 2021).
2. Williams et al., *Capitalism & Slavery*; Padraic X. Scanlan, *Slave Empire: How Slavery Built Modern Britain* (London: Robinson, 2020).
3. Scanlan, *Slave Empire*; Paul Finkelman, "The American Suppression of the African Slave Trade: Lessons on Legal Change, Social Policy, and Legislation," *Akron Law Review* 42, no. 2 (2009): 431–68.
4. Scanlan, *Slave Empire*; Williams et al., *Capitalism and Slavery*.
5. Isabel Wilkerson, *The Warmth of Other Suns: The Epic Story of America's Great Migration*. 1st ed. (New York: Vintage, 2010).
6. Andrew Edmund Kersten, *Race, Jobs, and the War: The FEPC in the Midwest, 1941–46* (Urbana: University of Illinois Press, 2007).
7. Ibid.
8. Ibid.
9. Ibid.
10. Federal Security Agency, *Second Annual Report*, 1941, 10.
11. Kersten, *Race, Jobs, and the War*.
12. Ibid.
13. Ibid.

14. Philip A. Randolph to Walter White, March 18, 1941.
15. Philip A. Randolph to Mrs. Franklin D. Roosevelt, June 5, 1941, Franklin D. Roosevelt Presidential Library & Museum; Philip A. Randolph to Fiorella H. LaGuardia, June 5, 1941, Office of Civilian Defense, National Archives, Identifier 7859715.
16. Letter from Randolph to Mrs. Roosevelt; Memorandum of Robert P. Patterson, Secretary of War, June 13, 1942.
17. Merl Elwyn Reed, *Seedtime for the Modern Civil Rights Movement: The President's Committee on Fair Employment Practice, 1941–1946* (Baton Rouge: Louisiana State University Press, 1991).
18. Memorandum from Robert P. Patterson, Secretary of War, to Mrs. Franklin D. Roosevelt, June 23, 1941.
19. American Bar Association, "What Is an Executive Order?," January 25, 2021, www.americanbar.org/groups/public_education/publications/teaching-legal-docs/what-is-an-executive-order-/.
20. Ibid.
21. Ibid.
22. Ibid.
23. "Executive Order 8802 of June 25, 1941, Reaffirming Policy of Full Participation in the Defense Program by All Persons, Regardless of Race, Creed, Color, or National Origin, and Directing Certain Action in Furtherance of Said Policy," *Code of Federal Regulations*, title 3 (1941); Unsigned Letter Eleanor Roosevelt to Philip A. Randolph from Campobello Island, June 26, 1941.
24. "Executive Order 8801 of June 24, 1941, Exemption of Archie W. Davis From Compulsory Retirement for Age," *Code of Federal Regulations*, title 3 (1941).
25. Reed, *Seedtime*.
26. Lawrence W. Cramer to Mrs. Franklin D. Roosevelt, August 20, 1942.
27. Reed, *Seedtime*.
28. Sidney Milkis and Katherine Rader, "The March on Washington Movement, the Fair Employment Practices Committee, and the Long Quest for Racial Justice," *Studies in American Political Development* 38, no. 1 (2024): 16–35.
29. Ibid.
30. Ibid.
31. "Executive Order 9981 of July 6, 1948, Establishing the President's Committee on Equality of Treatment and Opportunity in the Armed Services," *Code of Federal Regulations*, title 32 (1948).
32. Ibid. It was not until the passage of Title II of the Civil Rights Act of 1964 that other establishments like hotels, motels, and restaurants were desegregated; Gina-Gail S. Fletcher and H. Timothy Lovelace, Jr., "Corporate Racial Responsibility," *Columbia Law Review* 124, no. 2 (2024).
33. Richard M. Dalfiume, "The Fahy Committee and Desegregation of the Armed Forces," *The Historian* 31, no. 1 (1968): 1–20.
34. Louis Lauhtier, "Truman Goal Disputes Bradley: President Envisions End of Segregation; Royall Says Chief Didn't Flout Order," *Negro Press*, August 3, 1948, Newspaper Clippings Files, 1948–1950, National Archives.
35. "Balto Afro-American, Truman Has Mind of Own," *Negro Press*, July 31 (n.d.), Newspaper Clippings Files, 1948–1950, National Archives.
36. Ernest K. Lindley, "Equal Rights in the Armed Services," week of May 22, 1950, National Archives, Letters on Final Report, Record Group 220: Records of Temporary Committees, Commissions, and Boards.

37. Robert Frederick Burk, *The Eisenhower Administration and Black Civil Rights* (Knoxville: University of Tennessee Press, 1984).
38. Ibid.
39. 347 U.S. 483 (1954).
40. Aldon D. Morris, *The Origins of the Civil Rights Movement: Black Communities Organizing for Change* (New York: Free Press, 1984).
41. Telegram to the Governor of Arkansas in Response to His Request for Assurance Regarding His Action at Little Rock, 1 Pub. Papers 659 (Sept. 5, 1957); see also W. H. Lawrence, "Eisenhower 'Disappointed' By Impasse at Little Rock," *New York Times*, September 20, 1957.
42. Lawrence, "Eisenhower 'Disappointed'."
43. Henry Hampton and Steve Fayer, *Voices of Freedom: An Oral History of the Civil Rights Movement from the 1950s through the 1980s* (New York: Bantam Books, 1990).
44. Ibid.
45. Ibid.
46. Morris, *Origins of the Civil Rights Movement*.
47. Michael J. Klarman, "How Brown Changed Race Relations: The Backlash Thesis," *Journal of American History* 81, no. 1 (1994): 81–118. The first bus boycott occurred in Baton Rouge, Louisiana, in 1953.
48. William Henry Chafe, *Civilities and Civil Rights: Greensboro, North Carolina, and the Black Struggle for Freedom* (Oxford: Oxford University Press, 1980).
49. "Executive Order 10925 of March 6, 1961, Establishing the President's Committee on Equal Employment Opportunity," *Code of Federal Regulations*, title 41 (1961).
50. Randall L. Patton, *Lockheed, Atlanta, and the Struggle for Racial Integration* (Athens: University of Georgia Press, 2019), 52.
51. Susan E. Reed, *The Diversity Index: The Alarming Truth about Diversity in Corporate America ... and What Can Be Done about It* (Seattle: Amazon Publishing, 2011), 70.
52. Ibid.
53. "Executive Order 9808 of December 5, 1946, Establishing the President's Committee on Civil Rights," National Archives, Harry S. Truman Library Museum.
54. Reed, *Diversity Index*, 69.
55. Jennifer Delton, *Racial Integration in Corporate America, 1940–1990* (Cambridge: Cambridge University Press, 2009), 178.
56. Reed, *Diversity Index*, 69.
57. Ibid.
58. Ibid.
59. Ibid.
60. Patton, *Lockheed*, 50.
61. Albert Riley, "Lockheed Given $1 Billion Order Providing 5,000 Jobs at Marietta: Jet Transport Program May Last for 15 Years," *Atlanta Constitution*, March 14, 1961, 1.
62. Reed, *Diversity Index*, 70; Lockheed, *Twenty-Ninth Annual Report* (December 25, 1960), 1–2.
63. Reed, *Diversity Index*, 70.
64. Ibid.
65. Lockheed, *Thirtieth Annual Report* (December 31, 1961), 1.
66. Ibid., 2.
67. Ibid.
68. Ibid.
69. Marion Gaines, "Georgians Hail Boost in Economy," *Atlanta Constitution*, March 14, 1961, 1.

70. Peter Braestrup, "Lockheed Signs Equal-Jobs Pact: Agrees to a Plan Advancing Negro Opportunities," *New York Times*, May 26, 1961.
71. Ibid.
72. "Re-examination of Lockheed Plant Contract Urged," *Atlanta Daily World*, April 2, 1961; Judson MacLaury, "President Kennedy's E.O. 10925: Seedbed of Affirmative Action," *Federal History* 48 (2010): 42–57.
73. "U.S. to Act to End Segregation at Lockheed; Firms with Gov't. Contracts to Face Similar Move," *Atlanta Daily World*, April 12, 1961.
74. Ibid.
75. Patton, *Lockheed*, 89.
76. Ibid., 83.
77. Hugh Davis Graham, *The Civil Rights Era: Origins and Development of National Policy* (New York: Oxford University Press, 1990), 51–52.
78. Troutman was President Kennedy's roommate at Harvard Law School. Kennedy and Johnson asked Troutman to spearhead the Plans for Progress program to see if the major companies of American industry and the largest employers would be onboard to address employment discrimination against Black people. Robert Troutman Jr., oral history interview, February 2, 1965, transcript, JFK Presidential Library, 128–129.
79. Ibid.
80. Lockheed Aircraft Corporation and the President's Committee on Equal Employment Opportunity, "Joint Statement on 'Plan for Progress,'" undated, Harris Wofford Files, Box 8, JFK Library, 1.
81. Ibid.
82. Ibid.
83. Ibid., emphasis added.
84. Ibid.
85. "Lockheed Pledges Job Equality at Plants," *Atlanta Daily World*, May 26, 1961.
86. Ibid.
87. Ibid.
88. Ibid; "Lockheed Ending Race Bias, Says U.S.: Marietta Plant Taking Steps, Johnson Says After Meeting," *Atlanta Constitution*, May 3, 1961; A. H. Raskin, "Negro Makes Job Gain in South Under Initial Drive at Lockheed: Negroes Gaining in Lockheed Jobs," *New York Times*, June 18, 1961.
89. "Advanced Copy of Statement to be Presented by Mr. R. J. Cordiner, General Electric Company," July 12, 1961, Harris Wofford Files, Box 8, JFK Library, 1.
90. Douglas Aircraft Company Inc., and the President's Committee on Equal Employment Opportunity, "Joint Statement 'Equal Employment Opportunity Plan for Progress,'" July 12, 1961, Harris Wofford Files, Box 8, JFK Library, 1.
91. "Major American Firms Sign Plans for Progress," *Atlanta Daily World*, May 10, 1964, A1. One example was American Motors, whose chief executive officer reported that the company joined to focus "the problem of equal employment opportunity for our people …. Plans for Progress has been good because it has made us concentrate on the problem of minority employment"; see National Industrial Conference Board, *Company Experience with Negro Employment*, vol. 1 (New York: National Industrial Conference Board, 1966), 58.
92. Delton, *Racial Integration*, 178.
93. Frank Dobbin, *Inventing Equal Opportunity* (Princeton: Princeton University Press, 2009), 49.
94. U.S. President, Proposed Regulation, "Plans for Progress Program, 1965," *Federal Register* 30, no. 183 (September 22, 1965): Section 4-12.5119-1(a).

95. "Joint Statement on 'Equal Employment Opportunity Plan for Progress,'" North American Aviation, Inc., and the President's Committee on Equal Employment Opportunity, July 12, 1961, Harris Wofford Files, Box 8, JFK Library, 1.
96. Edelman, *Working Law*, 109.
97. Ibid.
98. President's Committee on Equal Employment Opportunity, *Report to the President*, 6; "Executive Order 10925," Sec. 103.
99. "Executive Order 10925," Sec. 312(f).
100. Ibid; Peter Braestrup, "Lockheed Drafts Equal-Jobs Plan: Federal Aides Begin Talks with Aircraft Concern," *New York Times*, May 14, 1961, 76.
101. "Executive Order 10925," Sec. 312(f).
102. Ibid.
103. Sovern, *Legal Restraints*, 105–127.
104. Dobbin, *Inventing Equal Opportunity*, 73.
105. Alvin Spivak, "Eight Defense Contract Sign Non-Discrimination Government Job Agreements: President Kennedy Hails Ceremony as a Historic Step," *Atlanta Daily World*, July 13, 1961, 1.
106. "33 More Firms Pledge Equal Employment Plan," 1.
107. President's Committee on Equal Employment Opportunity, *Report to the President*, 2.
108. Ibid.
109. Alexander and Doriot, *Management of Racial Integration*, 102.
110. Ibid.
111. Plans for Progress continued to diffuse across companies in the late 1960s through meetings and conferences, but also through advertisements in trade journals. E. G. Mattison, Advisory Council on Plans for Progress, and President's Committee on Equal Opportunity Employment, *Implementing Plans for Progress: A Selection of Resumes of Experiences of Plans for Progress Companies in Implementing Their Programs--Intended for Use by Other Interested Plans for Progress Companies* (Washington, DC: Advisory Council on Plans for Progress, June 1964). For example, one advertisement stated that 350 corporations had formed Plans for Progress, a voluntary organization, willing to help companies turn their unskilled labor to skilled labor: "How long does it take to train a man to be a welder, machinist, bookkeeper, draftsman, assembler, molder? A few months." "The Skilled Labor Shortage. It's Amazing How Fast You Could Change It," *Business Management* 31, no. 6 (March 1967).
112. Sovern, *Legal Restraints*, 117.
113. Ibid; Alexander and Doriot, *Management of Racial Integration*, 19.
114. Sovern, *Legal Restraints*, 117; "33 More Firms Pledge Equal Employment Plan."
115. Graham, *Civil Rights Era*, 52.
116. Sovern, *Legal Restraints*, 117.
117. Ibid; Other examples include, "Joint Statement on 'Equal Employment Opportunity Plan for Progress,'" The Boeing Company and the President's Committee on Equal Employment Opportunity, July 12, 1961, Harris Wofford Files, Box 8, JFK Library, 1; "Joint Statement on 'Equal Employment Opportunity Plan for Progress,'" The Martin Company and the President's Committee on Equal Employment Opportunity, July 12, 1961, Harris Wofford Files, Box 8, JFK Library, 1; "Advanced Copy of Statement by Mr. R. J. Cordiner," 1. This is an example of a format that deviates from the Lockheed plan; Peter Braestrup, "U.S. Panel Split Over Negro Jobs: Johnson Committee Tries to Reconcile 'Voluntary' and 'Compulsory' Programs; Johnson's Committee on Jobs for Negroes Is Divided over a 'Voluntary' Program: N.A.A.C.P. Fears Drive May Falter

but Vice President's Aides and Labor Secretary Are Untroubled by Dispute 65 Per Cent Settled Finds Value in Threats Decries Integration 'Fuss' May Discuss Proposal Publicity Value Stressed Asks Data on Complaints," *New York Times*, June 18, 1962, 1. The *New York Times* described General Electric's plan as "unspecific and little more than a polite response to the panel's invitation to cooperate." Many companies had never examined their statistics until signing up for Plans for Progress. The availability of statistics not previously available was surely an advantage of the Plans for Progress Program. For example, the Michigan Bell Telephone Company signed a Plan for Progress in June 1962. The company's president recalled that "top management thought [it was] doing well … then the statistical reports prepared under the Plan for Progress began to come in. These shocked us." National Industrial Conference Board, *Company Experience*, 19.

118. Ibid., 12.
119. This number was lower than the combined total number of 2,095 complaints received by the previous President's Committee on Government Contracts, and President's Committee on Government Employment Policy that were in existence from 1953 to 1960, and 1955 to 1960 respectively. "'Significant Progress' Is Johnson Note," *Atlanta Daily World*, April 11, 1962, 2.
120. In other cases, the Committee dismissed complaints as being without cause, lacking in jurisdiction, or failing to provide necessary information. Ibid.
121. Ibid.
122. Ibid.
123. Ibid.
124. Dobbin, *Inventing Equal Opportunity*, 48.
125. Nancy MacLean, *Freedom Is Not Enough: The Opening of the American Workplace* (Cambridge, MA: Harvard University Press, 2008).
126. Edelman, *Working Law*, 109.
127. Sovern, *Legal Restraints*, 107.
128. In Sovern's discussion, he relies on 41 CFR section 60-1.24(c) from 1964. Ibid., 108.
129. Ibid., 110.
130. President's Committee on Equal Employment Opportunity, *Report to the President*, 11.
131. Ibid.
132. John D. Pomfret, "2 Concerns Draw Job Bias Penalty: U.S. Bars Companies from Contracts Until They Halt 'Discriminatory' Hiring 2 Concerns Face Contract Ban by U.S. over Hiring Practices," *New York Times*, April 18, 1962, 1.
133. Ibid.
134. Special to the New York Times, "U.S. Lifts Charge of Hiring Bias: Comet Rice Mills Is Eligible for Federal Contracts," *New York Times*, May 3, 1962, 22; Special to the New York Times, "Federal Ban Lifted on Machine Concern," *New York Times*, May 19, 1962, 27.
135. President's Committee on Equal Employment Opportunity, *Report to the President*, 11.
136. Ibid., 11.
137. Richard P. Nathan, *Jobs & Civil Rights: The Role of the Federal Government in Promoting Equal Opportunity in Employment and Training*, Clearinghouse Publication No. 16, 1969, 141.
138. "Johnson Urged to Probe Job Bias in General Motors," *Atlanta Daily World*, December 2, 1962, 5.
139. Ibid.
140. Ibid.

141. "Progress Has Been Made, but Negro Has Long Way to Go, President States," *Atlanta Daily World*, December 25, 1963, 3.
142. Ibid.
143. Ibid.
144. John D. Pomfret, "Negro-Job Pledge Is Found Flouted: 24 Branches of Big Companies Are Studied," *New York Times*, April 17, 1963, 1.
145. Armand J. Thieblot, *The Negro in the Banking Industry* (Philadelphia: University of Pennsylvania Press, 1970), 140.
146. Ibid.
147. "Lockheed Increasing Racial Opportunities," *Atlanta Daily World*, January 27, 1962, 1.
148. Ibid.
149. "U.S. Plan Speeding Gain for Negro Jobs," *New York Times*, January 26, 1962, 14.
150. "Job Equality Drive Spurs Negro Hiring," *New York Times*, February 7, 1962, 40.
151. Sylvestre C. Watkins, *Negro Heritage* (Reston, VA: Watkins, 1963), 23.
152. Ibid.
153. Bernard E. Anderson, *The Negro in The Public Utility Industries*, Report No. 10 (Philadelphia, PA: University of Pennsylvania Press, 1970), 203.
154. President's Committee on Equal Employment Opportunity, *Plans for Progress: A Report, January 1966–August 1967*, 27.
155. Edelman, *Working Law*, 49.
156. Thieblot, *Negro in the Banking Industry*, 140.
157. Nathan, *Jobs & Civil Rights*, 135.
158. Ibid.
159. Dobbin, *Investing Equal Opportunity*, 49; Edelman, *Working Law*, 110.
160. Sovern, *Legal Restraints*, 119.
161. Silberman discusses how demonstrations in Birmingham represented a major event in the history of race relations, and their impact on Black employment as Black people protested for jobs. The article also documents the dire experiences of Black households with significant unemployment and abysmal wages. Charles E. Silberman, "The Businessman and the Negro," *Management Review* 52 (1963): 17–20.
162. Graham, *Civil Rights Era*, 70.
163. Sovern, *Legal Restraints*, 119. This was certainly the criterion for success that the Southern Regional Council attempted to study in 1963. Its focus was to examine whether the employment of Black people and other minorities had increased, and whether they were being placed in nontraditional job categories. Southern Regional Council, *Atlanta Survey*, 2.
164. Alexander and Doriot, *The Management of Racial Integration in Business*, 8.
165. Pomfret, "Negro-Job Pledge," 1.
166. Nathan, *Jobs & Civil Rights*, 139.
167. Anderson, *The Negro in The Public Utility Industries*, 201.
168. This is an example of the responsibilities of a "fair employment coordinator." National Industrial Conference Board, *Company Experience*, 22.
169. Nathan, *Jobs & Civil Rights*, 140.
170. Ibid.
171. Ibid.
172. Sovern, *Legal Restraints*, 104.
173. Ibid.
174. Civil rights leaders dismissed OFCC's approach as "tough talk from the top unsupported by a willingness or determination to apply the necessary sanctions." Nathan, *Jobs & Civil Rights*, 103.

175. Economic Opportunity Act, Pub. L. No. 88-452, 78 Stat. 508 (1964).
176. Allen J. Matusow, *The Unraveling of America: A History of Liberalism in the 1960s* (Athens, GA: University of Georgia Press, 1984), 244.
177. Delton, *Racial Integration*, 228.
178. Matusow, *Unraveling of America*, 250.
179. Matusow, *Unraveling of America*, 251.
180. Delton, *Racial Integration*, 229; A. James Rubin. "The Dark Legacy of Henry Ford's Anti-Semitism," *Washington Post*, October 10, 2014, www.washingtonpost.com/national/religion/the-dark-legacy-of-henry-fords-anti-semitism-commentary/2014/10/10/c95b7df2-509d-11e4-877c-335b53ffe736_story.html.
181. Delton, *Racial Integration*, 229.
182. Ibid.
183. Ibid.
184. Robert A. Wright, "From Overalls to the Attaché Case: A Symbol of Negro Goals in Business," *New York Times*, January 6, 1969, 71.
185. Ibid.
186. Ibid.
187. David A. Thomas and John J. Gabarro, *Breaking Through: The Making of Minority Executives in Corporate America* (Boston, MA: Harvard Business School Press, 1999).
188. Ibid.
189. Title VII of the Civil Rights Act, 42 U.S.C. §§ 2000e – 2000e17 (as amended).
190. Edelman, *Working Law*, 49.
191. Ibid; Ruth G. Shaeffer, *Nondiscrimination in Employment: Changing Perspectives, 1963–1972* (New York: The Conference Board, 1973), 6.
192. During meetings sponsored by NAM and Plans for Progress, OFCC representatives explained that appropriate steps to comply might include special recruiting and training programs, which are now generally known as diversity programs. Shaeffer, *Nondiscrimination in Employment*, 11; Dobbin, *Inventing Equal Opportunity*, 73.
193. Richard Nixon, "Statement on the Merger of the National Alliance of Businessmen and Plans for Progress, June 13, 1969," in *The American Presidency Project*, eds. Gerhard Peters and John T. Woolley, www.presidency.ucsb.edu/node/239441; Theodore L. Cross, *Black Capitalism: Strategy for Business in the Ghetto* (New York: Atheneum, 1974), 250.
194. Nixon, *Statement on the Merger of the National Alliance of Businessmen and Plans for Progress*.
195. Delton, *Racial Integration*, 231.
196. For example, Philip Morris participated in both Plans for Progress and NAB. Philip Morris Incorporated, *1968 Annual Report*, 7.
197. Gavin Wright, *Sharing the Prize: The Economics of the Civil Rights Revolution in the American South* (Cambridge, MA: Harvard University Press, 2018).
198. Ibid.
199. Cross, *Black Capitalism*, 244.
200. Western Electric, *1971 Annual Report*, 10.
201. Ibid.
202. President's Committee on Equal Employment Opportunity, *Plans for Progress: A Report*, 11.
203. Braestrup, U.S. Panel Split over Negro Jobs, *New York Times*, 2.
204. Southern Regional Council, *Atlanta Survey*, 15.
205. Edelman, *Working Law*.
206. Ibid.

2

Race-Conscious Disclosures, Image, and Reputation

This chapter argues that corporate words and actions about race are directed toward building reputational capital and managing reputational risk. The chapter centers on how corporations used public statements about race, which I refer to as "race-conscious disclosures" to build reputational capital between 2020 and 2024. It also addresses the distinction between racial progress in employment as defined by corporations, versus true racial progress that gives people of color agency, mobility, power, and decision-making authority.

The summer of 2020 was the stimulus that aided corporations to build a "race-conscious image." Corporations began to experience pressure from shareholders and stakeholders, including customers, employees, and the public to take steps to show their support for Black communities and other communities of color. Companies began to make race-conscious disclosures systematically in order to create race-conscious public images that would benefit them at the time.

Race-conscious disclosures are multifaceted. They include public declarations regarding a company-wide or societal need to take steps toward tackling racial inequality; disclosures regarding the racial compositions of boards of directors, executives, and employees; and pledges to hire, retain, and promote people of color by a certain time, to fund minority-owned businesses and nonprofits that address race equity or serve communities of color, and to racially diversify corporate suppliers. Companies made race-conscious disclosures to derive increased benefits from customers, prospective employees, employees, and shareholders who favor companies that say something and appear to do something about racial discrimination and racial inequality.

In this chapter, I examine Amazon and Chevron as case studies to illustrate how companies constructed their race-conscious public images between 2020 and 2024. I chose these companies for a few reasons. Amazon is an obvious choice to examine this phenomenon. It is the second largest private employer in the United States – employing 1.54 million people in 2023.[1] In 2022, at least 72 percent of Americans shopped at Amazon, which means that the company has a large influence on consumers.[2] Amazon also has a large global footprint with more than 200 million Prime members worldwide in 2024.[3]

By contrast, Chevron may not seem like an obvious choice, but its operations have implications for environmental justice, making it an ideal case for examining race-conscious image construction, particularly because of growing public awareness about the relationship between environmental hazards and environmental justice.[4] Viewed together, Amazon and Chevron have a combined revenue of over $700 billion, with activities that touch issues of racial, social, economic, and environmental justice.[5]

Methodologically, I rely on press releases, website statements, voluntary sustainability and diversity reports, 10-K annual reports,[6] shareholder proposals, and news articles published between 2018 and 2024 to tell the story of how both companies set about constructing their public images using race-conscious disclosures and then used those constructed public images to make it seem like the issues of racism, racial discrimination, and the disproportionate impact of "business as usual" on communities of color were unimportant or resolved.

CONSTRUCTING A RACE-CONSCIOUS PUBLIC IMAGE

Race-conscious image construction is about a company's use of public statements to develop a perception that the company is taking steps to tackle racial inequity. Companies constructed their race-conscious images for positive perception, and to establish or boost their reputations as entities that addressed racial inequality in the minds of shareholders, employees, potential employees, customers, other stakeholders, and the public.

To develop and maintain an image that portrays a company as one that addresses racial inequality, a firm must influence the expectations, attitudes, and feelings shareholders and stakeholders have about its focus on being racially conscious.[7] This process then translates to a positive reputation for companies. Reputation – the subjective evaluation of a firm's quality or standing on a particular dimension – is an important asset bestowed on a company by its audiences.[8] In this context, reputation involves an assessment of a company's relative status as being race-conscious.[9] The building blocks for establishing a firm's reputation starts with making consistent disclosures.[10] Shareholders and stakeholders then judge a firm's interest in attending to racial inequality based on those disclosures.

As a general matter, disclosures, or making facts or information known to a regulatory body or the public, are a staple of publicly traded companies. Public companies – whose shares are traded freely on stock exchanges – are required to periodically disclose information about their financial and operational conditions to the US Securities and Exchange Commission (SEC) – a federal government agency that regulates companies – to aid investors in making informed investment decisions.[11] Disclosures made to the SEC, which are publicly available, must not be inaccurate, false, or misleading, or a company may be subject to sanctions.[12]

Beyond regulatory mandates, however, public companies – along with private companies that do not have shareholders and are not required to make public disclosures – choose to voluntarily disclose information to the public from time to time. Companies are under pressure to meet societal and investor expectations to engage in social change, or at a minimum, show that they are responsible citizens.[13] Companies therefore make voluntary disclosures about issues such as the risks of climate change, human rights, economic inequality, philanthropy, the communities in which they operate, ethics, diversity, equity and inclusion, gender inequality, and racial inequality, among others, because they believe that these disclosures influence how they are perceived by shareholders, customers, employees, potential employees, and the public.[14]

Between 2020 and 2024, companies disclosed information about race because they wanted prospective and current employees to perceive them as attractive places to work, or for customers to view them as companies that pay attention to racial inequality – perceptions that boost talent, revenue, and profit, and have an overall positive impact on a company's financial well-being.[15]

In addition, global media, technology, shareholders, stakeholders, including employees, consumers, advocacy groups, and younger generations who tend to demand novel commitments from business, have fueled the need for corporations to be transparent.[16] One study on consumers found that they value transparency on race and ethnicity from companies.[17] Companies have internalized this expectation, adopting the belief that their stakeholders want them to be transparent and want to associate with firms that share their values. For stakeholders to know whether a firm shares their values, the firm needs to disclose information about those values. One company explained in its 2020 voluntary disclosures that, similar to disclosures about its finances and operations, disclosures about race was "material to [its] business, helpful to [its] stakeholders, and increasingly expected by investors."[18] Being known as a company that addresses racial inequality became a valuable reputation for companies in 2020.

Interviews with companies' chief sustainability officers (CSOs) and chief diversity officers (CDOs) between 2022 and 2024 reflect the importance of transparency as a business issue on par with revenue and its role in maintaining credibility with stakeholders. The CDO of one company explained that there was "[an] evolution, which is … about how you treat this the same way you treat other business problems. And so, revenue is a very important business issue, and there's a revenue top projects meeting that happens with all the people that care about that issue. And so, we started a diversity, inclusion, belonging top projects meeting. And what that allowed us to do is really say, what are these big issues, and what are we going to do about them?"[19] Another CDO expressed that "customer obsession has a lot to do with trust. And trust … is linked to transparency and disclosure of the work we were prioritizing all those years. It is important … that customers understand what we feel … was the right thing to do and the right investment." For another CDO, the point is that "communication lends credibility to the tactics people are using to tackle equity and climate change," while another said that "communication … and how information gets shared ... is really important because [it] speaks to the retention, the recruitment, and the aspect of how the company [values these issues] across the board." Finally, another CDO declared that

> these are issues that are so critical. They're not things that a company should do and check the box and then never speak about them. We need to talk about them to create ... an obligation. The public should expect us to do these things, so if we talk about them, then we're expected to do them ... we should be obligated to constantly tell our stories and prove that we are having a positive impact.

Therefore, stakeholder expectations of transparency had a major influence on the proliferation of race-conscious disclosures between 2020 and 2024.

To be sure, companies were making voluntary disclosures about race and ethnicity long before 2020. In 2016, legal scholar and sociologist Lauren Edelman's research showed how companies symbolically disclosed antidiscrimination policies to signal compliance with laws that make it illegal to discriminate on the basis of gender or race, while continuing to maintain discriminatory practices.[20] Sociologist Ellen Berrey's work similarly described in 2015 how one company disclosed diversity statements, which often includes some numerical measure of the proportional representation of minorities within a firm.[21]

What makes race-conscious disclosures after 2020 distinct from prior forms of symbolic performance by companies? Three factors. The first is the systematic way in which most American and multinational companies – public and private – made similar race-conscious disclosures. Prior to 2020, race-conscious disclosures were much more variable in content and extent. The second is a noticeable change in what companies said and how they said it. Race-conscious disclosures became less vague and more likely to target and name specific racial and ethnic groups. Prior to 2020, race-conscious disclosures were uncommon and largely relied on vague language. But the need to construct a race-conscious public image drove companies to make disclosures about specific racial and ethnic groups and the problems of racial inequality and injustice. The third shift that occurred in 2020 was moving away from making race-conscious disclosures for legal compliance and toward using them as a tool for building reputational capital to satisfy a wide range of shareholders and stakeholders. As sociologist Patricia Banks has argued in the philanthropy context, companies portrayed an image to the public to strengthen their corporate interests, and not in response to law or government pressure to address racial inequality.[22]

There was no legislation, regulation, or policy that uniformly required companies to make race-conscious disclosures. What did exist were weak government attempts in the United States to require the disclosure of information about race among other identity characteristics, and regulations in other countries requiring the disclosure of information related to sustainability, discussed further in Chapter 6.[23]

The SEC and Congress made four weak attempts between 2009 and 2021 to make disclosures related to race mandatory: (1) a 2009 regulation that requires companies

TABLE 2.1 *Race-conscious disclosures*

General statements	Statistics on racial composition	Racial targets	Philanthropy
Statements to address racial inequality, increasing racial diversity, general statements about people of color and corporate and societal racial inequality.	Racial composition of boards of directors, executives, managers, and employees.	Plans or aspirations to hire, retain, or promote people of color.	Funding minority groups and causes with focus on business transactions.

to disclose whether and how they consider diversity in their board nominations but allows firms to define diversity as broadly as they wish and does not require them to adopt a diversity policy;[24] (2) a 2020 regulation requiring human capital disclosures, which many companies interpreted to include race-conscious disclosures between 2020 and 2023; (3) a 2021 rule requiring Nasdaq-listed companies to disclose the names of two diverse board members, including one person of color, or explain why they lack diversity, which the United States Court of Appeals for the Fifth Circuit struck down in December 2024; and (4) the 2021 Environmental, Social and Governance (ESG) Disclosure Simplification Act, a bill that, if it ever became law, would require companies to disclose board and employee diversity, among other things. These attempts are weak because they were either inexplicit in their mandates of race-conscious disclosures (1–4), did not apply uniformly to all publicly traded companies (3), or are either no longer law or unlikely to become law because of political polarization (3, 4).[25]

Despite the limited reach of these attempts, as shown on Table 2.1, between 2020 and 2024, public and private companies systematically made four major types of race-conscious disclosures: (1) general statements about racial inequality, which are wide ranging and include statements about people of color, commitments to racial equity or tackling inequality that impacts racial minorities, and increasing racial diversity in a company's workforce. General statements are broadly about race and ethnicity, with companies naming racism, racial injustices, institutional racism, racial inequality, Black people, and other racial minorities; (2) statistics about past or current racial compositions of boards of directors, executives, managers, and employees; (3) racial targets, or plans to hire, retain, or promote people of color; and (4) pledges about philanthropy or funding minority groups and causes, with a particular focus on minority businesses and transactions.

RACE-CONSCIOUS DISCLOSURES BEFORE 2020

Prior to 2020, Amazon, Chevron, and many other large companies regularly made general statements, often including cursory references to race. In 2019, for example,

Amazon's diversity, equity, and inclusion statement on its website noted that "[the company's] diverse perspectives come from many sources including gender, race, age, national origin, sexual orientation, culture ... as well as professional and life experience."[26]

Like Amazon, prior to 2020, Chevron's public statements often focused on broad notions of diversity. In 2019, Chevron's CDO stated that: "[the company's] aim [was] to improve workforce demographics ... by providing equal opportunity through recruitment, development and promotion without regard to gender or race [and] where everyone can do their best, everyone can participate, everyone can feel included."[27] However, unlike Amazon and most other companies, since at least 2012, Chevron made its yearly Employer Information Report, or EEO-1, publicly available. Employers with at least 100 employees and federal contractors with at least 50 employees are required to complete and submit EEO-1 data, which includes information about employees' job categories, ethnicity, race, and gender, to the Equal Employment Opportunity Commission (EEOC) and the US Department of Labor every year.[28] The EEOC keeps the disclosures confidential and makes only aggregated data available to the public.[29] An officer of a firm must certify EEO-1 disclosures as accurate.[30] Unlike Amazon and many other companies,[31] Chevron chose to make its own EEO-1 data available to the public prior to 2020, although it too significantly increased its race-conscious disclosures in 2020.

Therefore, before 2020, race-conscious disclosures were infrequent, largely vague, and often lumped race together with other factors.

RACE-CONSCIOUS DISCLOSURES AFTER 2020

Amazon, Chevron, and thousands of other large companies, many of which are less well known than these behemoths, began to voluntarily make systematic race-conscious disclosures as soon as the cell phone video of George Floyd's murder was publicized.

Amazon

In 2020, Amazon's sustainability reports included race-conscious disclosures in all four categories described in Table 2.1. The company's general statements about institutional racism and racial inequality were specific and impassioned:

> The inequitable and brutal treatment of Black and African Americans is unacceptable. Black lives matter and Amazon stands in solidarity with our Black employees, customers, and partners. We are committed to helping build a country and a world where everyone can live with dignity and free from fear.[32]

Amazon also disclosed the statistics of its workforce at the time, highlighting the percentages of racial and ethnic minorities among its employees and managers.

It also made disclosures about its racial philanthropy: "Amazon and our employees—through a donation match program—were able to donate more than $27 million to organizations working to bring about social justice and improve the lives of Black and African Americans .... We plan to continue building our relationships with these organizations and supporting movements for racial equity."[33]

In 2021, Amazon continued to make impassioned statements, including a statement that it needed to do better and "directly confront how institutional racism and racial inequality is hurting people, including how marginalized communities face disproportionate negative environmental impacts."[34] It also made numerous further disclosures about racial philanthropy:

> Amazon donated $10 million to organizations working to bring about social justice and improve the lives of Black and African Americans .... This initial donation was followed by a successful employee donation matching program that resulted in an additional $17 million going to these organizations in 2020. While it will take years of thoughtful focus and partnership to make the progress needed, Amazon is committed to being part of the solution.[35]
>
> In January 2021, Amazon launched the Housing Equity Fund, a commitment of more than $2 billion to preserve and create more than 20,000 affordable homes in three communities where we have a high concentration of employees.... The Housing Equity Fund helps create inclusive housing developments and ... grants to non-traditional and traditional housing partners, public agencies, and minority-led organizations.[36]

In addition, for the first time in 2021, Amazon made race-conscious disclosures that fully disaggregated the statistics of its workforce at the time into categories of employees, managers, field and customer support, and senior leaders. This breakdown highlighted the severe lack of racial diversity among managers and leaders and showed that people of color were overrepresented among low-wage field and customer support workers.

In 2021, Amazon also made racial targets, disclosing statistics of its plans to hire and promote people of color by declaring that it had "set a goal to increase [the] hiring of US Black employees in Level 4 through Level 7 positions by at least 30% year over year from 2020 hiring [and] the number of US Black software development engineer interns by at least 40%."[37]

Chevron

Like Amazon, Chevron also made impassioned general statements about confronting racial inequities in 2020, with a particular focus on Black communities:

> In 2020, Chevron evolved our long-term approach to improve racial equity by increasing our support and investment in the ... development of Black talent and leadership. This approach is in response to a convergence of events that include the

spread of COVID-19, an economic downturn that led to massive unemployment, and social unrest growing out of the death of George Floyd and other Black citizens in the United States. These events sparked a movement to eliminate institutional racism and racial inequality, racial inequality and economic inequality that have disproportionately affected Black Americans and other people of color.[38]

We not only seek to achieve better representation and retention of Black employees, but also to increase our workforce's understanding of Black experiences and adopt or revise practices, policies, and programs to create greater racial equity.[39]

In 2021, Chevron also made disclosures about its philanthropic efforts:

Our racial equity approach includes a $15 million commitment that has four pillars: education, job creation, talent and leadership development, and community and small business partnerships. We are also working to expand our existing relationships with community, business, and educational partners such as K–12 science, technology, engineering, and mathematics (STEM) organizations and Historically Black Colleges and Universities (HBCUs).[40]

And, as was its usual practice, Chevron continued to make its EEO-1 disclosures publicly available to show the demographic statistics of its workforce.

BEYOND AMAZON AND CHEVRON

Chevron and Amazon are not unique. They are two of the over 2,000 companies I examined, 97 percent of which engaged in systematic race-conscious disclosures in both voluntary disclosures and their mandatory reports submitted to the SEC between 2020 and 2024. As described further in the Appendix, I examined hundreds of thousands of pages of voluntary and mandatory corporate reports using natural language processing. Voluntary reports are nonfinancial disclosures about sustainability, diversity and inclusion efforts, and other social issues. Mandatory reports are financial, operational, and financial risk disclosures that publicly traded companies are required to submit to the SEC quarterly or annually. Corporations are not required to make sustainability or diversity disclosures in mandatory SEC disclosures but often choose to do so to provide information to their shareholders.

This chapter documents companies' general statements and statistics about the composition of their workforces. Racial targets will be covered in depth in Chapter 3 and philanthropic efforts in Chapter 4. In 2023, 96.5 percent of the companies in my research made general statements about race in voluntary reports that they were not required to make public. These general statements about race and racial inequality increased by 27.6 percent from 2018 levels. To put these statistics into sharper relief, while only 363 companies mentioned anything about race in public voluntary disclosures in 2018, 1,561 did in 2023, as indicated in Figure 2.1. And as I discuss in Chapter 5, the percentage increased further to 97.7 percent in 2024, despite conservative backlash related to DEI policies and practices before Trump's second term.

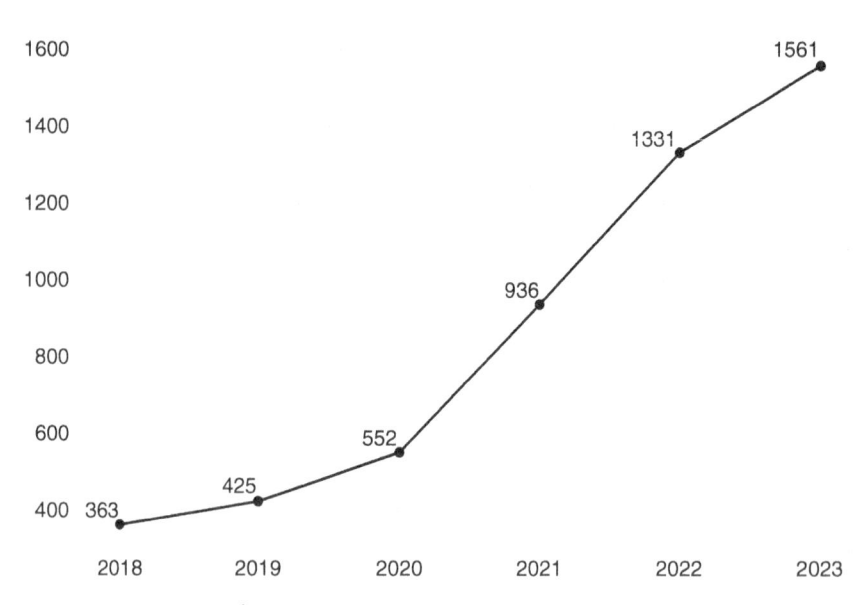

FIGURE 2.1 Voluntary reports with general race-conscious disclosures

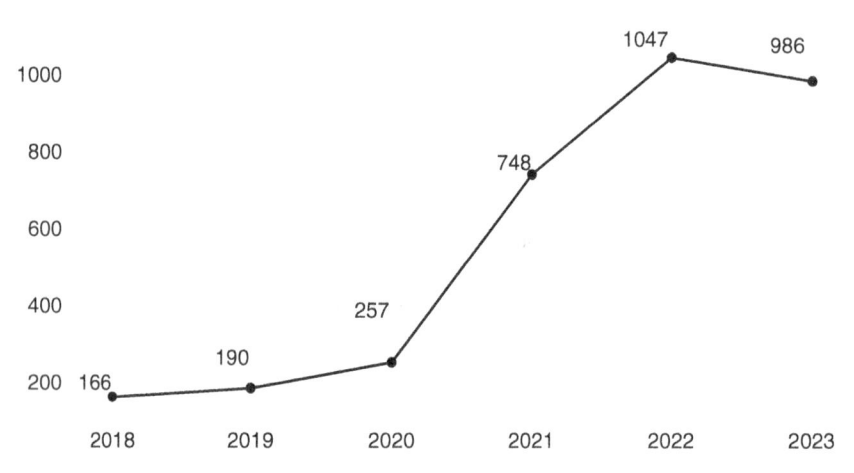

FIGURE 2.2 Mandatory reports with general race-conscious disclosures

A similar but more dramatic trend can be seen in mandatory reports companies filed to the SEC, as shown in Figure 2.2.[41] Unlike unverified and unaudited voluntary reports, companies file their annual 10-K reports with the SEC.[42] Laws prohibit companies from making materially false or misleading statements or omitting material information in their annual 10-Ks.[43] The Sarbanes-Oxley Act of 2002, which was passed in response to several accounting scandals in the early 2000s, also requires a company's chief executive officer (CEO) and chief financial officer (CFO) to certify the accuracy of the 10-K.[44] Until 2020, less than 200 companies included any

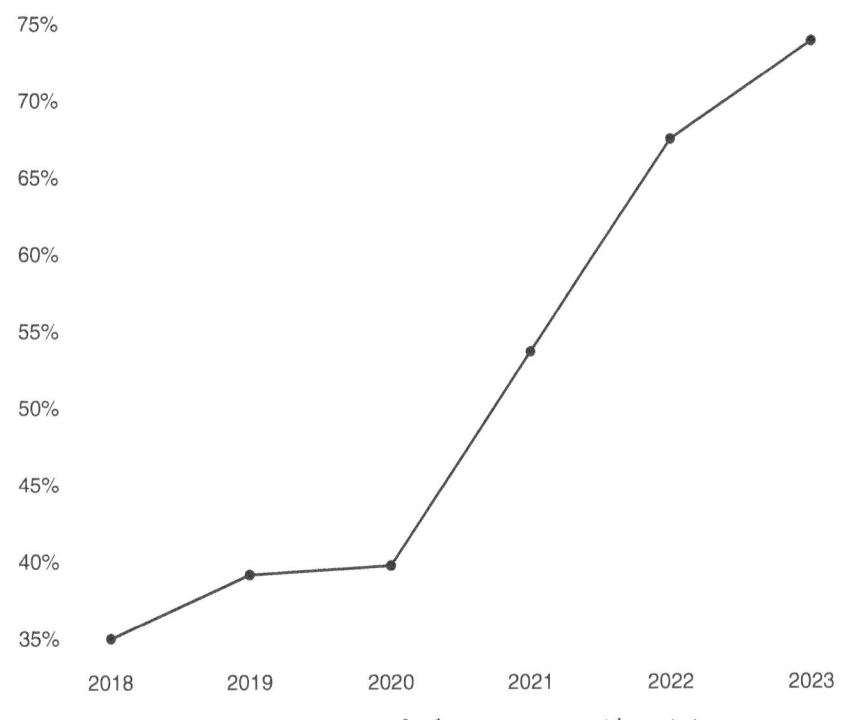

FIGURE 2.3 Percentage of voluntary reports with statistics

form of race-conscious disclosure in their 10-K reports. However, still without any legal requirement to disclose, general statements about confronting racial inequality increased by unprecedented levels, reaching 1,047 out of 1,330 or 79 percent of companies' 10-Ks. Since the SEC requires companies to make material disclosures in their annual reports, in 2022, 79 percent of the companies in my research made race-conscious disclosures because they believed such disclosures were material to their businesses alongside mandatory disclosures about their finances and operations. That number dropped only slightly to 986 out of 1,539 or 64 percent in 2023.

These companies also made other types of race-conscious disclosures, including those involving workplace composition statistics and racial targets. Figure 2.3 shows that race-conscious disclosures that include workplace composition statistics remained under 40% in voluntary reports until 2020. They increased to 53.6% in 2021 and then to 73.8% by 2023. So, by 2023, seven out of every ten companies voluntarily disclosed some type of statistics about race and ethnicity. As shown in Chapter 5, race-conscious disclosures with statistics increased to 83.1% in 2024.

Starting in 2020, companies were also more likely to specify racial or ethnic groups in their disclosures than in the past. As shown in Figure 2.4, prior to 2020, the prevalence of statistical disclosures about Native Americans, Asian individuals, Black people, and Latino people remained below 30 percent. Those numbers

58   *Race-Conscious Disclosures, Image, and Reputation*

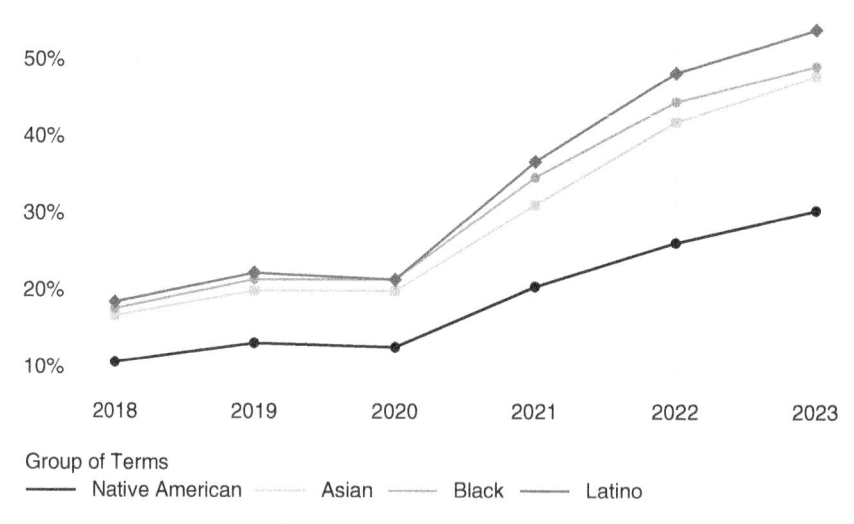

FIGURE 2.4 Percentage of voluntary reports with statistics by racial or ethnic group

increased significantly by 2023. For example, while 17.5% or only two out of every ten companies disclosed statistics about Black people in 2018, 53.9% or five out of every ten companies made statistical disclosures specifically about Black people in 2023. That is the highest prevalence of any racial or ethnic group. For Asian and Latino people, it was 47.9% and 49.3%, respectively, in 2023.

Significantly, race-conscious disclosures are not limited to public companies. As shown in Figure 2.5, at least 100 of the largest private companies in the United States, which are not required to make disclosures to the SEC or the public, also made race-conscious disclosures between 2020 and 2023.[45]

Figure 2.6 shows increases similar to those in public companies, with private companies also naming specific racial and ethnic groups. Black people were the most prominent in 2023, with 52.8 percent of private companies disclosing statistics specifically related to Black people. Statistics about Asian and Latino people were at 35.8% and 39%, respectively, in 2023.

Why did privately held companies who typically do not make SEC disclosures, and are generally not expected to do so by the public, make race-conscious disclosures that mirror those of public companies? Interviews with private companies reveal that they too hold a belief that transparency is expected of them by their stakeholders – employees, prospective employees, customers, and advocacy groups. As one CSO of a private company explained:

> The primary audience is our customers. We are a privately owned company … so the primary audience will be our customers and other stakeholders. There are community groups that we interact with. Other industry businesses groups. So we are thinking about each of these categories of stakeholders. Ultimately it is internal too. The stakeholder list is quite broad. So, I would say we're not targeting any

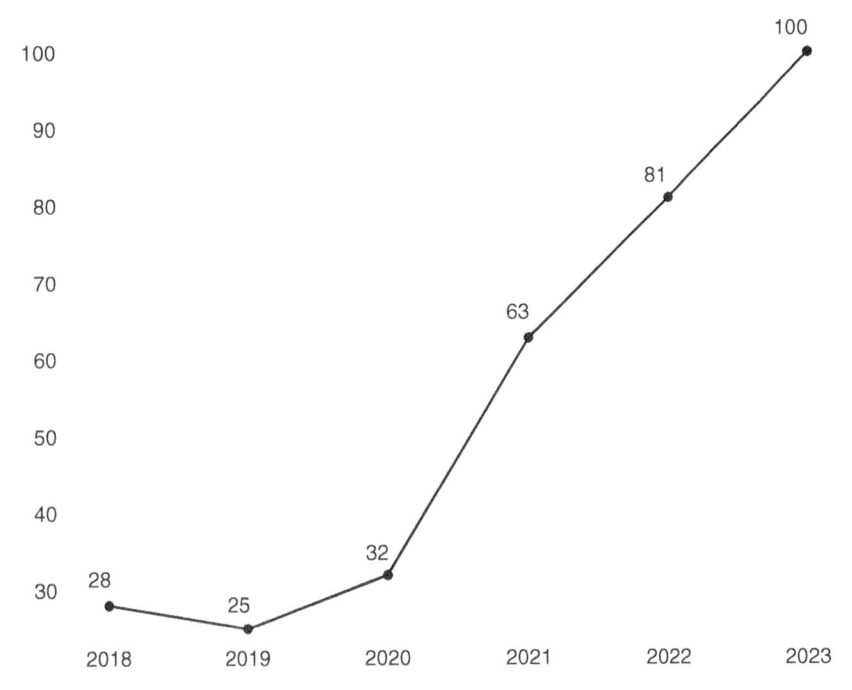

FIGURE 2.5 Voluntary reports with general race-conscious disclosures (private companies)

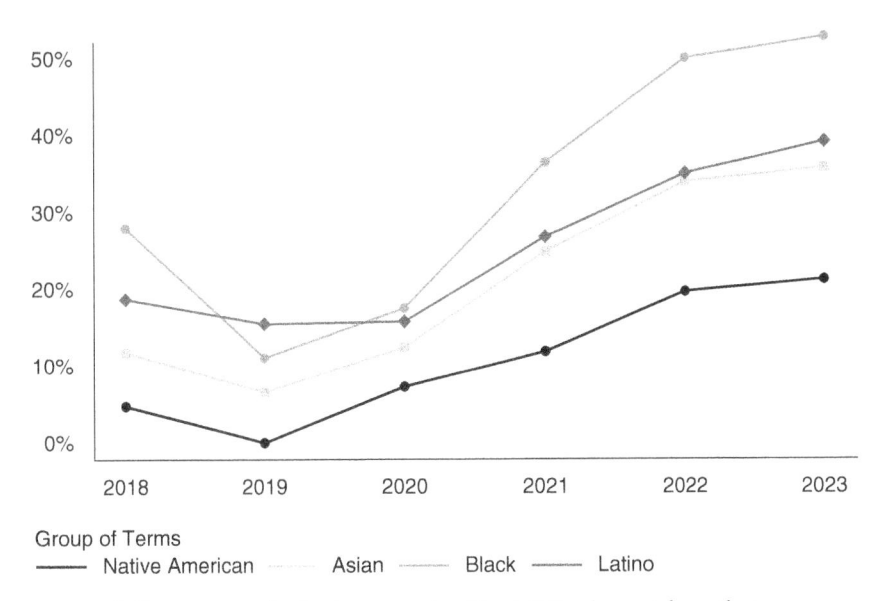

FIGURE 2.6 Percentage of voluntary reports with statistics by racial or ethnic group (private companies)

particular stakeholder group, it's going to be a very ... integrated comprehensive message that each stakeholder group will find their piece of interest.

Transparency is the linchpin of race-conscious disclosures that seek to build reputational capital. Companies made race-conscious disclosures to establish their public images as businesses that tackled racial inequality, or at a minimum, did not ignore racial inequality or the plight of people of color in their firms and in society. And as in previous historical contexts, corporations did not do this because of a moral obligation, but in response to societal pressures and reputational risk calculus.

INVESTORS, RACIAL EQUITY AUDITS, PROPOSALS, AND RISKS

While customers, prospective employees, and employees have pressured companies to make race-conscious disclosures, the most intense pressure to say and do something about race has come from institutional shareholders or investors – entities like credit unions, mutual funds, hedge funds, venture capital funds, insurance companies, and pension funds – that invest other people's money, as opposed to individual shareholders who invest their own money in companies. Institutional investors have pressured companies to express support for doing something about racial inequality, including by publicly disclosing the composition of their workforces disaggregated by race, ethnicity, gender, job category, and income levels. They have also pressured companies to seek more racial diversity on corporate boards, to examine and address how their business activities might disproportionately affect communities of color, and to assess the efficacy of their existing racial diversity programs.[46] Institutional investors are often motivated to become shareholder activists in this way because of their own constituents. A small but significant group of institutional investors have used shareholder proposals as a vessel to present a broad range of demands to companies, often asking companies to conduct racial equity audits to further illuminate claims and suspicions of racial discrimination and racial bias in their businesses.[47] These shareholder pressures have been catalysts for more race-conscious disclosures because corporations used words to convey their support for shareholders' demands. Corporations also used words, however, to reject shareholder demands, invoking their own previous words as evidence of their action.

Since 2020, shareholders have used shareholder proposals as their primary instrument to pressure companies to address racial inequalities related to their business activities. Under SEC Rule 14a-8,[48] shareholders of public companies are permitted to present corporations with proposals on a wide range of social issues to draw attention to and pressure management to respond.[49] SEC rules require corporations to include eligible shareholder proposals in their proxy materials. Shareholders then vote on proposals at annual meetings or in proxy statements. Shareholder proposals tend to also receive substantial publicity beyond the shareholder meeting, such as

Negotiation

```
                Pre-Proposal              Successful
Shareholder ─────────────→ Company ────────────────→ Withdraw
                Post-Proposal
```

Disagree

```
                                                              Yes    Omit
                 Proposal                                   ┌──────→
Shareholder ──────────────→ Company ──→ File SEC No Action Letter
                                   └──→ Disagree without SEC action
                                                              No     Vote
                                                            └──────→
```

Agree

```
                 Proposal
Shareholder ──────────────→ Company ──────────────→ Vote
```

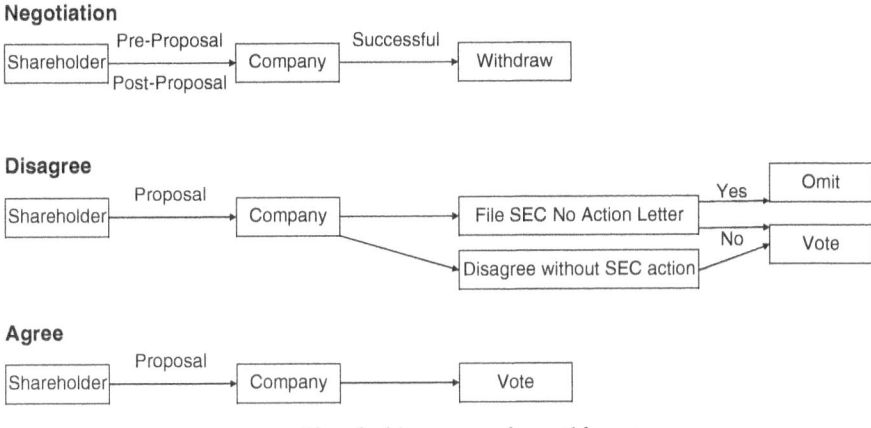

FIGURE 2.7 Shareholder proposal possible outcomes

when 98 percent of Costco's shareholders voted against what they considered to be a shareholder proposal against diversity, inclusion, and community in January 2025.[50]

When a shareholder submits a proposal or asks a company to examine its business for racial inequality or the disproportionate impact of its business activities on people of color, the corporation has at least four options at its disposal. One option, as shown in Figure 2.7, is to settle with shareholders either before or after the proposal is filed by agreeing to give the request serious consideration or implementing the proposal (this is a common outcome for pension fund proposals).[51] This often results in the withdrawal of the proposal. Ultimately, the managers of a company decide which shareholder proposals warrant this level of responsiveness.[52]

The second option is for the company to challenge the legality of the request by filing a "no-action letter" request with the SEC to seek the SEC's informal and nonbinding opinion on whether it agrees that there is a legal basis to exclude the shareholder proposal from the company's proxy statement under Rule 14a-8.[53] Depending on the SEC's response, the company can then either omit the proposal or include it and make a recommendation for shareholders to vote for or against the proposal.

The third option is for the company to include the proposal in its proxy statement, oppose it, and recommend that shareholders vote *against* the proposal. The fourth option is for the company to include the proposal in its proxy statement and recommend that shareholders vote *for* the proposal.

I examined sixty-nine no-action letter requests related to disclosures about race, racial equity audits, or racial inequality that companies submitted to the SEC between 2020 and 2022. About 76 percent of the associated shareholder proposals were submitted by institutional investors. As shown in Figure 2.8, companies rejected the proposals and asked the SEC for no-action letters for a variety of reasons, including that the proposals interfered with the company's ordinary business operations (47.8%), that they had implemented whatever the request was about in prior *disclosures* (not

Proposal Request

- 6 (10.9%)
- 29 (52.7%)
- 20 (36.4%)

Disclosures about race
Racial Equity Audit/Civil Rights Audit
Business impact on POC

Grounds for Rejection

- 23 (9.2%)
- 120 (47.8%)
- 77 (30.7%)

Interferes with Ordinary Business Decisions
Implemented Through Disclosures
Prior Similar Proposal
Implemented Through Prior Action
Micromanagement
Leave to Legislature

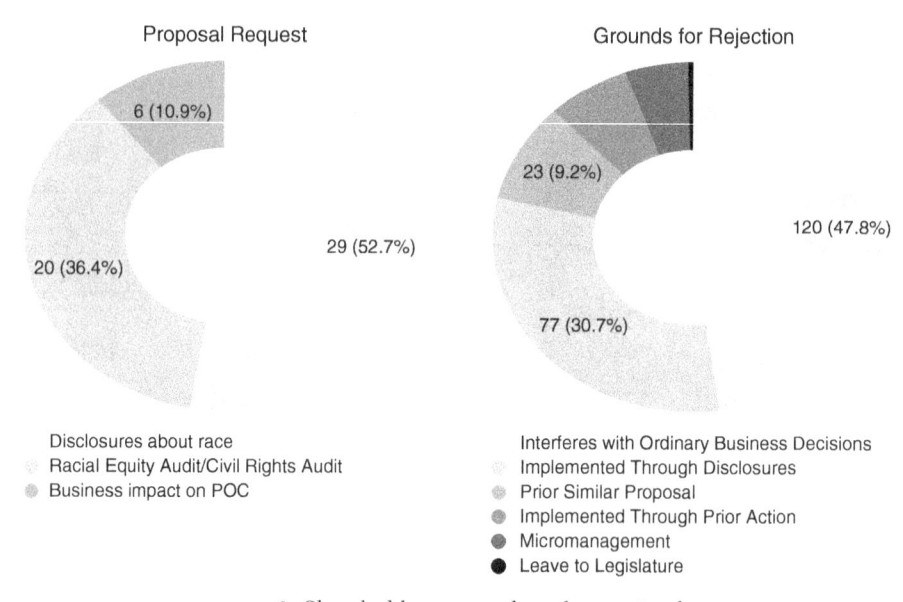

FIGURE 2.8 Shareholder proposals and no-action letters

action) (30.7%), that they had done something else to implement the request (6.8%), that the request constituted micromanagement (5.2%), that the proposals were vague, false, or misleading, that the proposals violated certain laws, such as insurance laws, or that policies on racial equity should be addressed by the legislature.

For instance, a 2020 shareholder proposal to Comcast Corporation urged the company to publish the process that the board follows for assessing the effectiveness of its diversity, equity and inclusion programs, as well as the board's assessment of program effectiveness, as reflected in any goals, metrics, and trends related to its promotion, recruitment, and retention of protected classes of employees, including people of color. The company submitted a no-action letter request to the SEC to exclude the proposal from its 2021 annual shareholders' meeting on the basis that the proposal related to the company's ordinary business operations and litigation strategies.

A 2021 shareholder proposal by SOC Investment Group, a nonprofit accountability group, to McDonald's urged the company's board to oversee a racial equity audit analyzing the adverse impact of the company's policies and practices on the civil rights of employees above and beyond legal and regulatory matters, and to provide recommendations for improving the company's civil rights impact.[54] McDonald's responded by submitting a no-action letter request to the SEC to exclude the proposal from its 2022 annual shareholders' meeting on the basis that the proposal related to the company's ordinary business operations and litigation strategies. The SEC ultimately rejected the company's argument for exclusion. McDonald's had to present the proposal for a vote at its 2023 shareholder meeting,[55] and shareholders ultimately voted for the company to conduct the audit.[56] Without the shareholder vote, McDonald's would have quashed the racial equity audit.

Assuming a proposal makes it to a shareholder vote, it still has an uphill battle to obtain enough shareholder support to pass. The McDonald's proposal for a racial equity audit passed by 55 percent.[57] Of the 251 proposals about racial diversity or racial equity submitted by shareholders between 2020 and 2022, only twenty received a vote of approval from shareholders. That is about 7.9 percent of all proposals about race. Despite the difficulty of obtaining support from other shareholders for a proposal to address racial inequality, companies do not want proposals on race to even make it to the point where shareholders can vote on them because of the risk that they would be approved like McDonald's, and the attendant media coverage of the issues shareholders raise.

Research by Stavros Gadinis and Amelia Miazad, involving discussions with over three hundred asset managers, investment banks, pension funds, proxy advisors, hedge funds, investors and sustainability advocates, suggests that companies use ESG activities, which include taking up racial inequality, to manage their reputations.[58] Establishing a public image that conveyed engagement with taking up an issue, here, racial inequality, readies a company to avert any reputational fallout that may come if and when shareholders or stakeholders raise potential avenues for growth on that issue.

Racial Equity Audits

A racial equity audit, also known as a "civil rights audit" or "civil rights assessment," is an independent analysis of a company's business practices, policies, practices, and products designed to identify ways in which they may have discriminatory effects on customers, employees, suppliers, or other stakeholders.[59] Typically, corporations hire law firms or other auditors to conduct audits.

Racial equity audits seem to have first emerged in 2016 when Airbnb, with guidance from civil rights organizations, conducted an audit following allegations that hosts were discriminating against guests.[60] Before 2020, racial equity audits like the Airbnb one, were often proposed by civil rights leaders or groups rather than institutional investors through shareholder proposals. Starbucks and Facebook also conducted racial equity audits prior to 2020. Starbucks conducted its first racial equity audit after an employee called the police to arrest two Black men who were holding a meeting in a coffee shop in downtown Philadelphia in 2018.[61] Following the incident, Starbucks closed 8,000 stores nationwide to provide 175,000 employees with four hours of racial bias training.[62] The company then consulted with Sherrilyn Ifill, former president and counsel of the NAACP Legal Defense and Educational Fund and renowned civil rights lawyer, and Heather McGhee, a policy advocate, who together recommended an internal audit to examine bias within the company.[63] Starbucks conducted the racial equity audit in 2019, which it reported in its notice to its shareholders.[64] Like Starbucks, Facebook also conducted a racial equity audit in 2018 at the behest of civil rights leaders and some members of Congress.[65] The audit was then published in July 2020 after the murder of George Floyd.[66]

After 2020, institutional investors pressured many more companies to conduct racial equity audits or to examine racial pay gaps. One of those companies was Amazon. In 2021, shareholders submitted a proposal asking the company to conduct a racial equity audit to examine whether its hourly employees were experiencing disparities in pay and promotion. Amazon responded by asking other shareholders to vote against the proposal because, it argued, its prior disclosures had already shown its steps to address racial inequality, thus invalidating the need for an audit. In 2022, shareholders again asked Amazon to examine whether its health and safety practices give rise to any racial disparities in workplace injury rates among its warehouse workers. Again, Amazon's response invoked its previous actions, noting its broad diversity, equity, and inclusion goals in addition to workplace programs to promote safety in its warehouses. A similar scenario played out at Chevron in 2022, when the company's shareholders asked it to examine whether its oil refineries disproportionately harm communities of color. Chevron pointed to its prior disclosures as proof that it did not need to conduct a racial equity audit.

When Amazon and Chevron's shareholders made proposals asking the companies to conduct racial equity audits, both companies explicitly asked their shareholders to vote *against* the audits. In Amazon's case, the US House of Representatives reprimanded the company, which forced it to agree to conduct the audit. There was no such reprimand by a government entity in the Chevron case, and consequently no racial equity audit. In both cases, the companies treated the possibility of having to conduct a racial equity audit as a risk to the race-conscious reputations they had so assiduously built through race-conscious disclosures. They responded by using their public images – based on their disclosures – as a strong basis for not needing to assess their business dealings for racial inequality.

Other companies have used the same or similar methods to squelch shareholder proposals asking companies to examine how their businesses might disproportionately impact communities of color. Rather than take steps to address concerns about the disproportionate impact of business activities on people of color as employees or in their communities – with or without public declarations about doing so – companies asserted that their unregulated public statements show their commitments to racial equity. Corporations used the public image they had constructed with these statements as leverage in maintaining that they did not need to address racial inequality even before conservative pushback toward race-conscious retraction discussed in Chapter 5.

In the 2020 proxy season, shareholders submitted fifty-three proposals related to racial diversity or equity concerns.[67] In 2021, shareholders more than doubled their efforts and submitted 128 proposals about racial diversity or equity concerns.[68] There was a slight drop in 2022, when shareholders submitted ninety-seven such proposals about racial diversity or equity concerns. In the 2023 proxy season, shareholders submitted only twenty-nine proposals relating to racial diversity and equity concerns.[69] My examination of Institutional Shareholder Services (ISS) shareholder proposal data reveals that there were 251 shareholder proposals related to racial diversity or equity between 2020 and 2022.[70] The topics or requests of these proposals ranged from adopting a board diversity policy, to examining and reporting on racial pay gaps, to conducting a racial equity audit.

Among these 251 proposals, I examined 71 proposals related specifically to racial equity audits and pay gap assessments brought between 2020 and 2022. I found that in only 4 out of 71 proposals did the boards of directors of the companies involved support the proposals. And in those four cases, the proposing shareholders had already received overwhelming support from other shareholders. In 93% of racial equity audit requests, and 100% of pay gap analysis requests, boards of directors asked shareholders to vote against the proposals.

To be sure, this is not an unusual board response to shareholder proposals in general.[71] However, rejecting proposals requesting racial equity audits and the like is inconsistent with the construction of race-conscious public images.

Reputational and Litigation Risks

Business risk comes in many different forms. There are financial risks, security risks, compliance risks, operational risks, litigation risks, and reputational risks. The primary actors behind risks can vary widely to include shareholders, advocacy groups, employees, prospective employees, consumers, suppliers, regulators, politicians and other government officials, and the media.[72]

Between 2020 and 2024, employees, shareholders, consumers, and advocacy groups were the primary drivers of reputational risks to companies on matters related to climate change, sustainability, and racial inequality. These actors have used different forms of activism, including protests, direct communication with management, indirect communication through the press or social media, letters to the board, and shareholder proposals, to pressure companies to act.[73]

The risk of litigation is another type of risk that drives corporate words and behaviors on race, and it is a complex issue. Regarding race-conscious disclosures (and not retraction), corporations may have been concerned about derivative lawsuits – legal action filed by shareholders on behalf of corporations, against corporate directors or officers, alleging that they have breached their fiduciary duties and caused harm to those companies – by shareholders claiming that corporations have not done enough to tackle racial inequality. Corporations may have believed that more race-conscious disclosures would deter some progressive leaning shareholders from bringing derivative lawsuits because of their constructed public images indicating that they were already tackling racial inequality. So, by asking shareholders to vote against proposals or asking the SEC to weigh in on whether they could exclude shareholder proposals seeking to address racial inequality, corporations used their constructed race-conscious reputation to shield themselves from potential litigation, including derivative lawsuits claiming discrimination against racial and ethnic minorities.

It may indeed be accurate that responding this way was the optimal path toward preventing litigation. As discussed in Chapter 5, corporations may be concerned that while succumbing to progressive-leaning shareholders and making race-conscious disclosures signals that they are doing something about racial inequality, this effectively opens them up to litigation from conservative groups. However, while the risk of litigation is a fair and legitimate concern for some corporations, companies simultaneously open themselves up to litigation and reputational risks by *not* supporting what they claim to, and, more importantly, actually impeding the racial progress they claim to support. Moreover, risk calculations that tend to elevate litigation above other kinds of risks and employ strategies that do not prioritize tackling racial inequality as race-conscious disclosures say they would, can have negative long-term consequences for corporations as well.

Regardless of whether Amazon, Chevron, or other companies choose to address racial inequality in their businesses, using their public images to push back on shareholder requests to tackle racial inequalities will further shut out communities of color from economic, social, and environmental justice. Legal scholar Lisa Fairfax has argued that corporate hypocrisy – when companies fail to follow through on public statements – can enable stakeholders to make better decisions about a corporation by taking into account the ways in which corporate actions may differ from their words; and can lead to companies altering their behavior, increasing the possibility that future behavior will be more closely aligned with specific corporate statements.[74] There are surely potential benefits to corporate disclosures even when companies do not follow through on their disclosures. I have written about the ways in which employee and shareholder activists can use corporate disclosures instrumentally to push companies to increase corporate diversity.[75] However, corporate hypocrisy that leaves claims about institutional racism and racial inequality unheard altogether robs people of color of the ability to call corporations to account for their words and actions and thus constrains racial progress.[76]

CONSTRAINING RACIAL PROGRESS

Corporations constrain racial progress with their public statements in three important ways. The first is by failing to acknowledge past shortcomings. The second is the use of disclosures to push back against inquiries about racial inequality in business, or potential measures to achieve racial progress. The third is by engaging in race-conscious retraction.

Failing to acknowledge or only minimally acknowledging past shortcomings vis-à-vis race, and the continued relevance of race for the present structure of opportunities within companies constrains racial progress. Without past race-conscious disclosures, corporations have extensive leeway to define the meaning of racial progress in the present for their firms and the rest of society. It is particularly in relation to past corporate action or inaction that more race-conscious disclosures would be useful to stakeholders and others, because it would provide useful context for other race-conscious disclosures. But even here, disclosures about past shortcomings can be used to constrain racial progress if corporations use them as evidence that they are attentive to racial inequality.

The lack of race-conscious disclosures about the past also has direct impact on the backlash on diversity, equity, and inclusion and its influence on race-conscious retraction. Conservative groups' claim that their campaigns against DEI are in support of racial progress have probably gained traction because of the general lack of knowledge about the role of corporations in perpetuating and also alleviating racial discrimination and inequality in the past. Race-conscious disclosures about the past can serve as reminders about the historical racial discrimination and racial inequality that people of color have experienced. For example, in its almost a century and a half history, Chevron has engaged in many activities and sanctioned policies that disproportionately impacted people of color. Disclosure of some of those activities and policies and their influence on the present can help the company define racial progress for the future. Virtually no corporation has made disclosures to that effect.

The second form of constraint to racial progress is the use of disclosures to push back against any potential measures to achieve racial progress. It is noteworthy that about 30 percent of companies' grounds for rejecting shareholder proposals about racial inequality or the disproportionate impact of business on racial minorities between 2020 and 2022 was having previously made prior disclosures that addressed the issue, even if those disclosures did not fully cover shareholders' requests in their proposals.

In 2021, after the Treasury Department found that Bank of America offered disproportionately fewer home loans to racial minorities than white applicants in Philadelphia, and after finding that only 8 percent of the bank's executives were Black, the company's shareholders asked for a racial equity audit to examine its operations.[77] Bank of American's board, in turn, asked other shareholders to vote against the racial equity audit because "[Bank of America's] actions and focus in making progress on the issue of racial equality and reporting on [its] progress regularly, renders the proposal's requested audit unnecessary."[78] The company then referenced its racial philanthropy, among other race-conscious disclosures, as further evidence of this. Specifically, it argued, its "$1 billion commitment to supporting minority-owned businesses, job initiatives, and affordable housing programs" indicated that more is not needed from the company.[79] Shareholders ultimately voted against the audit, and the bank won.

Companies including Alphabet (Google's parent company), Amazon, Bank of America, Comcast, Chevron, Citigroup, Goldman Sachs, JP Morgan, Nike, The Home Depot, and Wells Fargo have used disclosures to respond to claims that their businesses or operations perpetrate racial discrimination or have disproportionate impact on racial and ethnic minorities by either asking shareholders to vote against proposals seeking the collection of information or measures to address those concerns or requesting "no-action" letters from the SEC to seek its input for excluding those proposals from shareholder proxy materials.

These strategies are harming the cause of racial equity in two important ways. The first is that they send a strong signal that the issues a company supported and made commitments to as it constructed its race-conscious image were perhaps never important or are no longer important to the company. This is a particularly insidious form of hypocrisy that sends a powerful message to shareholders, stakeholders, and the public about what corporations value. Second, these approaches often put an end to inquiries about the role of racial inequality in a company's operations and help to continue the cycle of racial discrimination and inequality in business. Both elements are problematic and have long-term consequences for tackling social and economic inequality.

Amazon

As of June 2023, institutional investors held 59.2 percent of Amazon's outstanding shares, giving those investors significant advantage in influencing the company's direction.[80] As I discussed above, in 2021 some of Amazon's institutional shareholders requested a racial equity audit citing alleged discrimination against the company's Black and Latino workers, as evidenced by their low wages and exposure to dangerous working conditions.[81] In response, Amazon publicly declared that its race-conscious disclosures – which included "funding historically Black colleges and universities, running leadership programs for underrepresented minorities and channeling tens of millions of dollars to help close the racial wealth divide" – should excuse it from completing a racial equity audit to reveal whether its products and policies discriminate against people of color.[82]

Amazon's response de-emphasized the importance of correction if, in fact, the company's products and policies have disproportionate impact on communities of color. If Amazon's plants are disproportionately making members of certain neighborhoods sicker than others, for example, then those neighborhoods are at a disadvantage economically and in terms of overall health. Using its race-conscious disclosures as leverage for not attending to the disproportionate impact of its business on communities of color constrains racial progress. Amazon, like other companies, used those disclosures to reap benefits from customers, employees, shareholders, and the public, who likely believed that the company's values espoused racial equity. Research has confirmed that these kinds of disclosures result in financial benefits for companies.[83]

In May 2022, Amazon reluctantly agreed to conduct a limited third-party-led racial equity audit to measure any disparate racial impacts on its hourly employees only.[84] While the audit was extremely limited, Amazon may not have considered it at all if the SEC had not denied its request to keep the proposal off the ballot at its annual meeting.[85] The SEC had recently rescinded a first-term Trump-era policy that helped company executives exclude shareholder proposals on social issues from their annual proxy statements, providing companies with fewer valid grounds to exclude a shareholder proposal from the ballot.[86]

In 2022, former Attorney General Eric Holder, who in his capacity as senior counsel at Covington & Burling LLP, has helped companies conduct racial equity audits,[87] said that a company's refusal to approve a racial equity audit could generate reputational risk "if an unrecognized and unaddressed problem surfaces" later.[88] After the SEC weighed in, Amazon quickly agreed to the audit and significantly narrowed its scope. The audit Amazon ultimately agreed to was not focused on claims of racial discrimination or disproportionate treatment that result in environmental and economic inequalities.[89] It is also unclear who would require Amazon to address any problems raised in its narrowly focused audit, or whether the audit would lead to any meaningful change at all. Ultimately, Amazon was able to decide that allowing the audit was the least risky choice at the time, precisely given how limited its scope ended up being and the lack of any clear requirements regarding accountability or follow-up.

Nonetheless, there are also some ways in which racial equity audits themselves can be self-serving. They satisfy shareholders and often result in more race-conscious disclosures that can boost a company's financial standing. Some companies have conducted racial equity audits that primarily serve to appease shareholders and further better their reputations, rather than as a tool to address racism and racial inequality.[90] For example, following Starbucks's 2018 racial equity audit, the company began making more race-conscious disclosures.[91] The public announcement of the audit and related race-conscious disclosures appeared to rehabilitate Starbucks's public image after the store manager called the police on two Black men, so much so that in 2021, RBC Capital Markets, an investment bank, found Starbucks to be the "most popular restaurant stock on the S&P 500 with actively managed funds that are dedicated to ESG investing."[92] At that point, Starbucks's shares had been up by 58 percent over a two-year period.[93]

For companies, determining whether to conduct a racial equity audit is about assessing and managing reputational and litigation risks. Between 2020 and 2023, companies seemed to pick and choose racial equity audits they wanted to oppose or allow depending on the predicted impact on their reputational capital and other financial gains, which depends on the specifics of the audit and other circumstances. This is similar to how companies either expand or rein in their use of race-conscious disclosures depending on the political, social, and environmental circumstances and how those circumstances shape the anticipated reputational benefit or reputational or litigation risks of making such disclosures.

Chevron

In May 2022, some of Chevron's shareholders filed a proposal calling for an independent racial equity audit analyzing if and how Chevron's policies and practices discriminate against or disparately impact communities of color.[94] The shareholders asked that "the report … clearly identify and recommend steps to eliminate business activities that further institutional racism and racial inequality, environmental injustice, threaten civil rights, or present barriers to diversity, equity, and inclusion."[95] The proposal asked Chevron to include input from impacted workers, community members, customers, and other relevant stakeholders.[96]

Among other things, Chevron's shareholders were particularly concerned about the residents who live closest to Chevron's Richmond, California, oil refinery.[97] Chevron's oil refinery has been in Richmond for over a century. More than 80 percent of the nearby residents are low-income people of color. Environmental justice activists have argued that the refinery has long threatened public health in Richmond and have called for it to be shut down, especially after it spilled about 750 gallons of diesel fuel into the San Francisco Bay in February 2021.[98] Many other dangerous incidents have occurred throughout the years, including in 2012, when a corroded pipe leaked and exploded, sparking a major fire that sent 15,000 residents to seek treatment for respiratory problems.[99] Richmond is in the ninety-ninth percentile of cities for asthma risk, with about twice the rate of other surrounding counties.[100] The city also has high rates of other respiratory illnesses, cancers, autoimmune disorders, and other ailments.[101]

The shareholders' concerns were dire, as demonstrated by research that shows that regardless of income, Black individuals are exposed to, on average, higher levels of pollution, associated with lung disease, heart disease, and premature death than people of any other race.[102] Richmond has a large Black population of 19.5%, second only to the 42.5% Latino population in the city.[103]

However, in response to public outcry and shareholder proposals about the impact of its activities on people of color, Chevron used its constructed public image to oppose the request for an audit.[104] Chevron's board of directors asked shareholders to vote against the proposal for a racial equity audit because "Chevron's actions in support of racial equity are described in detail in numerous publications," which it then enumerated.[105] The descriptions the board referenced were Chevron's prior race-conscious disclosures, which were unrelated to the specific racial and environmental justice concerns that motivated the calls for an audit. Ultimately, 52.5 percent of Chevron's shareholders rejected the proposal as the board had recommended, and the proposal did not pass.[106] This meant that Chevron continued business as usual while the communities of color in Richmond continue to suffer. Occurrences like this reveal the very real, material stakes of regulating race-conscious disclosures.

The third form of constraint to racial progress is the retraction of race-conscious disclosures, which is the subject of Chapter 5. Race-conscious retraction shows how corporations continue to use disclosures to define and determine the shape of racial progress.

NOTES

1. Blake Morgan, "Walmart vs. Amazon: Who Wins the Retail Battle in 2023?," *Forbes*, July 10, 2023, www.forbes.com/sites/blakemorgan/2023/07/10/walmart-vs-amazon-who-wins-the-retail-battle-in-2023/?sh=2ac98b7968fe.
2. Statista, "Share of People Who Shopped at Amazon in the United States in 2022, by Age," www.statista.com/statistics/480351/people-who-shopped-at-amazon-within-the-last-3-months-usa/.
3. Morgan, "Walmart vs. Amazon"; Statista, "Amazon Prime – Statistics & Facts," www.statista.com/topics/4076/amazon-prime/#editorsPicks. Amazon Prime subscribers are people who pay for a subscription to Amazon's paid service, which provides access to additional services, including free and expedited shipping.
4. Anthony Nicome, Philip M. Alberti, and Carla S. Alvarado, AAMC, Center for Health Justice, June 25, 2024, www.aamchealthjustice.org/news/polling/down-to-earth.
5. Statista, "Number of Amazon.com Employees from 2007 to 2021," www.statista.com/statistics/234488/number-of-amazon-employees/; Statista, "Net Revenue of Amazon from 1st Quarter 2007 to 3rd Quarter 2022," www.statista.com/statistics/273963/quarterly-revenue-of-amazoncom/; Statista, "Number of Employees of Chevron from 2008 to 2021," www.statista.com/statistics/277064/number-of-chevron-employees/; Statista, "Operating Revenue of Chevron from 2008 to 2021," www.statista.com/statistics/269079/revenue-of-chevron/.
6. Form 10-K is an annual report that publicly traded companies submit to the SEC, detailing their financial performance and business operations. It includes audited financial statements, management's discussion and analysis, risk factors, and other important disclosures they consider material to their business. Corporations mostly began making race-conscious disclosures in 10-Ks in 2020.
7. David M. Furman, "The Development of Corporate Image: A Historiographic Approach to a Marketing Concept," *Corporate Reputation Review* 13, no. 1 (2010): 63, 68.
8. Geoffrey E. Love and Matthew Kraatz, "Character, Conformity, or the Bottom Line? How and Why Downsizing Affected Corporate Reputation," *Academy of Management Journal* 52 (2009): 314.
9. Donald Lange, Peggy Lee, and Ye Dai, "Organizational Reputation: A Review," *Journal of Management* 37, no. 1 (2011): 1353, 1357.
10. Toyah Miller and Maria Del Carmen, "Demographic Diversity in the Boardroom: Mediators of the Board Diversity–Firm Performance Relationship," *Journal of Management Studies* 46 (2009): 755–86.
11. Securities Act of 1933, Pub. L. No. 73-22, 48 Stat. 74 (1933); Securities Exchange Act of 1934, Pub. L. No. 73-291, 48 Stat. 881 (codified as amended at 15 U.S.C. § 77g (1984)); 15 U.S.C. § 78n(a) (2000).
12. 15 U.S.C. § 77q(a) (2006); 15 U.S.C. § 78j(b) (2006); 17 C.F.R. § 240.10b-5 (2010).
13. Laura Sanderson and Sarah Galloway, "Activating Sustainability in the Boardroom," *Harvard Law School Forum on Corporate Governance*, January 4, 2023, https://corpgov.law.harvard.edu/2023/01/04/activating-sustainability-in-the-boardroom/.

14. Lucian A. Bebchuk and Roberto Tallarita, "Will Corporations Deliver Value to All Stakeholders?" *Vanderbilt Law Review* 75, no. 4 (2022): 1031–91, 1038–39.
15. Abby Corrington, Naomi M. Fa-Kaji, Mikki R. Hebl, Eden B. King, Dillon Stewart, and Temi Alao, "The Impact of Organizational Statements of Support for the Black Community in the Wake of a Racial Mega-Threat on Organizational Attraction and Revenue," *Human Resource Management* (2022): 699–722; Maya Balakrishnan, Jimin Nam, and Ryan W. Buell, "Differentiating on Diversity: How Disclosing Workforce Diversity Improves Brand Attitudes," *Production and Operations Management* (2023).
16. Nancy Koehn, "The Time Is Right for Creative Capitalism," Working Knowledge: Business Research for Business Leaders website, Harvard Business School, August 20, 2008, https://hbswk.hbs.edu/item/the-time-is-right-for-creative-capitalism.
17. Balakrishnan et al., "Differentiating on Diversity."
18. Moody's, *Diversity, Equity, and Inclusion Report*, 2020.
19. A "top projects meeting" is a meeting where high-level decision-makers in a corporation discuss the status, progress, and key strategic aspects of the most important projects, often focusing on updates, potential risks, and resource allocation for those top priority projects.
20. Edelman, *Working Law*, 5.
21. Berrey, *The Enigma of Diversity*, 42.
22. Patricia A. Banks, *Black Culture, Inc.: How Ethnic Community Support Pays for Corporate America* (Stanford: Stanford University Press, 2022), 3.
23. The ESG movement, which is also currently under attack from conservative groups, transformed what it means for large companies to be good global, national, and local citizens. ESG encompasses a broad swath of activities but ultimately involves corporate leaders and investors assessing performance and objectives on environmental, social, and governance issues related or unrelated to maximizing profit. Environmental factors are about a company's stewardship of the environment and focus on issues such as waste and pollution, greenhouse gas emissions, deforestation, and climate change. The social aspect of ESG is where race-conscious disclosures would come in but is also the most varied because a range of factors get lumped into this category, including employee relations, racial, gender, LGBTQIA+, disability, age, and other forms of diversity, working conditions, philanthropy, local communities, human rights, and health and safety. See ADEC Innovations, "ESG Solutions What Is ESG?" www.esg.adec-innovations.com/about-us/faqs/what-is-esg/. Governance factors are about how a company is managed, including how its executives are compensated; see Pollman, "Origins and Consequences," 3. Despite intense political scrutiny, ESG investing has endured, and is likely to continue even if companies change their nomenclature; see Tom Lydon, "Some Positive ESG Trends Emerged in 2023," *Yahoo Finance*, December 28, 2023, https://finance.yahoo.com/news/positive-esg-trends-emerged-2023-142557774.html.
24. 17 C.F.R. § 229.407(c)(2)(vi); Dhir, *Challenging Boardroom Homogeneity*.
25. Devin Caughey, James Dunham, and Christopher Warshaw, "The Ideological Nationalization of Partisan Subconstituencies in the American States," *Public Choice* 176 (2018): 133–51; Thomas B. Edsall, "America Has Split, and It's Now in 'Very Dangerous Territory'," *New York Times*, January 26, 2022, www.nytimes.com/2022/01/26/opinion/covid-biden-trump-polarization.html.
26. Amazon, "Diversity, Equity and Inclusion at Amazon."
27. Priyansha Mistry, "Making Diversity Central to Success: Q&A with Chevron's Chief Diversity Officer," *The HR Digest*, August 1, 2019, www.thehrdigest.com/making-diversity-central-to-success-qa-with-chevrons-chief-diversity-officer/.
28. Equal Employment Opportunity Commission, "EEO-1 Data Collection," https://perma.cc/Y5Q7-QQRB.

29. Ibid.
30. "EEO-1 Component 1 Data Collection Instruction Booklet 2023," https://perma.cc/7HTF-NECB.
31. Since 2021, shareholders have increased their demand that companies make their EEO-1 data publicly available; see Lydia Beyoud and Andrew Ramonas, "Shareholders Up Demands for Workplace Diversity Data Seen by Few," *Bloomberg Law*, https://news.bloomberglaw.com/esg/shareholders-up-demands-for-workplace-diversity-data-seen-by-few.
32. Amazon, *Staying the Course on Our Commitment to Sustainability*, 2020.
33. Ibid.
34. Amazon, *Sustainability Report: Further and Faster, Together*, 2020.
35. Ibid.
36. Ibid.
37. Ibid.
38. Chevron, *Corporate Sustainability Report*, 2020.
39. Chevron, *Corporate Sustainability Report*, 2021.
40. Ibid.
41. In August 2020, the SEC amended Item 101(c) of Regulation S-K to require companies to make human capital disclosures in the "business" section of their annual 10-K reports, to the extent the information is material to an understanding of their business. It requires companies to provide "a description of [their] human capital resources, including the number of persons employed and any human capital measures or objectives that the [company] focus on in managing [its] business tailored to its unique business and workforce." 17 C.F.R. 229.101. (2020) [Release Nos. 33-10668; 34-86614]; File No. S7-11-19. One industry analysis of 451 S&P 500 companies that filed an annual 10-K report between November 2020 and July 2021 shows that 82 percent of 10-K reports included general discussions about diversity, equity, and inclusion, encompassing a range of identity factors. Of those, 35 percent included Type 2 race-conscious disclosures. Gibson Dunn, "Discussing Human Capital: A Survey of the S&P 500's Compliance with the New SEC Disclosure Requirement One Year after Adoption," November 10, 2021, www.gibsondunn.com/discussing-human-capital-survey-of-sp-500-compliance-with-new-sec-disclosure-requirement-one-year-after-adoption/.
42. SEC Office of Investor Education and Advocacy, "Investor Bulletin: How to Read a 10-K," www.sec.gov/files/reada10k.pdf.
43. Ibid.; 17 C.F.R. § 240.14a-9 (2001); 15 U.S.C. § 77q(a) (2006); 15 U.S.C. § 78j(b) (2006); 17 C.F.R. § 240.10b-5 (2010).
44. SEC Office of Investor Education and Advocacy, "Investor Bulletin."
45. Andrea Murphy, "America's Largest Private Companies," *Forbes*, November 14, 2023, www.forbes.com/lists/largest-private-companies/?sh=54ea24a8bac4.
46. Marcela Pinilla and Nandini Hampole, "Investors Are Committing to Action on Diversity. Now What?," *BSR*, October 7, 2020, www.bsr.org/en/blog/investors-are-committing-to-action-on-diversity-now-what.
47. Ibid.; Shareholders have also filed shareholder derivative lawsuits against directors and officers of Oracle Corp., Facebook Inc. and QualComm Inc., for among other things, authorizing false statements in proxy statements, including avowing a commitment to diversity, on which shareholders relied in reelecting the directors, approving executive compensation, and rejecting shareholder proposals concerning diversity issues. Francesca Odell, Victor Hou, and James Langston, "3 Cases Spotlight Shareholder Interest in Public Co. Diversity," *Law 360*, August 4, 2020.
48. 17 C.F.R. § 240.14a-8 (2012).

49. Myron P. Curzan and Mark L. Pelesh, "Revitalizing Corporate Democracy: Control of Investment Managers' Voting on Social Responsibility Proxy Issues," *Harvard Law Review* 93 (1980): 670, 671.
50. Anne D'innocenzio, "Costco Successfully Defends Its Diversity Policies as Other US Companies Scale Theirs Back," *Associated Press*, January 23, 2025, www.apnews.com/article/costco-shareholder-proposal-diversity-dei-0330f448741b35f2f788a36948ff3f95.
51. David Parthiban, Matt Bloom, and Amy J. Hillman, "Investor Activism, Managerial Responsiveness, and Corporate Social Performance," *Strategic Management Journal* 28, no. 1 (2006): 91–100. The Trump administration's SEC guidelines for Regulations 13D and 13G in 2025 has limited the behind-the-scenes process that occurs before proposals are submitted. The guidelines limit the ability for institutional shareholders with 5 percent or more in shares to inform a corporation's board of its voting direction because that kind of shareholder engagement may constitute "attempts to influence control" over management. Cooley Alert, "SEC Staff Adopts Significant New Guidance Affecting Shareholder Proposals and Engagement," February 14, 2025, www.cooley.com/news/insight/2025/2025-02-14-sec-staff-adopts-significant-new-guidance-affecting-shareholder-proposals-and-engagement.
52. Parthiban, et al., "Investor Activism."
53. In 2024, in an unprecedented move, ExxonMobil side-stepped the established SEC no-action process and sued two of its own investors, Arjuna Capital and Follow This, after they filed a climate shareholder proposal. The shareholders withdrew the proposal, but Exxon continued to pursue the litigation. The case was ultimately dismissed after the shareholders assured the court that they would not resubmit the proposal. Exxon Mobil Corporation v. Arjuna Capital, LLC et al Exxon Mobil Corporation v. Arjuna Capital, LLC et al, Docket No. 4:24-cv-00069 (N.D. Tex. Jan. 21, 2024).
54. SOC Investment Group is focused on shareholder activism through engaging with companies on behalf of union-backed pension funds and is affiliated with the Strategic Organizing Center (SOC), a labor advocacy group.
55. Kate Rogers, "McDonald's to Start Focus Groups with Owners as Part of Civil Rights Audit," *CNBC*, September 11, 2023, www.cnbc.com/2023/09/11/mcdonalds-to-start-focus-groups-with-owners-as-part-of-civil-rights-audit.html.
56. Ibid.
57. John J. Edwards, III, and Allison Nicole Smith, "McDonald's Seeks Assessment on Race after Shareholder Vote," *Bloomberg*, June 2, 2022, www.bloomberg.com/news/articles/2022-06-02/lowe-s-investors-ask-for-report-on-racial-and-gender-pay-gaps?embedded-checkout=true.
58. Gadinis and Miazad, "Corporate Law and Social Risk," 1401–78.
59. Berenblat and Gonzalez-Sussman, "Racial Equity Audits."
60. Valecia M. McDowell and Elena F. Mitchell, "Racial Equity Audits: The New ESG Frontier," *Bloomberg Law*, April 26, 2022.
61. Matt Stevens, "Starbucks C.E.O. Apologizes after Arrests of 2 Black Men," *New York Times*, April 15, 2018, www.nytimes.com/2018/04/15/us/starbucks-philadelphia-black-men-arrest.html.
62. Rachel Siegel and Alex Horton, "Starbucks to Close 8,000 Stores for Racial-Bias Education on May 29 after Arrest of Two Black Men," *Washington Post*, April 17, 2018, www.washingtonpost.com/news/business/wp/2018/04/17/starbucks-to-close-8000-stores-for-racial-bias-education-on-may-29-after-arrest-of-two-black-men/.
63. Jill Disis, "Starbucks Advisers Say the Company Needs to Do More to End Racial Bias," *CNN Business*, July 2, 2018, https://money.cnn.com/2018/07/02/news/companies/starbucks-racial-bias-report/index.html.

64. Starbucks Corporation, 2020 *Notice of Annual Meeting of Shareholders and Proxy Statement*; SEC, "Schedule 14A: Proxy Statement."
65. Facebook, *Facebook's Civil Rights Audit – Final Report*, July 8, 2020, https://about.fb.com/wp-content/uploads/2020/07/Civil-Rights-Audit-Final-Report.pdf.
66. Ibid.
67. Social proposals cover a wide range of issues, inclusion diversity-related issues, gender/racial pay gap, disclosure of board statistics, and reporting on human rights, workplace policies, and the opioid crisis. Environmental proposals include addressing climate change, recycling, and sustainability disclosures. Gibson Dunn, Client Alert, *Shareholder Proposal Developments during the 2020 Proxy Season*, August 4, 2020, www.gibsondunn.com/shareholder-proposal-developments-during-the-2020-proxy-season/. A proxy season is a period during which publicly traded companies hold their annual shareholder meetings, allowing shareholders to vote on various matters affecting the company's direction, such as electing board members or deciding on key strategic initiatives, by submitting their votes through a proxy, even if they cannot attend the meeting in person.
68. Ibid.
69. Francesca L. Odell, Jennifer Kennedy Park, and Charity E. Lee, "How Boards Should Be Thinking about the Supreme Court's SFFA Affirmative Action Decision," *Harvard Law School Forum on Corporate Governance*, February 14, 2024.
70. ISS Insights, https://insights.issgovernance.com/. ISS provides data, analytics, and insight on shareholders and corporations to empower shareholders on social and sustainability issues.
71. Yonca Ertimur, Fabrizio Ferri, and Stephen R. Stubbe, "Board of Directors' Responsiveness to Shareholders: Evidence from Shareholder Proposals," *Journal of Corporate Finance* 16, no. 1 (2010): 53, 54–55 n.4.
72. Ibid.
73. Deloitte CFO Program, "Activist Shareholders: How Will You Respond?," www2.deloitte.com/us/en/pages/finance/articles/cfo-insights-shareholder-investor-activism.html; David F. Larcker, Brian Tayan, and Stephen A. Miles, "Protests from Within: Engaging with Employee Activists," *Harvard Law School Forum on Corporate Governance*, March 24, 2021, https://corpgov.law.harvard.edu/2021/03/24/protests-from-within-engaging-with-employee-activists/ (reporting data from Marketing Scenario Analytica).
74. Lisa M. Fairfax. "ESG Hypocrisy and Voluntary Disclosure," *New York University Journal of Legislation and Public Policy* 26, no. 1 (2024): 127–71.
75. Adediran, "Disclosing Corporate Diversity."
76. Ibid., 3.
77. Sumagaysay, "Citigroup, Wells Fargo, Bank of America."
78. Bank of America Corporation, *2021 Proxy Statement*, 2021, 90.
79. Ibid., 91.
80. CNN Business, "Amazon.com," accessed July 26, 2024, https://money.cnn.com/quote/shareholders/shareholders.html?symb=AMZN&subView=institutional.
81. Del Rey, "Bias, Disrespect, and Demotions."
82. Kishan, "Amazon to Undergo Racial Audit."
83. C. M. Ekwueme, C. F. Egbunike, and C. I. Onyali, "Benefits of Triple Bottom Line Disclosures on Corporate Performance: An Exploratory Study of Corporate Stakeholders," *Journal of Management and Sustainability* 3, no. 2 (2013): 79–91.
84. Kishan, "Amazon to Undergo Racial Audit."
85. Hazel Bradford, "SEC Backs Amazon Proposal from New York State Common," *Pensions & Investments*, April 8, 2022, www.pionline.com/regulation/sec-backs-amazon-proposal-new-york-state-common.

86. Paul Kiernan, "SEC Rescinds Trump-Era Policy, Eases Path for Shareholder Proposals on Environmental, Social Issues," *Wall Street Journal*, November 3, 2021; Lydia Beyoud, "ESG Proxy Proposals Land on Easier Path for Vote after SEC Change," *Bloomberg Law*, November 9, 2021.
87. Danielle Walker and Casey Sullivan, "Inside the Growing Big Law Business of Racial Equity Audits, Where Big Companies Hire Outsiders to Investigate Their Impact on Civil Rights," *Business Insider*, December 20, 2021.
88. Andrew Ramonas, "ESG Investors Push More Racial Issues after Wins at Apple, J&J," *Bloomberg*, May 25, 2022, https://news.bloomberglaw.com/securities-law/esg-investors-push-more-racial-issues-after-wins-at-apple-j-j
89. Amazon Employees for Climate Justice, "How Amazon's Emissions Are Hurting Communities of Color," *Medium*, May 26, 2020, https://amazonemployees4climatejustice.medium.com/environmental-justice-and-amazons-carbon-footprint-9e10fab21138.
90. Anna A. Travis, "Why Racial Equity Audit Matters," LinkedIn post, April 24, 2021, www.linkedin.com/pulse/why-racial-equity-audits-matters-anna-a-tavis-ph-d/.
91. Berenblat and Gonzalez-Sussman, "Racial Equity Audits."
92. Kori Hale, "Starbucks Steps Up Its Racial Justice Outreach with $100 Million Pledge," *Forbes*, January 20, 2021, www.forbes.com/sites/korihale/2021/01/20/starbucks-steps-up-its-racial-justice-outreach-with-100-million-pledge/; Berenblat and Gonzalez-Sussman, "Racial Equity Audits."
93. Hale, *Starbucks Steps Up*.
94. SEC, "Schedule 14A: Proxy Statement."
95. Ibid.
96. Ibid.
97. Ibid.
98. Drew Costley, "Once Again, a Chevron Oil Spill Is Impacting a Community of Color," *Medium*, February 12, 2021, https://medium.com/future-human/once-again-a-chevron-oil-spill-is-impacting-a-community-of-color-1f55f09a0694.
99. Danielle Renwick, "'No Time for Inaction': How a California Refinery Disaster Created a Generation of Activists," *The Guardian*, August 7, 2022, www.theguardian.com/us-news/2022/aug/07/chevron-fire-richmond-pollution-activism.
100. Susie Cagle, "Richmond v. Chevron: The California City Taking on Its Most Powerful Polluter," *The Guardian*, October 9, 2019, www.theguardian.com/environment/2019/oct/09/richmond-chevron-california-city-polluter-fossil-fuel.
101. Lien, "Oil Giant."
102. Jonathan M. Colmer, Suvy Qin, John L. Voorheis, and Reed Walker, "Income, Wealth, and Environmental Inequality in the United States," *National Bureau of Economic Research*, Working Paper 33050, October 2024; Ihab Mikati, Adam F. Benson, Thomas J. Luben, Jason D. Sacks, and Jennifer Richmond-Bryant, "Disparities in Distribution of Particulate Matter Emission Sources by Race and Poverty Status," *American Journal of Public Health* 108 (2018): 480–85; Phil McKenna, "EPA Finds Black Americans Face More Health-Threatening Air Pollution – Inside Climate News," *Inside Climate News*, March 2, 2018, https://insideclimatenews.org/news/02032018/air-pollution-data-african-american-race-health-epa-research/.
103. Data USA, "Richmond, CA – Demographics Data," accessed June 4, 2024, https://datausa.io/profile/geo/richmond-ca/#demographics.
104. Ilana Cohen, "Chevron's 'Black Lives Matter' Tweet Prompts a Debate about Big Oil and Environmental Justice – Inside Climate News," *Inside Climate News*, June 20, 2020, https://insideclimatenews.org/news/20062020/chevron-black-lives-matter-twitter/.

105. SEC, "Schedule 14A: Proxy Statement." In January 2021, Chevron's filed a letter with the SEC stating its intent to exclude the proposal from its Annual Meeting of Stockholders because it related to pending litigation in a number of cases, including City of Oakland v. BP p.l.c. et al., No. 3:17-cv-6011, Dkt. 199 ¶ 135 (N.D. Cal. Apr. 3, 2018); State of Delaware v. BP Am. Inc. et al., No. N20C-09-097-AML CCLD, Compl. ¶ 239 (Del. Super. Ct. Sept. 10, 2020).
106. SEC, *Chevron Corporation Form 8-K*, 2022.

3

Racial Targets

Until this point in the book, I have described race-conscious disclosures as different categories of public statements about race and people of color. This chapter zeros in on "racial targets," a specific type of race-conscious disclosures focused on the hiring and retention of people of color. Racial targets are publicly disclosed nonbinding, voluntary goals, or aspirations – rather than mandatory requirements – to hire, retain, or promote people of color by a future point in time on a general institutional level, such as among employees, boards of directors, managers, and other leaders.[1] Publicly traded large, medium, and small companies, as well as some large private companies made extensive racial targets between 2020 and 2023.

Unlike general statements about race and people of color, racial targets have the potential to positively influence true racial progress by breaking cycles of subordination or relegation to lower wage positions, incorporating opportunities to move up the corporate ladder, and giving people of color agency and decision-making authority. No wonder conservatives, particularly since the beginning of Trump's second presidential term, have weaponized racial targets, calling them quotas, which are fixed proportions of opportunities reserved exclusively for certain minority groups in particular jobs. Most quotas are illegal in the United States.[2] Couching targets as quotas has resulted in many corporations getting rid of them altogether.[3] As I have written elsewhere, racial targets are legally defensible despite conservatives framing them as illegal quotas.[4]

But while companies made specific goals about hiring and promotion, they did not disclose how their past hiring trends may have limited opportunities for people of color, making targets necessary in the first place. Instead, corporations disclosed information regarding the racial composition of their workforce at the time and set goals to hire and promote people of color in the future. Ultimately, these goals limit racial progress because corporations retained the power to determine the floor and ceiling of hiring and promotions without assessing whether and how those parameters would propel people of color into leadership positions.

This chapter documents extensive racial targets corporations made between 2020 and 2023. It analyzes the types of racial targets corporations have made, how companies have used them, and how targets are part of the broader project of corporations using words to demonstrate concern for and action toward tackling racial inequality. Racial targets reveal how corporate words matter in practice and show the complicated relationship between positive aims and the challenges of moving toward true racial progress. Corporations did not need to use racial targets as part of race-conscious disclosures but chose to do so. If a corporation claims to want to achieve racial progress by establishing racial targets, it is important for the corporation to consider strategies that actually advance true racial progress, rather than those focused primarily on increasing the company's financial standing.

During the Nixon administration, the Business Roundtable – a consortium of the nation's leading corporations established in 1972 and still in existence – stated that "setting goals and using numerical measures are a basic fact of how business operates."[5] Corporations set goals by making disclosures and, historically, the setting of hiring goals has been crucial to increasing racial diversity in companies. A study from 1970 found that the primary reason the proportion of Black employees did not increase in public utility companies was because company managers did not consider Black employment to be important enough to "warrant the same kind of goal setting, program planning, and performance evaluation applied in other areas of company operations."[6] And when in 1985, President Reagan threatened to rescind President Lyndon Johnson's executive order calling for affirmative action in employment, companies vehemently promised to "continue goals and timetables no matter what the government does."[7] Indeed, in a 1985 survey of CEOs of Fortune 500 companies, more than 90 percent of participants, or 116 out of 127, said that the "numerical objectives" in their affirmative action programs were established partly to satisfy corporate objectives unrelated to government regulations.[8]

The history of corporate goal setting around race has parallels with the contemporary phenomenon of companies establishing racial targets starting in 2020. Corporations carefully crafted racial targets, seeking not to violate the laws that make racial quotas or mandates illegal. Importantly, there are three key distinctions between racial quotas and racial targets.

First, like other race-conscious disclosures, racial targets are private and voluntary statements of programs and policies unrelated to federal affirmative action. They were invented *by* companies *for* companies and have no state or government entity requiring them.

Second, while racial targets often include the specific numbers or percentages of people of color that a company aims to hire or promote, they tend to do so on a general institutional level and do not apply to specific occupations or jobs, unlike racial quotas. Racial targets are almost always general aspirations to increase the percentage of people of color among employees, leadership, or boards of directors. Therefore, if a company states a goal to have 20 percent of its leadership comprise of people of color, "leadership" can be so broadly construed that the 20 percent can be applied to a range of occupations, professions, or roles.

Third, racial targets are aspirations or goals rather than strict requirements. This means they are nonbinding. In 1972, the US Commission on Civil Rights distinguished goals from quotas by defining goals as "nothing more than a description of what the labor force would look like absent the effects of illegal racial or sexual discrimination, and the 'timetable' is the informed estimate of time needed to achieve the discrimination-free labor force without disrupting the industry or denying anyone the opportunity for employment."[9] Per this definition, a goal is a desired result rather than a strict plan that must be achieved. In this way, companies can choose to use racial targets as metrics of assessment rather than strict end results.[10]

RACIAL TARGETS AFTER 2020

Corporations set various types of goals, including financial ones, using specific, tangible metrics in response to different priorities.[11] Goals tend to derive from the values and philosophies of CEOs as well as shareholder and stakeholder expectations.[12] For publicly traded companies, goals also derive from shareholders' stock market responses to company performance.[13] All corporate goals are the result of both explicit and implicit trade-offs among competing interests.[14]

Like other race-conscious disclosures, racial targets were a response to reputational risk calculus. But unlike other types of race-conscious disclosures (except corporate racial philanthropy), they are important corporate words that do actually matter in terms of achieving corporate goals and impacting racial progress.

To show what corporations say when they make racial targets, I randomly selected publicly traded companies across a six-year period from 2018 to 2023 to analyze racial targets. To determine whether a company declared a racial target, I created a list of verbs that signal future intent, such as "commit," "grow," or "increase," as discussed in further detail in the Appendix. I used these verbs to identify when a company's statistics speak to what they plan to do in the future, as opposed to what they have done in the past or are doing in the present. For a company to count as making a racial target, it must use a verb that signals future intent in conjunction with the words "percent," "percentage," or the "%" symbol.

Companies rarely publicly disclosed racial targets prior to 2020. Table 3.1 and Figure 3.1 show that while only four or 13.3% of the thirty companies I examined for racial targets in 2018 made them, sixty-nine or 36.1% of the 191 companies I examined in 2021 made racial targets. By 2023, 167 or 39.4% of the 423 companies I examined had made racial targets.[15]

Figure 3.2 shows that companies were more likely to make racial targets about Black people in comparison to Asian, Latino, and Native American people. The year 2020 marks the beginning of this focus on racial targets in general, and on Black people in particular, for future hiring and promotions. In 2023, for every ten racial

TABLE 3.1 *Racial targets in public companies by year*

Year	Total reports examined	Companies with targets
2018	30	4
2019	55	15
2020	77	21
2021	191	69
2022	331	113
2023	423	167

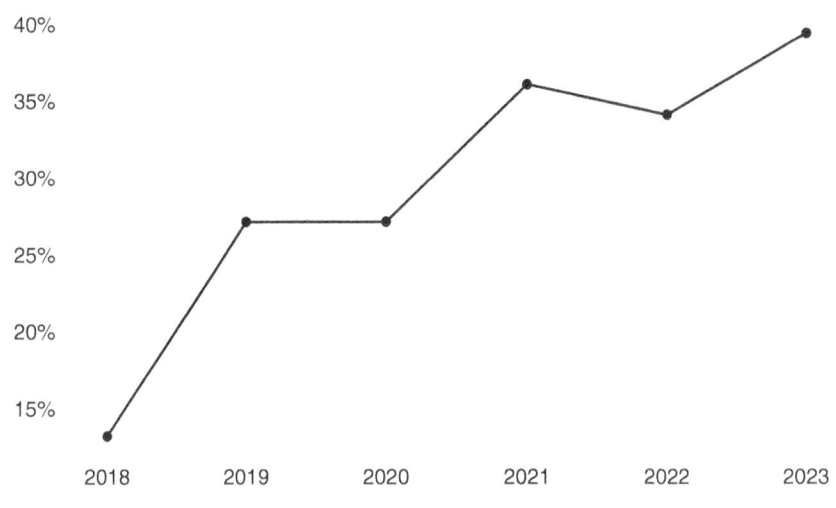

FIGURE 3.1 Racial targets in public companies by year

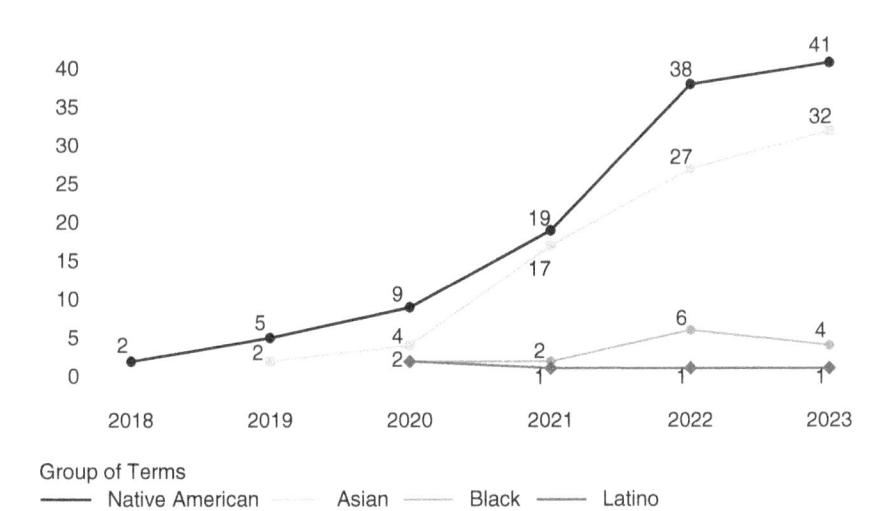

FIGURE 3.2 Racial targets in public companies by racial or ethnic group

targets that focused on particular racial and ethnic groups, approximately four to five were about Black people, three to four were about Latinos, one to two were about Asians, and zero to one were about Native Americans.

In addition, when companies made racial targets, eight out of ten times, the target was about increasing racial diversity among employees, management, and firm leadership.

Results are generally similar for the large private companies I examined, even though there are fewer of them. Private companies are not listed on stock exchanges and are not required to make public disclosures. Yet private companies used racial targets – for example, in 2023, twelve out of the twenty-nine private companies I examined made racial targets (Table 3.2; Figure 3.3). In previous work, I have argued that disclosures made by large private companies should be regulated much like those of public companies in the context of disclosures about racial, gender,

TABLE 3.2 *Racial targets in private companies by year*

Year	Total	Companies with targets
2018	3	1
2019	5	3
2020	5	4
2021	8	4
2022	20	8
2023	29	12
Total	70	32

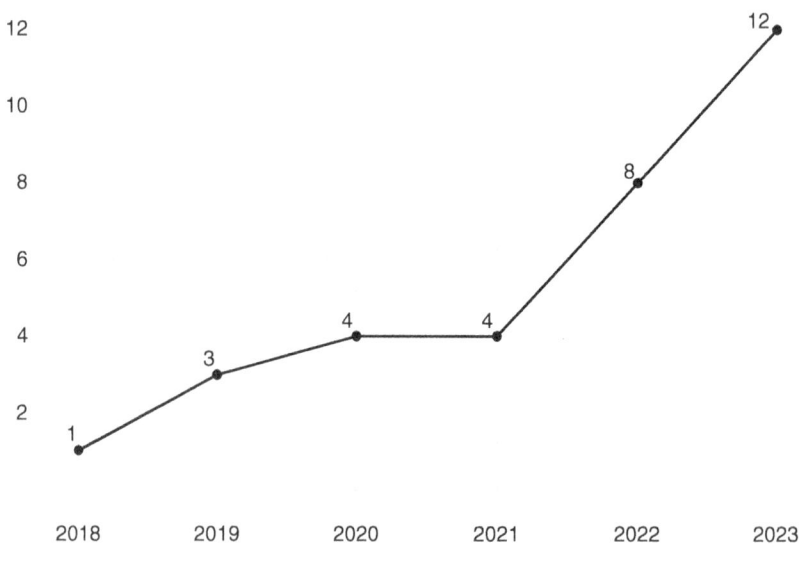

FIGURE 3.3 Racial targets in private companies by year

and other forms of diversity.[16] Chapter 6 focuses on regulating both public and private companies' race-conscious disclosures and retractions.

TYPES OF RACIAL TARGETS

To understand the substance and structure of racial targets, I conducted two levels of analysis. The first level was quantitative: I counted the prevalence of racial targets over time using Python, a programming software. The second was qualitative: I observed how companies made racial targets over a three-year period and found distinctions between them using manual coding and Atlas.ti, a qualitative text management software.

I identified two types of racial targets: closed-ended racial targets and open-ended racial targets. Closed-ended racial targets include a stated period by which a company intends to meet a goal; open-ended racial targets do not include such a stated period by which to meet the goal.

Closed-Ended Racial Targets

Closed-ended racial targets vary in language and specificity, but all closed-ended targets have two common elements: (1) a specific goal or aspiration to hire or promote a specified percentage of people of color and (2) a year or period by which the corporation intends to reach the goal. Racial targets made by the Bank of New York (BNY), Hartford Prudential Financial, Starbucks, Sysco, and Target are illustrative of closed-ended targets, as indicated by the following corporate statements (emphases added):

> By *year-end 2023*, [BNY] plans to achieve these levels by improving diverse outcomes in hiring, advancement and retention: Achieve a *15% increase* in Black representation *to 12%*. Achieve a *30% increase* in Black representation of senior leaders [] *to over 4%*. Achieve a *15% increase* in Latinx representation to *almost 8%*. Achieve a *30% increase* in Latinx representation of senior leaders [] to *over 5.5%*.[17]
>
> Hartford is on pace to reach our new representation goal of ... *20% people of color* in senior leadership roles *by 2030* because the actions critical to our success are now fully integrated into our business, compensation and talent strategies.[18]
>
> In December 2020, [Prudential Financial] committed to the following set of diversity goals for our senior and mid-level leaders to be attained *by 2023*: Increase overall diversity of our most senior leader population *by 10%* and increase our percentage of Black and Latinx employees *by at least 25%*. For our mid-level leaders, increase the percentage of people of color *by 8%* and increase our percentage of Black and Latinx employees *by at least 25%*.[19]
>
> [Starbucks has a goal of] at least *40%* BIPOC[20] representation ... in all retail roles, *by 2025* in the U.S. *At least 40%* BIPOC representation ... in all manufacturing roles *by 2025* in the U.S. *At least 30%* BIPOC representation ... for all enterprise roles, including senior leadership, *by 2025* in the U.S.[21]

> [*By 2025*, Sysco aims to] [i]ncrease total U.S. associate ethnic and gender diversity *to 62%*.²²
>
> As a first step forward, [Target is] planning to increase representation of Black team members across the company *by 20% by 2023* by sharpening our focus on advancement, retention and hiring.²³

The examples above show that companies were often specific about the actual percentage increase they intended to reach, and the year by which they intended to reach it. There were some exceptions. Some closed-ended targets used a range of years instead of a specific year. But like all closed-ended targets, they identified some point in time at which the company sought to meet a stated goal. State Street's and Truist's racial targets are illustrative of closed-ended targets with a range of years (emphases added):

> [State Street aims to] *triple* our Black and Latino leadership (Senior Vice Presidents and above) and *double* our percentage of Black and Latino populations *over the next three years*.²⁴
>
> [Truist's] target is to increase ethnic diversity of senior leadership *from 11.9% to 15% in three years* and promote pay equity by conducting regular external, independent, and expert equity reviews.²⁵

Among closed-ended racial targets, Starbucks's 2021 racial target comes closest to the specificity associated with racial quotas.²⁶ Specifically, Starbucks stated that its goal applied to "manufacturing," in addition to enterprise roles. However, in contrast to the language of quotas, Starbucks did not name a particular position, job, or occupation within the manufacturing industry. This is an important distinction that separates racial targets from quotas. Most companies' targets generally state an increase among employees and leadership positions, rather than in relation to specific jobs or occupations.

Open-Ended Racial Targets

At first, it is surprising that open-ended targets were relatively uncommon compared to closed-ended targets during this period, because open-ended targets provide more flexibility for unexpected circumstances that may require adjustments or changes in timeframe. If most companies had adopted open-ended racial targets, perhaps it would have been easier to defend them against conservative pushback. This is not because open-ended racial targets are more "legal" than closed-ended racial targets, but because they seem less specific and are therefore more fluid than closed-ended targets.

But perhaps corporations mostly relied on closed-ended racial targets because they already tend to set specific goals in their operations not explicitly related to race. Having closed-ended goals is likely simply more intuitive to business managers, and this includes racial targets. Research on DEI targets broadly also shows that specificity sets clear expectations and allows investors greater confidence in companies.²⁷

In general, racial targets are open-ended when companies provide a percentage without a set time frame in which a hiring goal or aspiration should be met. Procter & Gamble (P&G) and Pactiv Evergreen's racial targets are illustrative of the open-ended approach. Pactiv Evergreen's is also open-ended in terms of its goals:

> [P&G has declared an aspiration] to achieve 40% representation of multicultural employees at every management level of the Company.[28]
>
> In 2020, nearly 50% of total US [Pactiv Evergreen] employees were Black, Indigenous or People of Color. In 2021, we're working to revamp and accelerate our people strategy to make it more inclusive and representative.[29]

Like closed-ended racial targets, open-ended targets also tend to refer to the hiring and promotion of broad categories such as employees and management. They also include percentages but stop short of providing a year or timeframe by which the goals would be met. Despite this distinction, both open- and closed-ended racial targets are distinguishable from quotas because targets are goals or aspirations rather than requirements.

BENEFITS AND CHALLENGES OF RACIAL TARGETS

Historically, the setting of hiring goals was crucial to increasing racial diversity in companies, but those goals were rarely made public and thus could not be scrutinized to determine progress over time. In 1996, legal scholars David Wilkins and Mitu Gulati documented that leadership positions in firms was overwhelmingly white.[30] In 2023, legal scholar and sociologist, Kevin Woodson confirmed similar findings in his book, *The Black Ceiling: How Race Still Matters in the Elite Workplace*.[31] Because they are made publicly available, racial targets can be a useful mechanism for challenging racial inequality because they can put companies under the microscope for scrutiny. Some CDOs told me during interviews that their boards of directors and shareholders would not permit their companies to make baseless statements without the intention of actually meeting stated goals. Assuming corporate managers are held accountable by boards and shareholders for their racial targets, and Trump had not returned for a second term, racial diversity should have increased in those companies that set targets.

One way companies held executives accountable for addressing racial inequality was to incentivize them to prioritize it. After the murder of George Floyd, companies began to build incentive structures into racial targets. According to a 2022 industry report, at least half of all companies in each industry in the S&P 500 included an incentive for executives to make progress toward equity goals.[32] For example, in 2021, McDonald's Corporation established a human capital management metric to reinforce the importance of the company's values and hold executives accountable for making progress on DEI.[33] The metric gave executives a 15 percent short-term cash incentive.[34] By 2023, the program had been solidified with a checkbox on a form indicating whether a metric had been achieved.[35] In 2024, the company retained the program but became vague by simply noting that it continued to make progress toward increasing the representation of underrepresented minorities in senior director and above positions, although only a few directors had received the incentive.[36] In 2025, McDonald's bowed to conservative pressure to get rid of these kinds of incentive structures.[37] It is extremely likely that most if not all companies that retained these kinds of incentive structures in 2024 will get rid of them.[38]

Perhaps management incentives could have made a difference toward true racial progress. But we know the story is more complicated, because there are many obstacles that have prevented companies from fully meeting their racial targets, let alone achieving the kind of true racial progress that propels significant numbers of people of color outside of low-level positions into leadership. Those obstacles include limitations on the power and influence of shareholders (one of the constituencies most inclined to seek corporate accountability on this issue), as described in Chapter 2, the conservative backlash discussed in Chapter 5, and capitalist strategies that can incentivize hiring people of color, but also risk perpetuating racial inequality.

In terms of capitalist strategies that impeded the realization of racial targets, interviews with CDOs reveal three categories of companies, differentiated by the specific approach they took toward meeting their racial targets after making them. In the first category are companies that said they were on target to meet their goals but made limited changes toward reaching them before intense conservative backlash commenced. These companies made racial targets but mostly continuing with business as usual without making any fundamental changes around how they conducted hiring and promotions. Companies in this category were more likely to quickly accede to conservative backlash against DEI and adopt complete race-conscious retraction, as discussed in Chapter 5. And many of the same companies cut jobs and conducted layoffs that impacted a high proportion of people of color amid an economic downtown and backlash to corporate diversity that took off in 2023.[39]

The second category includes companies that set racial targets and followed through with hiring and promoting *some* people of color. Bloomberg Law examined eighty-eight S&P 100 companies, all of which are included in my database, for overall job growth in 2020 and 2021, and found that these companies increased their US workforces by 323,094 people, 94 percent of whom were people of color.[40] The share of Black managers and professionals increased at seventy of the eighty-eight companies.[41] This is a version of racial progress as these corporations hired many more people of color. But while some companies also increased the racial diversity of their executives, managers, and other professionals, the highest numbers of hires were made in low-paying job categories, such as sales and administration.[42] White individuals continue to hold a disproportionate proportion of high-paying jobs at S&P 100 companies.[43]

This is not the kind of racial progress that propels generations of people of color out of racial subordination.[44] Corporations have often taken the approach of hiring many people of color into low-paying jobs when pressured to do so. This was true in the 1960s as discussed in Chapter 1 and was also true between 2020 and 2024. This approach signifies racial progress on corporate terms. True racial progress, by contrast, would prioritize hiring and promoting people of color into executive and management positions where they can have agency and decision-making power within the corporation. At Amazon, for example, Black employees have claimed that they are often passed up for promotions that would get them to positions of power and decision-making.[45] In this way, corporations set racial targets and pointed to steps they took toward meeting them, yet remained focused primarily on hiring in low- and entry-level positions without clear prospects for advancement.

In the third category are companies that undertook hiring strategies that resulted in the hiring of large numbers of people of color, but with limited consideration of how those approaches might further exacerbate racial inequality in minority communities, or fail to yield true racial progress. The CSO of a company described how companies zeroed in on cities with large populations of people of color, like Atlanta, Georgia, "like vultures ... using the community to achieve ... corporate goals." Starting in 2020, many Fortune 500 companies opened branches in Atlanta seeking Black talent.[46] As urban studies scholar Dan Immergluck has documented, Atlanta has experienced a twentieth-century expansion through continuing reliance on public–private partnerships and state and regional planning.[47] Immergluck argues that Atlanta's expansion project caters to capital, often at the expense of predominantly Black and Latino communities.[48] Atlanta is a national leader in Black higher education with six historically Black colleges and universities.[49] The United States Census estimates the city's Black population to be 48.2 percent of the total population in 2022.[50] A large technology company that I interviewed for this book provided an example illustrative of the strategy to expand into these communities:

> One of the big things [is that] we're creating our second-largest office in Atlanta, period, globally, for the Black engineering talent that is coming in, and also, the richness and the diversity of that city. From the very beginning of its inception obviously, there's a lot of nuances to that history but it's the highest density of HBCUs with computer science programs. More diverse than a lot of the MITs of the world in terms of Black and brown engineers. And the number of distinguished engineers that are out of that office now has exploded, which I think is going to result in a lot of important developments for companies like ours moving into the future. *I do know a lot of other companies are having a similar approach in Atlanta* .... And then centering them in cities like Atlanta, cities like Detroit, cities like Miami for Hispanic talent if that's what folks are looking for. (emphasis added)

In a similar move, Autodesk, a software company, made public that it renamed its "Diversity and Inclusion" team the "Diversity and Belonging" team, and switched the location of a new office hub from Denver to Atlanta, to have a better shot at attracting Black engineering graduates there.[51]

These companies and many others expanded into cities with large numbers of people of color, in part, because of the belief that it would help them reach their racial targets.[52] Strategies such as this, while potentially resulting in the hiring of people of color, are often not focused on achieving true racial progress and can further exacerbate inequality, because unless a company takes specific steps, it will not necessarily integrate people of color into a company or its leadership. Many technology companies, for example, have their headquarters where their C-Suites, or top leadership positions, are located in cities like Seattle, WA, which is not racially diverse, with only 6.8 percent of its population being Black in 2022.[53] Members of the C-Suite, including the CEO and CFO, manage a company's affairs. Opening a second, third, fourth, or fifth office in cities like Atlanta is likely to create jobs but is unlikely to propel racial and ethnic minorities into leadership positions in the C-Suite or other senior management roles, especially when company's headquarters remain in predominantly white cities like Seattle, and they do not make plans to advance the people of color that are hired within the firm. Research by Revelio Labs, a workplace analytics firm, has found that Seattle has a high concentration of employees with prestige who also earn significantly higher wages than employees with the same positions in other parts of the country.[54]

Take Blackrock, the world's largest institutional asset manager, with its headquarters in New York City, for example. Blackrock opened its third largest office in Atlanta between 2020 and 2022. However, most if not all of the members of its C-Suite are located elsewhere. It is also unclear whether managers in the Atlanta office are racially diverse or imbued with the authority to make major decisions. But it does not have to be this way. When Visa opened its Atlanta office in 2023, it moved at least two members of its C-Suite to Atlanta to situate some decision-makers and signal the notion of agency and mobility in a city the corporation hopes can cultivate a lot of racially diverse talent.[55] Ensuring that important decision-makers are in offices located in predominantly minority cities, and taking steps toward advancing employees in those offices into leadership is true racial progress.

If racial targets are meant to address racial inequality, the strategy of focusing on Atlanta and similar cities should propel people of color into corporate decision-making positions, rather than hiring them as low-level employees and not creating clear plans toward advancement. If corporations seek to move beyond simply obtaining talent, building capital, and protecting against reputational risks related to racial discrimination or inequality, they can consider using racial targets to advance true racial progress that go beyond hiring and talent acquisition.

RACIAL TARGETS AS RACE-CONSCIOUS DISCLOSURES

Disclosureland is ultimately about the significance of corporate words and their impact on racial progress. Unlike demographic statistics and statements about people of color, racial targets are a defined, action-focused type of race-conscious disclosure. Companies have made racial targets in conjunction with other race-conscious disclosures and have used them as evidence of action toward racial equity in their businesses. Whether through making race-conscious disclosures or engaging in race-conscious retraction, companies have used racial targets to enhance or protect their bottom lines – by proclaiming their interests in addressing racial inequality or retracting previously made targets to protect themselves from reputational or litigation risks.

However, racial targets are a double-edged sword. Unlike general statements about race and demographic statistics about the racial composition of a company, racial targets (and racial philanthropy) can be an avenue for reaching true racial progress because they can incentivize companies to act. In a study of DEI targets in general, researchers found a positive association between companies disclosing DEI targets and the hiring of additional employees who are racial and ethnic minorities.[56] But racial targets can also provide a strong impression that a company is tackling racial inequality in its business, or taking steps toward true racial progress that prioritizes leadership for people of color, even when it is not, which means that racial targets are more likely to benefit companies in terms of their reputation and, ultimately, financial standing. One study found that US companies that articulate targeted and specific DEI commitments improved market performance because DEI targets set clear expectations, which improve investor confidence in companies' DEI strategies.[57]

Therefore, probably more than any other type of race-conscious disclosure, racial targets are the most likely to make a difference toward true racial progress but also carry the greatest risk of impeding it. Racial targets are also the most likely to trigger corporate litigation risk mitigation strategies because stakeholders and conservatives can scrutinize specific corporate goals and bring lawsuits against companies based on those goals.

NOTES

1. Atinuke O. Adediran, "Racial Targets," *Northwestern University Law Review* 118, no. 6 (2024): 1457.
2. Adediran, "Racial Targets," 1457.
3. Conor Murray and Molly Bohannon, "MLB Removes References to Diversity from Careers Website: Here Are All the Companies Rolling Back DEI Programs," *Forbes*, March 22, 2025, www.forbes.com/sites/conormurray/2025/03/22/mlb-removes-references-to-diversity-from-careers-website-here-are-all-the-companies-rolling-back-dei-programs/.
4. Atinuke O. Adediran, "Racial Targets," *Northwestern University Law Review* 118, no. 6 (2024): 1455–1502.
5. MacLean, *Freedom Is Not Enough*, 310.
6. Anderson, *The Negro in the Public Utility Industries*, 222.
7. Anne B. Fisher, "Businessmen Like to Hire by the Numbers," *Fortune*, September 16, 1985, 28.
8. Ibid.

9. MacLean, *Freedom Is Not Enough*, 110.
10. Veronica Root Martinez and Gina-Gail S. Fletcher, "Equality Metrics," *Yale Law Journal Forum* 130 (2021): 869, 875.
11. Gordon Donaldson, "Financial Goals and Strategic Consequences," *Harvard Business Review* (1985): 1, 6; Melissa Houston, "How to Set Financial Goals for Your Business in 2023," *Forbes*, December 28, 2022, www.forbes.com/sites/melissahouston/2022/12/28/how-to-set-financial-goals-for-your-business-in-2023/.
12. Donaldson, "Financial Goals."
13. Ibid.
14. Ibid.
15. Adediran, "Disclosing Corporate Diversity."
16. Ibid.
17. BNY Mellon, 2020 *Enterprise ESG Report*, 18; emphasis added.
18. Hartford, 2020 *Sustainability Highlight Report*, 5; emphasis added.
19. Prudential Financial Inc., *Environmental, Social and Governance Summary Report*, 2021, 5; emphasis added.
20. BIPOC means Black, Indigenous, and people of color. Sandra E. Garcia, "Where Did BIPOC Come From?," *New York Times*, June 17, 2020, www.nytimes.com/article/what-is-bipoc.html.
21. Starbucks, 2020 *Global Environmental & Social Impact Report*, 8; emphasis added.
22. Sysco, 2021 *Corporate Social Responsibility Report*, 10; emphasis added.
23. Target, 2020 *Corporate Social Responsibility Report*, 39; emphasis added.
24. State Street, 2020 *ESG Report*, 58; emphasis added.
25. Truist, *Corporate Social Responsibility*, 2019, 36; emphasis added.
26. Adediran, "Racial Targets," 1457.
27. Fei Li, Chris K. Y. Lo, and Christopher S. Tang, "Will Diversity Equity and Inclusion Commitment Improve Manufacturing Firms' Performance? A Signaling Theory Perspective on DEI Announcements," SSRN website, December 15, 2022, https://ssrn.com/abstract=4318187.
28. P&G, 2020 *Citizenship Report*, 70; emphasis added.
29. Pactiv Evergreen Inc., *Environmental, Social & Governance Update*, 2021, 21; emphasis added.
30. David B. Wilkins and G. Mitu Gulati, "Why Are There So Few Black Lawyers in Corporate Law Firms – An Institutional Analysis," *California Law Review* 84, no. 3 (May 1996): 493–626.
31. Kevin Woodson, *The Black Ceiling: How Race Still Matters in the Elite Workplace* (Chicago: University of Chicago Press, 2023).
32. Semler Brossy, *S&P 500, ESG + Incentives Report*, 2022.
33. McDonald's Corporation, 2021 *Notice of Annual Shareholders' Meeting and Proxy Statement*.
34. Ibid.
35. McDonald's Corporation, 2023 *Notice of Annual Shareholders' Meeting and Proxy Statement*.
36. McDonald's Corporation, 2024 *Notice of Annual Shareholders' Meeting and Proxy Statement*.
37. McDonald's Corporation, No Action Letter Request to the SEC, January 17, 2025, www.sec.gov/files/corpfin/no-action/14a-8/nlpcmcdonalds11725-14a8inc.pdf. McDonald's Corporation. 2025 *Notice of Annual Shareholders' Meeting and Proxy Statement*. 2025. The National Legal and Policy Center, a conservative organization, submitted a shareholder

proposal to McDonald's in 2025. The company subsequently filed a no-action letter request with the SEC to exclude the proposal from shareholder votes on the basis that the company had implemented the proposal, which it had by removing the incentives from consideration.

38. Patrick Temple-West, "Companies Drop DEI Targets from Bonus Plans on Pressure from Conservatives," *Financial Times*, July 21, 2024, www.ft.com/content/63ac21a5-9929-4bc3-9089-03299f023bcd.
39. Reyhan Ayas, Paulina Tilly, and Devan Rawlings, "Cutting Costs at the Expense of Diversity," *Revelio Labs*, February 7, 2023, www.reveliolabs.com/news/social/cutting-costs-at-the-expense-of-diversity/.
40. Green et al., "Corporate America."
41. Ibid.
42. Ibid.
43. Jeff Green, David Ingold, Raeedah Wahid, Cedric Sam, and Daniela Sirtori-Cortina, "Corporate America Promised to Hire a Lot More People of Color. It Actually Did," *Bloomberg*, September 25, 2023, www.bloomberg.com/graphics/2023-black-lives-matter-equal-opportunity-corporate-diversity/?utm_source=website&utm_medium=share&utm_campaign=copy.
44. Particularly without strong collective action or unionization processes, which corporations have historically opposed. Lawrence Mishel, Lynn Rhinehart, and Lane Windham. "Explaining the Erosion of Private-Sector Unions," *Economic Policy Institute*, November 18, 2020, www.epi.org/unequalpower/publications/private-sector-unions-corporate-legal-erosion/.
45. Del Rey, "Bias, Disrespect, and Demotions."
46. Frank Holland and Cait Freda, "Atlanta Is a Growing Hub for Top Tech Companies Like Apple and Microsoft to Find Black Talent," *CNBC Tech*, February 4, 2022, www.cnbc.com/2022/02/04/atlanta-is-a-growing-hub-for-top-tech-companies-like-apple-and-microsoft-to-find-black-talent.html; Metro Atlanta Chamber, "Metro Atlanta Welcomes Assurant as Newest Fortune 500 Company," Metro Atlanta Chamber website, July 17, 2023, www.metroatlantachamber.com/fortune-500-1000-company-assurant/.
47. Dan Immergluck, *Red Hot City: Housing, Race, and Exclusion in Twenty-First Century Atlanta* (Berkeley: University of California Press, 2022).
48. Ibid., 22.
49. Ibid.
50. United States Census, "Quick Facts: Atlanta City – Georgia," www.census.gov/quickfacts/fact/table/atlantacitygeorgia/PST045222.
51. Jennifer Miller, "Why Some Companies Are Saying 'Diversity and Belonging' Instead of 'Diversity and Inclusion,'" *New York Times*, May 16, 2023, www.nytimes.com/2023/05/13/business/diversity-equity-inclusion-belonging.html.
52. Holland and Freda, "Atlanta Is a Growing Hub."
53. United States Census, "Quick Facts: Seattle City – Washington."
54. Alvaro Carril, "Does Amazon Want Employees to Commute or Quit?," *Revelio Labs*, November 12, 2024, www.reveliolabs.com/news/business/does-amazon-want-employees-to-commute-or-quit/.
55. Ellen McGirt, "Visa Moved Part of Its C-suite to Atlanta to Diversify Company Ranks – But Making a Dent in the City's Income Inequality Problem Is an Uphill Battle," *Fortune*, April 4, 2023, https://fortune.com/2023/04/04/visa-atlanta-diversity-michelle-gethers-clark/.
56. Wei Cai, Yue Chen, Shiva Rajgopal, and Li Azinovic-Yang, "Diversity Targets," *Review of Accounting Studies* 29 (2024): 1–52.
57. Li et al., "Will Diversity Equity."

4

Corporate Racial Philanthropy

The McKinsey Institute for Black Economic Mobility estimates that by the end of May 2021, Fortune 1,000 companies had earmarked and publicly disclosed about $200 billion in funding for racial equity.[1] And in 2022, total corporate monetary public commitments to racial equity causes had risen to an unprecedented $340 billion.[2] By another estimate, fifty-four of America's largest public companies and their foundations publicly committed nearly $50 billion to racial equity over a range of years.[3] These monetary allocations were quite large. What is not apparent is that the funding was allocated in a manner that is unusual in traditional philanthropy. For those fifty-four companies, $45.2 billion or 90 percent of the commitments were allocated as loans or investments.[4] Only $4.2 billion was in the form of grants to tax-exempt organizations, as is often the case when for-profit entities or private foundations donate money for philanthropic causes.[5] Another estimate made by Candid, an organization that collects data on the nonprofit sector, found that corporate grant pledges to nonprofit organizations for racial causes went from about $341 million in 2019 to 8.8 billion in 2020, which was more than twenty-four times the amount in 2019.[6] Of that amount, another source found that only about $3.4 billion in actual grants or 38.6 percent were awarded to nonprofit organizations for racial causes.[7] And by 2021, corporate grants to nonprofit organizations for racial causes decreased from the $3.4 billion to $2.5 billion, and in 2022, they had decreased to $980.7 million. These numbers reveal two disparate results. On the one hand, corporate philanthropy for racial causes *increased* significantly between 2019 and 2022. On the other hand, corporate philanthropy to nonprofit organizations for racial causes *decreased* during the same period.

What explains this seeming discrepancy in corporate philanthropy? Why did corporate giving to racial causes increase, while grants to nonprofits for racial causes decreased? The answer is that corporations used disclosures to define the parameters of their engagement in racial causes, and defined philanthropy for racial causes around business activities, including supplier diversity programs and loans and investments, to reach communities of color.[8] As sociologist Patricia Banks has argued, corporate philanthropy to racial and ethnic minorities helps companies to develop positive racial images, which offer business advantages from stakeholders.[9] Corporate philanthropy to minority communities also provides financial benefits to companies through stakeholder goodwill, by signaling that a company not only cares for its community but also cares about particular racial groups or causes.[10]

This chapter empirically develops and advances the concept of "corporate racial philanthropy" (CRP) as the use of corporate disclosures to define the parameters of philanthropy as focused on business transactions and the strategic pursuit of financial gain by targeting minority groups. Corporate racial philanthropy is within the framework of business development initiatives that use philanthropy to tap new markets and generate profit.[11] In this way, it is just another form of strategic corporate philanthropy, the goal of which is to make profits for firms. However, CRP also provides an example of how corporations use race-conscious disclosures to constrain racial progress. With CRP, corporations defined engagement with causes that impact racial minorities largely from a transactional standpoint. Corporate racial philanthropy can be viewed as a response from good faith corporate actors to solve a credibility problem – namely, that corporate words are viewed by the public with suspicion as merely "cheap talk." Like racial targets, CRP disclosures seek to dispel this suspicion through specificity, providing details on what corporations intend to do with their philanthropic dollars.

This chapter argues that CRP cannot be dismissed as cheap talk because, like other forms of race-conscious disclosures, corporations have used CRP disclosures to reduce the significance of claims of racial inequality raised by shareholders and other constituents in other business contexts, while profiting from those words and transactions that accompany them.[12]

CORPORATE PHILANTHROPY

Corporate philanthropy was not an institutionalized or integrated aspect of most American companies until the 1960s.[13] Prior to that, philanthropy by corporations was sporadic, individualized, and limited by the emergence of private foundations and law.[14] The members of boards of publicly owned companies could not make charitable gifts that did not directly benefit their companies or that had no relation to their businesses, unless expressly authorized by statute or charter.[15] It was not until World War I, when corporations began to play a critical role in financing war efforts, including through fundraisers organized by the YMCA and the American Red Cross in 1917 to support servicemen, that corporate philanthropy started to expand.[16]

The Development of Corporate Philanthropy in the United States

Corporate philanthropy grew as companies grew in size, became major players in the wealth, health, and social problems of the communities in which they were located, and attempted to bear part of the responsibility for the welfare of those communities.[17] Progressive politicians in the 1920s also demanded greater social responsibility from corporations.[18] By 1936, revenue from US corporate giving reached $30 million and then plateaued at over $200 million every year between 1939 and 1944.[19] It then exceeded $300 million in 1951.[20]

This rapid increase can be attributed in part to changes in the law and in part to the Korean War, when a record number of corporate foundations were established.[21] In 1946, there were 172 corporate foundations in the United States.[22] By 1953, there were 620.[23] The ecosystem of corporate philanthropy became increasingly more developed as the surrounding social, legal, and political landscape changed. In 1949, the American Bar Association Committee on Business Corporations proposed a statute for incorporation that included a section allowing corporations to donate charitable gifts that have no relation to their businesses or direct benefits to companies.[24] In 1953, when shareholders of the A. P. Smith Manufacturing Company contested a $1,500 contribution the company made to Princeton University,[25] the New Jersey Supreme Court upheld the contribution and the state's legislation permitting it.[26] The US Supreme Court denied review, and the *A. P. Smith* case has effectively stood as the legal precedent allowing donations without a corporate benefit as legitimate business activity.[27] By 1959, corporations in forty-one states could donate to charity without needing to demonstrate that the contributions were tied to the nature of their businesses.[28]

By the 1960s, corporate philanthropy had increased significantly.[29] According to Scott Cutlip, a pioneer of public relations education, "the modern corporation had slowly, often reluctantly, come to accept the social responsibility that its power and place in society impose upon it, part of which is discharged through gifts to public causes."[30] In the early 1960s, annual corporate giving reached $500 million.[31] By the early 1970s, it exceeded $1 billion.[32] Separate from their companies, corporate foundations continued to account for a significant proportion of corporate giving, channeling about 25 percent of corporate contributions to nonprofit charities.[33] Indeed, by 1963, there were nearly 1,500 corporate foundations holding $1.3 billion in assets.[34]

In 1981, President Ronald Reagan's Task Force on Private Sector Initiatives urged companies to double their cash and noncash philanthropy over the following four years to a minimum of 2 percent of their pretax income, and to reassess programs to ensure that the most critical community needs were met.[35] Most executives at the time, however, believed that more efficient resource management was necessary and preferred to link contributions to business objectives.[36] In other words, by 1981, most executives had a preference for the pre-*A. P. Smith* era, when companies were prohibited from making contributions that were unrelated to their businesses.

The rise in corporate giving brought with it a shift in philanthropic ideology or the motivations underlying corporate giving – that is, whether companies pursue philanthropy for purely altruistic reasons, whether they are motivated by potential return on investments and competitive advantage, or whether they attempt to proactively align business interests with altruism.[37]

Strategic Corporate Philanthropy

By the 1980s, the alignment of altruistic interests with business interests began to gain prominence in the form of strategic corporate philanthropy. Strategic corporate philanthropy has been defined as identifying community issues that most align with a firm's goals and objectives and using the firm's resources and functions to meet those community objectives.[38]

Strategic corporate philanthropy is aligned with the profit-maximizing ethos of corporations, with a focus on firms' financial objectives. Firms gain profit by serving the community in such a way that aligns their charitable giving as closely as possible with their business operations.[39] Corporate self-interest is the dominant rationale for strategic corporate philanthropy, with some benefits also accruing to charitable organizations and, in turn, the communities and causes they serve.[40] Some firms, such as Amazon and General Motors, have even dissolved their corporate foundations and moved their grantmaking activities in house to facilitate better alignment between their businesses and charitable goals.[41] DreamWorks SKG created a program to train low-income students in Los Angeles to work in the entertainment industry.[42] Other strategies include making targeted charitable grants for specific purposes, donating companies' products to charities for use or donation during events, sponsoring charitable events, and employee giving programs that allow employees to donate money to specified charitable organizations.[43] These strategies are geared toward helping communities where companies already operate their businesses, thus helping companies market their brands, and increasing employee satisfaction.[44] In a 2003 survey of 126 corporate giving managers in US companies, 98 percent confirmed a strategic focus in their approaches to philanthropy.[45] Several Fortune 500 companies, including AT&T, IBM, and Microsoft, have recognized that successful strategic philanthropic initiatives yield both social impact and financial returns for their businesses.[46] In a 2008 survey conducted by McKinsey and the Committee Encouraging Corporate Philanthropy, 86% of surveyed chief executive officers indicated that they considered both business and social impact when funding corporate philanthropy programs, and 55% believed business needs should be given equal or greater weight than social impact.[47]

Yet even with strategic corporate giving, firms have difficulty aligning charitable objectives with business ones and with measuring the social impact and financial returns to the company.[48] The 2008 survey mentioned above also showed that less than 20 percent of CEOs believed their company was efficient in aligning business and philanthropic ventures.[49] When business impact is measured, it is often about things like the effects of philanthropic programs on employee motivation.[50] This lack of alignment has prompted a lot of practical suggestions for businesses and nonprofits to take toward alignment.[51]

Legal scholars Dana Brakman Reiser and Steven Dean have defined strategic corporate philanthropy more broadly, sidestepping the often-controversial inquiry of how to align a firm's charitable objectives with its business objectives. For these scholars, strategic corporate philanthropy is about perceiving a more general connection between altruism and business and between the interests of shareholders and stakeholders.[52]

Corporate Giving in the United States

In 2023, the total estimated charitable giving in the US reached $557.16 billion, of which $36.55 billion came from corporations, a growth of 3 percent from 2022 levels.[53] Corporate giving – strategic or otherwise – has become a significant aspect of business operations in most corporations, especially with increasing numbers of chief sustainability officers (CSOs) now overseeing the sustainability and philanthropic departments in large companies.

In the United States, corporate contributions account for about 7 percent of all charitable giving – a seemingly small but important portion of US contributions to charitable nonprofits every year.[54] Nancy Koehn, a business historian has argued that "[n]o other set of institutions – not religious organizations, not the nation-state, not individual NGOs – has the resources or the breadth and on-the-ground depth of business to deal with [the social and economic problems in society today]."[55]

CORPORATE ENGAGEMENT IN RACE-CONSCIOUS PHILANTHROPY

As corporate giving began to emerge as a visible form of philanthropy in the 1960s, many may have expected that developments like the Plans for Progress program and the civil rights movement discussed in Chapter 1 would have mobilized corporate support for racial causes. But companies were not major supporters of racial causes during the early part of the civil rights movement and only started giving after summers of urban rioting.[56] When companies began to financially support organizations focused on advancing the plight of Black people, they did so primarily to pacify Black communities, particularly in urban centers; this was framed as accommodating "manageable Black demands."[57]

What did thrive during the civil rights era and beyond was race-focused philanthropic giving by private foundations, such as the San Francisco Foundation's funding of the Urban League.[58] And in the wake of the urban uprisings in the 1960s, some large companies donated to the National Association for the Advancement of Colored People (NAACP), the United Negro College Fund, and the Urban League.[59]

After the passage of the 1964 Civil Rights Act, the federal government pressured companies to increase Black employment in technology and management.[60] While historically Black colleges and universities (HBCUs) saw this as an opportunity for greater financial support from corporations, corporate funding did not exceed

20 percent of their revenues, with an average gift size of between $5,000 and $10,000.[61] The majority of HBCUs' corporate funding came from large national companies, as opposed to local or regional ones, because most HBCUs were in the South, where local and regional companies were averse to giving their money to pay for the education of "rowdy" students.[62]

Pre-2020 Corporate Engagement with Race and Philanthropy

Companies were interested in race in philanthropy in limited ways before 2020 but did not feel the need to devote resources to addressing racial inequities. Historically, Black-led nonprofit organizations were funded at significantly lower levels by corporate and foundation grants than white-led nonprofits.[63] An analysis of early-stage nonprofit organizations in 2020 showed that, on average, the revenues of Black-led organizations were 24 percent smaller than the revenues of their white-led counterparts.[64] The figures are even more stark with private unrestricted funding, which comes with fewer strings attached, with the unrestricted net assets of the same Black-led organizations being 76 percent smaller than those of white-led nonprofits in 2020.[65] The stark disparity in unrestricted assets is particularly startling as such funding often represents a proxy for trust. Minority-led organizations and those that primarily serve minority populations are also more likely to be smaller in terms of staff and volunteers and rely on funding from government sources, which comes with more restrictions in reporting and utilization.[66] Black-led organizations are also more likely to be precarious and impacted by cycles in politics and the economy.[67]

Nneka Logan, a scholar of communications and race, and legal scholars Gina-Gail S. Fletcher and H. Timothy Lovelace, Jr., have argued that because corporations have historically contributed to a racial order of oppression and white supremacy, they are obligated to play a role in encouraging racial justice. For Logan, Fletcher, and Lovelace, companies have a responsibility to proactively use their dollars to give voice to racial issues and heighten public awareness of racism in order to foster a more just, egalitarian, and harmonious society.[68] This responsibility includes but is not limited to philanthropic efforts.[69]

Logan uses Starbucks, AT&T, and Ben and Jerry's as examples of corporations that have attempted to take on this corporate responsibility vis-à-vis race.[70] In 2015, responding to demands by employees, Starbucks partnered with USA Today newspaper to launch the Race Together Initiative to foster a national dialogue on race relations following police-involved deaths of unarmed Black men in Ferguson, Missouri.[71] In a clear use of race-conscious disclosures even at the time, Starbucks dispersed print and online materials educating individuals about racial inequality and trends in diversity, made commitments to hire 10,000 young people, mainly Black and Latino youth, and pledged to open new stores in low-income neighborhoods.[72] The following year, in a 2016 speech to employees, AT&T's CEO Randall Stephenson discussed the importance of dealing with countrywide racial tensions and expressed support for the Black Lives Matter movement.[73] And in 2016, at least one of Ben & Jerry's blog posts supported Black Lives Matter. While most of these did not constitute philanthropy at the time, they do show that some companies were starting to take on a particular responsibility with regard to race.

Post-2020 Corporate Racial Philanthropy

If corporate efforts to take some responsibility for racial equity and to use race-conscious disclosures constituted only a trickle prior to 2020, public outcry following the murder of George Floyd led to a wave of race-conscious disclosures, including disclosures regarding CRP. In response to nationwide protests and demands for social justice, corporations initiated unprecedented levels of racial philanthropy,[74] emerging as formidable funders of causes and organizations advancing racial and social justice. By 2022, corporate pledges to give to minority led or serving organizations surpassed foundation and individual giving.[75]

Crucially, corporations' newfound support of racial causes could have taken many forms. Corporations could, for example, have reached out to communities to help design charitable support that put the communities' interests first, not necessarily the companies' business interests. State laws, including Delaware's – where most corporations are incorporated – do not generally constrain corporate philanthropy.[76] The "business judgement rule," which protects corporate directors from liability for decisions they make in good faith, also gives corporate directors the authority to design their philanthropic endeavors as they deem fit.[77] Unsurprisingly, however, corporations chose to constrain their definition of philanthropy in a way that prioritizes business transactions over support to nonprofits. This prioritizing of business transactions is not necessarily a bad thing, but it is another way in which corporate communications delimit racial progress.

I examined corporations' race-conscious disclosures in a two-stage process to show how, and to what extent, corporations' communications have constrained the parameters and impact of philanthropy to racial causes. All sustainability reports have a section devoted to philanthropy, so in the first stage, research assistants and I hand-coded the reports for the over 2,000 companies in my database for discussions about race and philanthropy. The coding process revealed the most common terms and phrases corporations use to describe racial philanthropy – namely, "Black," "minority business," and "diversity owned." Minority business and diversity owned are specifically geared toward business and transactions. Notably, none of the most common phrases are about giving to nonprofit organizations or grantmaking. What they show is the prevalence of Black people and minority businesses in companies' discussions about philanthropy and an outsized focus on the public images they wanted to project at the time. Other prevalent terms are "American," "community," "women," "support," and "supplier."

Corporate Engagement in Race-Conscious Philanthropy

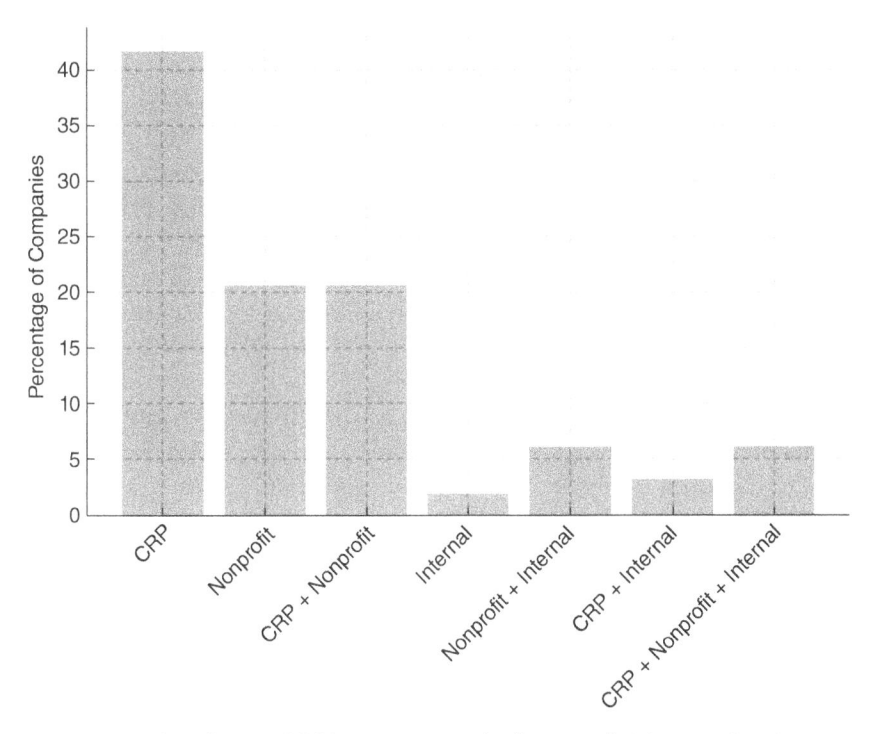

FIGURE 4.1 Prevalence of CRP in corporate disclosures of giving to minority causes

One CSO explained this trend in one company:

> With George Floyd and ... COVID ... we became very intentional about focusing on Black communities as a whole initiative on supporting and enabling economic development and empowerment of Black employees and individuals. And a supplier procurement component ... related to that as well, so that was a big change.

In the second stage of my analysis, I purposefully selected 233 companies with the most robust racial philanthropy disclosures between 2018 and 2023.[78] These companies account for 9 percent of the companies in my dataset for those years. As shown in Figure 4.1, I group their disclosures into three broad categories: nonprofit, CRP, and internal initiatives. CRP encompasses all race-conscious disclosures about business transactions in philanthropy, including loans to minority-owned businesses, business incubators, and supplier diversity. I include supplier diversity in the CRP category, because supplier diversity is about the expansion of racially inclusive suppliers of products and services, and corporations included supplier diversity in their broad category of philanthropy related to race.

I arrived at the three categories by coding the companies' discussions of their philanthropic efforts related to race. The respective categories are explained further below. As shown in Figure 4.1 with the "+" symbol, some companies combined some or all categories. For example, companies combined nonprofit and internal initiatives, and CRP and internal initiatives.

Of the 233 companies I examined, 71 percent made CRP disclosures whether by itself or with other forms of philanthropy as shown in Figure 4.1. That is seven out of every ten companies, which is consistent with media observations indicating that most corporate philanthropic dollars for racial equity went to things like loan programs, while few went to grants to nonprofits.[79] This is also consistent with research showing that the ability of minority-owned groups to obtain funds from private capital sources increases significantly during periods of high racial awareness when media appearances around racial discrimination or inequality are high (between 2020 and 2023 in this sample).[80]

This is not to say that corporations are not engaged in racial philanthropy outside of business transactions. Of the corporations I examined, 20.6 percent focused almost exclusively on nonprofit giving to racial equity causes in cash or kind. And while it is relatively uncommon for a company to have internal initiatives – internal programs established by companies or their employees to meet the needs of external nonprofit organizations – as its only form of philanthropy, 2.6 percent of the 233 companies I closely examined did.

More common with internal initiatives, though, are companies that combined it with other forms of philanthropy, including CRP. Traditionally, companies have facilitated philanthropy among employees by instituting payroll deduction for charitable deductions, implementing matching gifts programs, and/or institutionalizing employee voluntarism.[81] The response to the murder of George Floyd expanded the range of philanthropic options, and this included accelerating internal initiatives as corporations and their employees raced to establish internal programs that would have external impact on racial equity. Internal initiatives began with corporate programs through which companies and their employees supported an external organization. Estee Lauder's employee donation matching, and VMware's Foundation's Matching Gift program are illustrative of internal initiatives.[82]

In addition to the standalone CRP, nonprofit, and internal initiatives philanthropy approaches, nineteen corporations combined philanthropy to nonprofits with internal initiatives, sixty-five combined philanthropy to nonprofits with CRP, ten combined CRP with internal initiatives, and nineteen combined CRP, philanthropy to nonprofits, and internal initiatives.

Therefore, this sample of the staunchest supporters of racial minority causes through disclosures between 2020 and 2023, reveals that many, although not most, companies combined two or more types of philanthropy. Some companies combined multiple types in the same program or adopted multiple programs of different types. However, CRP was the most prevalent form of corporate philanthropy to racial causes.

CRP'S FOCUS ON BUSINESS TRANSACTIONS

Corporate racial philanthropy appears to be about economic inclusion, opportunity, and mobility in communities of color and was therefore treated by companies as philanthropic in nature. In corporate disclosures, discussions of economic opportunity through business philanthropy and transactions tended to appear alongside other forms of philanthropy. Corporate racial philanthropy tends to mirror business goals and operations much more closely, such as when a bank financially supports a Minority Depository Institution (MDI), a financial institution that serves underserved communities and is majority owned and operated by people of color as defined by the Federal Deposit Insurance Corporation (FDIC).

Corporate racial philanthropy reflects a trend identified by scholars like Brakman Reiser and Dean in which, "[p]ractices, players and norms native to the business sector are migrating into philanthropy, muddying the distinction between commerce and charity."[83] Brakman Reiser and Dean's observation refers to developments such as limited liability companies, donor-advised funds sponsored by investment company giants, and strategic corporate philanthropy programs that align charitable giving to business objectives.[84]

As part of this trend, CRP is a transactional engagement wherein philanthropy and business are one and the same. With CRP, companies partner with other businesses for a variety of purposes and frame the relationship as philanthropic in nature. The CSO of one company explained that after the murder of George Floyd, there was an inclination to "focus heavily on fulfilling [the] commitment around entrepreneurship and economic development in Black communities and with Black individuals, [and] working with the businesses to support their work around increasing their business and their work with Black communities, and areas where there's majority Black populations."

Other examples are from Micron Technology and Wells Fargo, both of which established loan programs for minority-owned businesses:

> Throughout 2020, Micron allocated $250 million in cash and cash equivalents to be managed by minority-owned firms, which has a multiplying effect in the economies of underrepresented communities. This effort includes allocating ... $100 million under Ramirez Asset Management, Inc., an affiliate of Samuel A. Ramirez & Company, Inc. which is the oldest and largest Hispanic-owned investment bank in the U.S. A final $50 million allocation to RBC Global Asset Management will support an impact investment strategy that aims to reduce wealth gaps in predominantly Black neighborhoods and increase access to homeownership, affordable rental housing, community facilities and small business loans.[85]

> Minority Depository Institutions (MDIs) serve a vital role in the U.S. financial ecosystem by providing ready access to capital and credit in minority and underserved communities, supporting neighborhood revitalization, and driving

economic opportunity. Wells Fargo is proud to build on our recent commitment of up to $50 million to African American MDIs by signing the Project Reach MDI Pledge.[86]

Corporate racial philanthropy became a driver of conservative backlash to philanthropic endeavors targeted toward racial minorities.[87] The Federalist Society, a conservative and libertarian legal organization, has referred to when corporations engage in CRP through third parties as "woke laundering," or offloading social justice agendas to outside groups.[88] For example, Visa's Entrepreneurship Program created for Black and African American entrepreneurs was managed by a third-party public benefit corporation incorporated in the state of Delaware.[89] Because Visa itself did not manage the program, conservatives couched Visa's involvement as a backdoor way of engaging in racial equity causes.

Supplier diversity is a form of CRP that is worth elaborating on. Supplier diversity alone (without other forms of business engagement) accounted for 95 out of 233 companies that discussed racial philanthropy in corporate communications. Supplier diversity involves the expansion of pools of suppliers of products and services to become more inclusive of businesses owned by racial and ethnic minorities. Supplier diversity not only served the purpose of increasing corporate suppliers but became the largest and most expansive form of CRP. Companies touted their inclusive suppliers, including minority-owned businesses, women, LGBTQ+, and veteran-owned businesses. Like their response to racial targets, a significant number of companies have engaged in race-conscious retraction on their supplier diversity initiatives in response to threats and pushback from conservative groups and the Trump administration.

The CSOs or heads of corporate foundations may disagree with the classification of supplier diversity as a form of philanthropy. However, the ways in which corporations talked about supplier diversity makes it at least arguable that it is a component of CRP. In race-conscious disclosures, supplier diversity was often discussed alongside community engagement, giving back, and funding nonprofit organizations engaged in equity work.[90] Ameren Corporation's discussion is illustrative: "Part of how we support our communities is by helping businesses grow …. As a major purchaser of materials and services, Ameren plays a significant role in the growth and development of diverse suppliers. We make sure qualified diverse suppliers are encouraged and given the opportunity to do business with us."[91]

Supplier diversity programs have been around since the civil rights era of the 1960s, with a notable early instance occurring in the US auto industry in the wake of the 1968 Detroit race riots.[92] The Small Business Act of 1978, which redefined minority firms as socially and economically disadvantaged small businesses, further expanded the programs to include federal contractors.[93] Supplier diversity programs expanded in 2020, and corporations began to reframe them as philanthropic in nature, an approach few companies took prior to that time. Rockwell Automation is an example of a corporation that framed supplier diversity as part of philanthropy as early as 2016.[94] In Rockwell Automation's voluntary disclosure, it discussed supplier diversity as part of sustainability and community, and in the same category as giving and partnerships with nonprofits in higher education.[95]

After 2020, corporations framed supplier diversity as an economic inclusion activity, and a way to promote diversity and inclusion and generate opportunities through partnerships with minority-owned businesses. As with other race-conscious disclosures, corporations touted the percentage of their suppliers who were minority-owned businesses and publicized goals to increase supplier diversity over the years, along with associated dollar amounts.

The quotes below provide examples of supplier diversity programs. Robert Half launched its program in 2004, and Sonos launched its program in 2021, targeting a range of underrepresented groups:

> [Robert Half's] supplier inclusion initiative supports the promotion, growth, and development of small businesses and minority-, woman-, veteran-, disabled veteran-, and LGBTQ-owned firms. This initiative was launched in 2004. A diverse business enterprise refers to a business that is at least 51% owned by a member of a minority group, including African Americans, Asian Americans, Hispanic Americans, Native Americans, LGBTQ, veterans, and disabled veterans.[96]
>
> In [financial year 2021], [Sonos] launched our new supplier diversity program to improve representation across our vendor base. Through this program, we will proactively identify and engage suppliers owned by members of underrepresented groups including women, members of the LGBTQIA+ community, diverse racial and ethnic backgrounds, persons with disabilities and veterans.[97]

Robert Half's supplier diversity program dates back two decades but was reframed after 2020. When it reported its supplier diversity efforts in 2019, the company framed them largely in terms of diversity and inclusion. Supplier diversity occupied a distinct page titled "supplier diversity," which used the word "community" only once. By 2022, the company had transformed its discussion of supplier diversity by placing it under the heading "our community, clients and partners" in a section reserved for volunteer programs, philanthropic programs, and social impact. The supplier diversity program [also became] part of the company's larger ESG disclosures as it "seek[s] to work with suppliers who conduct business in ways that align with [its] values and ESG objectives."[98]

A key question is why, exactly, companies would treat supplier diversity like philanthropy, or at least as an economic inclusivity strategy that signals that companies are doing good. Could it be that companies define philanthropy as intentionally making business opportunities available to people and businesses that have previously been left out of business partnerships and opportunities? That supplier diversity is a means of fueling diverse businesses, which makes it seem philanthropic? Companies may well view supplier diversity as akin to so-called diversity fellowships, whose goals include providing opportunities for people of color who were previously left out of opportunities because of racial discrimination or bias, institutional racism, or lack of networks resulting from geographical desegregation. Supplier diversity in this view would be an avenue to fund programs that allow minority businesses to get started or potentially compete with businesses owned by white individuals and businesses.

Yet it is puzzling to think of supplier diversity in any of these terms because supplier diversity squarely benefits corporations and their for-profit suppliers or similar businesses. In addition to benefits that companies obtain from the general use of suppliers to advance their businesses, supplier diversity has the added benefit of boosting companies' reputational and financial capital, especially when corporations also use words to describe what they are doing. Unlike corporate philanthropy to nonprofits, supplier diversity as a form of philanthropy appears to be a win–win situation for companies. Companies receive goods and services, profit from doing business, and get to disclose how much they are helping communities of color through philanthropy and reap the benefits from race-conscious disclosures.

Some might object that corporations may in fact not "win" by engaging in CRP. Imagine a business transaction that starts from the premise that a corporation will consider minority business enterprises as suppliers because it wants to promote Black businesses, even though it could potentially receive its goods and services cheaper from more established, majority-white suppliers. While it is possible that some transactions may not make as much profit as they potentially might with more established, often white suppliers, the corporation would still make profit. In addition to quantifiable financial gain, the corporation is also gaining goodwill and reputational gains that will likely translate to financial gain in the long run, through consumers, shareholders, or employees as it makes race-conscious disclosures about those transactions.

CRP as Philanthropy

In 2008, as an advice to businesses at the World Economic Forum in Davos, Bill Gates promoted the notion of "creative capitalism," urging businesses to use profit incentives in philanthropy whenever possible.[99] When profit incentives are unavailable, Gates encouraged companies to seek market-based incentives of recognition, which enhances corporate reputation and appeals to stakeholders.[100]

It appears that many corporations have adopted Gate's creative capitalism by engaging in CRP, as a tactical approach to benefit their corporate economic standing, partner with businesses, and advance a reputation for advancing racial equity. In the spirit of Gate's creative capitalism, CRP probably makes it easier for companies to make a case to shareholders about engaging in philanthropy, as it is closely related to operational efforts and likely to enhance measurable financial gain.[101] With supplier diversity, corporations can measure how many minority suppliers they have, how many they intend to have in the future, how much revenue they obtain from minority suppliers, and perhaps how much revenue those minority suppliers obtain in partnership with those companies. This level of data and information can incentivize shareholders' support for CRP above less measurable types of philanthropy.

A skeptic may question whether CRP is philanthropy at all. Perhaps it is just companies making decisions that benefit their bottom lines – maybe it's just capitalism. I would argue that CRP does constitute philanthropy under a broad definition of philanthropy. One definition that seems to capture this broad approach is espoused by renowned philanthropy scholars Robert Payton and Michael Moody, in their book, *Understanding Philanthropy: Its Meaning and Mission*: They define philanthropy broadly and simply as "voluntary action for the public good."[102] While CRP is largely about corporate interests, it still falls under the Payton and Moody definition because it is voluntary and considered by companies to achieve a public good and may in fact achieve some good. In other words, although primarily oriented around meeting profitmaking ends, corporations also want benefits to accrue to the communities to which they extend CRP.

Some scholars may also perceive CRP to be a form of corporate social responsibility (CSR). CSR is a very broad and much-criticized concept that encompasses the role of business in doing good in society.[103] Much like the idea of subsuming race into the concept of ESG or DEI, subsuming CRP into CSR would not only create confusion but also make CRP susceptible to CSR's criticisms, including that it is overbroad with multiple iterations, and a form of capitalist ideology, intended to blind people from the true inner workings of business operations.[104]

Recommendations for Improving CRP toward Racial Progress

There is no doubt that CRP can generate some benefits – large or small – to individuals or entities outside of the firm. And one does not need to agree that CRP is philanthropy to recognize that CRP can be a good thing for communities of color because it can provide opportunities for some businesses to start up or scale by receiving loans, other investments, or supplying goods or services to large corporations. However, if corporations want to maximize CRP for the benefit of communities of color, they should set aside the goal of corporate financial gain and drive their decisions based on what would fully benefit those communities and perhaps use tools like "participatory philanthropy" to get there.

The field of philanthropy has been grappling with how to take inclusive approaches to fundraising and philanthropic giving.[105] Participatory philanthropy "aims to create broader communal involvement and benefit ... expand the circle of those who participate in shaping ... decisions, and ... center philanthropy in community, rather than in managerial efficiency and effectiveness."[106] In the corporate context, internal initiatives that involve employees are a step toward participatory philanthropy, because they engage and can empower employees to direct and guide philanthropic choices and strategies. But there is still much room for improvement.

When corporations establish CRP as an area of philanthropy, they should center racial progress as the goal in both the design and implementation of the programs. Companies should prioritize inclusivity among CRP decision-makers. Companies should consider including minority-owned businesses, suppliers, and communities in their CRP decision-making. For example, in making decisions about a type of business venture, companies should inquire from groups in the community regarding what kinds of business ventures are most needed. And once a choice is made to, for example, build additional bank branches in a neighborhood with few banks, open a grocery store in a neighborhood with limited stores, provide energy supply in a minority neighborhood, or expand a supplier program, corporations should continue to include members of the community – and not just corporate employees – in the process. To be sure, companies would need to first define who is included in the community. They would also need to be careful not to prioritize some voices over others because the former seem more legitimate or respectable. But overcoming these minor challenges would be worth it to think about who decides what racial progress looks like.

There is more than ample evidence that the leadership of the nonprofit sector primarily consists of white individuals – about 74 percent – and corporate sustainability and philanthropy are also primarily led by white individuals.[107] Because CRP is ostensibly meant to serve racial and ethnic minority communities and interests, it may be useful for companies to hire people of color as the CSOs and philanthropic leaders and managers (and not just staff) that guide the philanthropic arms of their firms. People of color are more likely, although not exclusively likely, to have authentic relationships with communities that companies intend to support in their philanthropic endeavors.[108] More racial and ethnic diversity in corporate philanthropic leadership would go a long way toward ensuring that CRP focuses on true racial progress, rather than only strategically benefiting companies. And because CRP is really a business project, corporations should continue to work hard to diversify their business leadership positions (as discussed in Chapter 3) that get to make decisions about CRP programs. A long-term view of CRP is therefore important to ensure that the philanthropy and business sides of firms can provide necessary guidance on how corporations talk about and engage in CRP.

CRP AND CONSTRAINING RACIAL PROGRESS

Just because CRP is philanthropy does not mean it is faultless. Like other forms of race-conscious disclosures, corporations have used CRP to constrain racial progress in two ways. The first is by limiting the parameters of philanthropy related to racial causes to focus largely on business transactions. Almost seven out of every ten companies I examined have chosen to engage with causes related to racial minorities in this narrowly defined way, which has not been established as the best way to engage in causes that impact people of color.

The second is that even if CRP can propel us toward racial progress, like other forms of race-conscious disclosures, corporations have used CRP to suppress other concerns about racial inequality in their operations. Let's assume for a moment that at a future time, thousands of corporations make CRP disclosures of various types and benefit financially from the programs themselves and from the disclosures about them, through employee retention and satisfaction, shareholder approval, business generation, excellent suppliers, and enhanced marketing and branding opportunities. Should they also be able to use their CRP as evidence of taking up racial inequity in other contexts?

To consider this question, I will return to the Richmond, California example I first discussed in Chapter 2. Recall that Chevron used disclosures about its CRP, along with other race-conscious disclosures, to dismiss shareholder inquiries about the damaging environmental impact of its business activities on Richmond, a majority racial minority community. Should Chevron's board of directors be permitted to recommend that shareholders vote against a proposal asking the company to examine how its operations make the members of that community sick, on the basis that the company has made "extensive disclosures and action" on CRP, which it outlines in its disclosures?[109] I assert that companies should not be able to use CRP to shield themselves from accountability for racial inequality or disparate racial impact in philanthropy or in other contexts. As I discuss in Chapter 6, regulation can help minimize corporate constraint on racial progress.

Finally, some of the corporations I examined as CRP exemplars also make political donations to conservative politicians who oppose racial progress, including supporting the Trump administration. The interconnectedness of CRP with political support of conservatives further complicates corporate engagement in CRP. When corporations say that they want to or are working toward racial progress, yet, at the same time, use those same words to diminish inquiries about how their operations perpetuate racial inequality, or give money to political groups that seek to diminish such inquiries, there is clearly need for assessing what these contradictory corporate moves mean for achieving racial progress.[110]

In sum, this chapter calls on corporations to apply principles of participatory philanthropy to CRP by including minority-owned businesses, suppliers, and communities in their CRP decision-making and racially diversifying their CSO and other leadership positions. It also highlights the role of CRP within the broader project of using corporate communications to constrain racial progress by defining progress in ways that limit corporations' roles in advancing communities of color. It also raises the question of the implication of corporate political donations on racial progress.

NOTES

1. Megan Armstrong, Eathyn Edwards, and Duwain Pinder, "Corporate Commitments to Racial Justice: An Update," *McKinsey Institute for Black Economic Mobility*, February 21, 2023, www.mckinsey.com/bem/our-insights/corporate-commitments-to-racial-justice-an-update#/.
2. Ibid.
3. Tracy Jan, Jena McGregor, and Meghan Hoyer, "Corporate America's $50 Billion Promise," *Washington Post*, August 23, 2021, www.washingtonpost.com/business/interactive/2021/george-floyd-corporate-america-racial-justice/.
4. Ibid.

5. Ibid.
6. Candid, "Racial Equity, United States," Foundation Maps by Candid website, https://shorturl.at/ol8PY; Malkia Devich Cyril, Lyle Matthew Kan, Ben Francisco Maulbeck, and Lori Villarosa, *Mismatched: Philanthropy's Response to the Call for Racial Justice*, Philanthropic Initiative for Racial Equity (2021), 32, https://racialequity.org/mismatched/.
7. Cyril et al., *Mismatched*, 32.
8. Indiana University Lilly Family School of Philanthropy, *Giving USA*, 133.
9. Banks, *Black Culture*.
10. Ibid.
11. Dana Brakman Reiser, "Corporate Philanthropy: Development Tool or Profitable Strategy?," in *Handbook on Philanthrocapitalism*, eds. Steph Haydon, Tobias Jung, and Shona Russell (Cheltenham: Edward Elgar, 2025).
12. An important caveat is in order. This chapter is not about philanthropy by private foundations, including household names such as the Carnegie Foundation, Bill and Melinda Gates Foundation, and the Ford Foundation. It is about philanthropy conducted by companies such as Amazon, Best Buy, and Sonos separately and through corporate foundations, or nonprofit organizations created and financially supported by corporations.
13. F. Emerson Andrews, *Corporation Giving* (New York: Russell Sage Foundation, 1952), 91.
14. Craig Smith, "The New Corporate Philanthropy," *Harvard Business Review* 72 (1994): 107; Shruti Rana, "Philanthropic Innovation and Creative Capitalism: A Historical and Comparative Perspective on Social Entrepreneurship and Corporate Social Responsibility," *Alabama Law Review* 64 (2013): 1133; Mark Sharfman, "Changing Institutional Rules: The Evolution of Corporate Philanthropy, 1883–1953," *Business and Society* 33, no. 3 (December 1994): 243.
15. Davis v. Old Colony Railroad Company, 131 Mass. 258 (June 28, 1881); Sharfman, "Changing Institutional Rules," 249.
16. Sharfman, "Changing Institutional Rules," 246; "$291,500 in Profits for the Red Cross: Five More Companies Declare Special Dividends to Aid $100,000 Fund," *New York Times*, June 16, 1917.
17. Andrews, *Corporation Giving*, 15.
18. Lenore T. Ealy and Steven D. Ealy, "Progressivism and Philanthropy," *The Good Society* 15, no. 1 (2006): 39; Kim Nevin-Gattle, "Predicting the Philanthropic Response of Corporations: Lessons from History," *Business Horizons* 39, no. 3 (1996): 16.
19. Andrews, *Corporation Giving*, 23.
20. Ibid.
21. Natalie J. Webb, "Tax and Government Policy Implications for Corporate Foundation Giving," *Nonprofit and Voluntary Sector Quarterly* 23, no. 1 (Spring 1994): 44.
22. Ibid.
23. Marianna O. Lewis, ed., *The Foundation Directory*, 3rd ed. (New York: Russell Sage Foundation, 1967): 29.
24. Sharfman, "Changing Institutional Rules," 254.
25. A. P. Smith Mfg. Co. v. Barlow, 98 A.2d 581 (1953).
26. Ibid; Sharfman, "Changing Institutional Rules," 255.
27. Sharfman, "Changing Institutional Rules," 255–56.
28. Ralph L. Nelson, "Economic Analysis of Corporate Giving" in *Economic Factors in the Growth of Corporation Giving* (New York: National Bureau of Economic Research, 1970), 49.
29. Marybeth Gasman and Noah Drezner, "White Corporate Philanthropy and Its Support of Private Black Colleges in the 1960s and 1970s," *International Journal of Educational Advancement* 8 (2008): 79–92.

30. Scott M. Cutlip, *Fundraising in the United States: Its Role in America's Philanthropy* (New Brunswick, NJ: Rutgers University Press, 1965), 151.
31. Hayden W. Smith, "Panel One: An Introduction to Corporate Philanthropy: History, Practice, and Regulation: If Not Corporate Philanthropy, Then What," *New York Law School Law Review* 41 (1997): 759.
32. Ibid.
33. Ralph L. Nelson, "Company-Sponsored Foundations" in *Economic Factors in the Growth of Corporation Giving* (New York: National Bureau of Economic Research, 1970), 75.
34. Ibid.
35. "Executive Order 12329 of October 14, 1981, President's Task Force on Private Sector Initiatives," Code of Federal Regulations, title 5 (1981); "Remarks on Private Sector Initiatives at a White House Luncheon for National Religious Leaders," April 13, 1982, www.reaganlibrary.gov/archives/speech/remarks-private-sector-initiatives-white-house-luncheon-national-religious-leaders.
36. J. M. Logsdon, M. Reiner, and L. Burke, "Corporate Philanthropy: Strategic Responses to the Firm's Stakeholders," *Nonprofit and Voluntary Sector Quarterly* 19, no. 2 (1990): 93–109, 94.
37. Arthur Gautier and Anne-Claire Pache, "Research on Corporate Philanthropy: A Review and Assessment," *Journal of Business Ethics* 126, no. 3 (February 2015): 346; Michael E. Porter and Mark R. Kramer, "The Competitive Advantage of Corporate Philanthropy," *Harvard Business Review* 80, no. 12 (December 2002): 57; Smith, "New Corporate Philanthropy," 106.
38. David H. Saiia, Archie B. Carroll, and Ann K. Buchholtz, "Philanthropy as Strategy When Corporate Charity 'Begins at Home'", *Business and Society* 42, no. 2 (June 2003): 181.
39. Ibid.
40. Logsdon, Reiner, and Burke, "Corporate Philanthropy," 95.
41. Amazon, "Amazon Closing AmazonSmile to Focus its Philanthropic Giving to Programs with Greater Impact," January 18, 2023, www.aboutamazon.com/news/company-news/amazon-closing-amazonsmile-to-focus-its-philanthropic-giving-to-programs-with-greater-impactMelissa; Burden, "GM to End Foundation, Redirect Its Charitable Giving," *Detroit News*, June 12, 2017.
42. Porter and Kramer, "Competitive Advantage," 61.
43. Ibid.
44. Ibid; Saiia, Carrol, and Buccholtz, "Philanthropy as Strategy," 171.
45. Saiia, Carrol, and Buccholtz, "Philanthropy as Strategy," 181.
46. Brandon Vaidyanathan, "Corporate Giving: A Literature Review" (working paper, Center for the Study of Religion and Society, University of Notre Dame, 2008), 16.
47. Terence Lim, *Measuring the Value of Corporate Philanthropy: Social Impact, Business Benefits, and Investor Returns* (New York: Committee Encouraging Corporate Philanthropy, 2010), 28.
48. Vaidyanathan, "Corporate Giving," 7; Kellie Liket and Karen Maas, "Strategic Philanthropy: Corporate Measurement of Philanthropic Impacts as a Requirement for a 'Happy Marriage' of Business and Society," *Business & Society* 55, no. 6 (2016): 889–921.
49. Lim, *Measuring the Value of Corporate Philanthropy*.
50. An example is National Grid's measure of the effects of its philanthropic programs on employee motivation and the social impact of its community investments. Liket and Mass, "Strategic Philanthropy," 895.
51. Lim, *Measuring the Value*; Stephanie Burns, "How to Incorporate Social Impact into Your Business," *Forbes*, April 13, 2020, www.forbes.com/sites/stephanieburns/2020/04/13/how-to-incorporate-social-impact-into-your-business/?sh=73a17bee1eaf; Logsdon, Reiner, and Burke, "Corporate Philanthropy," 103–06.

52. Dana Brakman Reiser and Steven A. Dean, *For-Profit Philanthropy: Elite Power & the Threat of Limited Liability Companies, Donor-Advised Funds, & Strategic Corporate Giving* (New York: Oxford University Press, 2023).
53. Indiana University Lilly Family School of Philanthropy, *Giving USA: The Annual Report on Philanthropy for the Year 2023.*
54. Indiana University Lilly Family School of Philanthropy, Giving USA: The Annual Report on Philanthropy for the Year 2023. It should be noted that these statistics does not account for types of CRP where business aligns with business.
55. Koehn, "Time Is Right."
56. Herbert H. Haines, "Black Radicalization and the Funding of Civil Rights: 1957–1970," *Social Problems* 32, no. 1 (1984): 39.
57. Ibid., 41.
58. Jiannbin Lee Shiao, *Identifying Talent, Institutionalizing Diversity: Race and Philanthropy in Post-Civil Rights America* (Durham, NC: Duke University Press, 2005).
59. Banks, *Black Culture.*
60. Gasman and Drezner, "White Corporate Philanthropy," 84.
61. Ibid.
62. Ibid.
63. Adediran, "Disclosures for Equity," 865–922; Young, Black & Giving Back Institute, "Grassroots, Black & Giving: How Philanthropy Can Better Support Black-Led and Black-Benefiting Nonprofits," Young, Black & Giving Back Institute, Research Report, 2023.
64. Cheryl Dorsey, Jeff Bradach, and Peter Kim, "Racial Equity and Philanthropy: Disparities in Funding for Leaders of Color Leave Impact on the Table," Report by Echoing Green and The Bridgespan Group (2020), 11, www.bridgespan.org/insights/disparities-nonprofit-funding-for-leaders-of-color.
65. Ibid.
66. Adediran, "Disclosures for Equity," 865–922.
67. Ibid.
68. Nneka Logan, "Corporate Personhood and the Corporate Responsibility to Race," *Journal of Business Ethics* 154 (2019); Fletcher and Lovelace, "Corporate Racial Responsibility."
69. Logan, "Corporate Personhood," 982–95.
70. Ibid.
71. Ibid.; Starbucks, "What 'Race Together' Means for Starbucks Partners and Customers," *Inclusion, Diversity & Belonging*, March 16, 2015, https://about.starbucks.com/stories/2015/what-race-together-means-for-starbucks-partners-and-customers/.
72. Logan, "Corporate Personhood," 982–95.
73. Ibid.
74. Jan et al., "Corporate America."
75. Indiana University Lilly Family School of Philanthropy, *Giving USA*, 131.
76. John A. Pearce, II, "The Rights of Shareholders in Authorizing Corporate Philanthropy," *Villanova Law Review* 60, no. 2 (2015): 251–82; Stephen M. Bainbridge. *Corporate Law and Economics.* New York: Foundation Press, 2022; DGCL § 122(9). For more information about why most publicly traded corporations are incorporated in Delaware, see, for example, Robert IV Anderson, "The Delaware Trap: An Empirical Analysis of Incorporation Decisions," *Southern California Law Review* 91 (2018).
77. Pearce, *The Rights of Shareholders in Authorizing Corporate Philanthropy*; Delaware's business judgement rule in the philanthropy context is still geared toward shareholder interests. Some states, such as New York, permit philanthropy "irrespective of corporate benefit." BSC § 202.

78. By robust, I mean corporations that made the most substantive disclosures about philanthropy. To be included in this category, a company must make at least three paragraphs of disclosures about race and philanthropy in its voluntary disclosures.
79. Jan et al., "Corporate America."
80. Johan Cassel, Johan, Josh Lerner, and Emmanuel Yimfor, "Racial Diversity in Private Capital Fundraising," Working Paper 30500, *National Bureau of Economic Research*, September 2022, www.nber.org/papers/w30500.
81. Eugene Barman, "The Social Bases of Philanthropy," *Annual Review of Sociology* 43, no. 1 (2017): 271–90.
82. Estee Lauder's program includes dollar-for-dollar matching and dollars-for-hours volunteered matching. https://doublethedonation.com/matching-gifts/the-estee-lauder-companies; Ken Johnson, "VMware Loves Service & Givin – The VMware Foundation," Product Announcement, December 19, 2019, https://blogs.vmware.com/vsphere/2019/12/vmware-service-charity-giving.html.
83. Brakman Raiser and Dean, *For-Profit Philanthropy*, 1.
84. Ibid.
85. Micron, *Fast Forward, Sustainability Report*, 2021.
86. Wells Fargo, *Social Impact and Sustainability Highlights*, 2021.
87. Daniel Lennington, "How Corporations Launder Their Race Discrimination through Third Parties," *Federalist Media*, March 6, 2023.
88. Ibid.
89. Ibid.
90. Ameren, *Leading the Way to a Sustainable Energy Future Environmental, Social & Governance (ESG)*, 2021.
91. Ameren, *Our Sustainability Story: Customers at the Center, Ameren Sustainability Report*, 2020.
92. Philip Baker, "The New Business Mandate," University of Chicago Professional Education website, June 12, 2024, https://professional.uchicago.edu/stories/inclusive-business-and-supplier-diversity-strategies/new-business-mandate?language_content_entity=en.
93. The Small Business Act of 1978, Public Law 95–507.
94. Rockwell Automation, *Corporate Responsibility Report*, 2016.
95. Ibid.
96. Robert Half, *Corporate Citizenship Report*, 2019.
97. Sonos, *Listen Better Report, Environmental, Social and Governance at Sonos*, 2021.
98. Robert Half, *Leading with Integrity, Environmental, Social and Governance Report*, 2021, 35.
99. Michael E. Kinsley, *Creative Capitalism: A Conversation with Bill Gates, Warren Buffett, and Other Economic Leaders* (New York: Simon & Schuster, 2010), 10. The World Economic Forum's Annual Meeting in Davos is a gathering of world leaders from business, politics, science, and culture to discuss global issues.
100. Ibid.
101. Victor Brudney and Allen Ferrell, "Corporate Charitable Giving," *University of Chicago Law Review* 69 (2002): 1191–96.
102. Robert L. Payton and Michael P. Moody, *Understanding Philanthropy: Its Meaning and Mission*, Philanthropy and Nonprofit Studies (Bloomington: Indiana University Press, 2008), 27; Alexander Dahlsrud, "How Corporate Social Responsibility Is Defined: An Analysis of 37 Definitions," *Corporate Social Responsibility and Environmental Management* 15 (2008): 1–13.
103. Gail Hanlon and Peter P. Fleming, "Updating the Critical Perspective on Corporate Social Responsibility," *Sociology Compass* 3 (2009): 937–48; Dahlsrud, "How Corporate Social Responsibility."

104. Hanlon and Fleming, "Updating the Critical Perspective," 937–48.
105. Lisa Schohl, "How to Create a Culture of Inclusive Fundraising," *Chronicle of Philanthropy*, March 2021.
106. The Faculty of the Lilly Family School of Philanthropy, "Inclusive Philanthropy," *Stanford Social Innovation Review*, September 2020, https://ssir.org/articles/entry/inclusive_philanthropy; Katy Love and Jody Myrum, "Practicing Participatory Philanthropy: Five Key Findings," *Nonprofit Quarterly*, October 10, 2023, https://nonprofitquarterly.org/practicing-participatory-philanthropy-five-key-findings/.
107. Associated Press, "The Larger the Nonprofit, the More Likely It Is Run by a White Man, Says New Candid Diversity Report," *U.S. News*, May 16, 2024; Weinreb Group, *The Chief Sustainability Officer 10 Years Later: The Rise of ESG in the C-Suite*, Weinreb Group Report, 2021, https://weinrebgroup.com/wp-content/uploads/2021/05/Weinreb-Group-Sustainability-and-ESG-Recruiting-The-Chief-Sustainability-Officer-10-years-Later-The-Rise-of-ESG-in-the-C-Suite-2021-Report.pdf; Atinuke O. Adediran, "Nonprofit Board Composition," *Ohio State Law Journal* 83 (2022): 357–421.
108. Cheryl Dorsey, Peter Kim, Cora Daniels, Lyell Sakaue, and Britt Savage, "Overcoming the Racial Bias in Philanthropic Funding," *Stanford Social Innovation Review*, May 4, 2020, https://ssir.org/articles/entry/overcoming_the_racial_bias_in_philanthropic_funding.
109. SEC, *Schedule 14A, Proxy Statement*.
110. For further discussion of this phenomenon in the context of climate risks, see Thomas P. Lyon and William Mandelkorn, "Measuring Corporate Political Responsibility," in *Corporate Political Responsibility*, ed. Thomas P. Lyon, 62–97 (Cambridge: Cambridge University Press, 2023).

5

Race-Conscious Retraction

President Barack Obama's presidency is tethered to the history of race in America. Obama's ascendance produced a huge backlash that was undeniably racist in nature. In his book, *Post-Racial or Most-Racial?: Race and Politics in the Obama Era*, political scientist Michael Tesler argues that society became more polarized by racial attitudes because President Obama was elected in 2008.[1] This is not to say that racial polarization was an Obama-era development. On the contrary, racial polarization has been a part of America's history since slavery, the American Civil War, the Jim Crow era, and the civil rights era.[2] What makes the Obama presidency significant is that it was a manifestation of the fear of a changing racial makeup in the United States – specifically, the idea that there are fewer white individuals and an increasing number of racial minorities, with the latter gaining political power in the Democratic Party.[3]

The zeal to protect white identity, interests, and privileges has led to the election of President Donald Trump twice.[4] Trump, a white Republican who is derisive of racial and ethnic minorities, has made it clear that he would protect white interests and privileges. As political scientist Ashley Jardina has described, many white individuals see themselves as "outnumbered, disadvantaged, and even oppressed."[5] For many white individuals, particularly white Republicans, an erosion of majority status and the election of Obama as America's first Black president, signal a challenge to the absoluteness of white dominance.[6] Indeed, in their study, political scientists Nathan Kalmoe and Lilliana Mason found that white Republicans who fail to recognize racial disparities are most likely to despise Democrats because racial resentment is consistent with the Republican party's identity.[7] In other words, white Republicans vilify Democrats in defense of a racist system.[8] Google searches for "republican racism," which were largely nonexistent before Obama, spiked in 2008 and increased throughout Obama's presidency.[9] This well-documented rise in the levels of racial resentment set the stage for the political backlash resulting in the January 6, 2021, insurrection, in which thousands of white Republicans, urged on by Donald Trump, violently attacked the Capitol.[10] It also led to the election of Trump for a second presidential term in office, and the implementation of Project 2025 through his many executive orders. Project 2025 is a conservative blueprint to among other things, dismantle racial equity programs and policies in government and other institutions.[11]

Conservative backlash against corporations that make race-conscious disclosures or attempt to deal with racial inequality is geared toward maintaining white dominance in America. It seems to operate alongside other strategies, such as book bans, lawsuits, threats of lawsuits, targeting racial minorities in positions of power as illegitimate, and gerrymandering among other tactics.

Between 2020 and 2024, companies used disclosures about race to systematically construct a public image indicating that they were attempting to alleviate racial inequality. This project was designed with corporate financial benefit as the goal rather than the quest to truly address racial inequality and tended to be largely ineffective at addressing racial inequality even by corporate standards. Through race-conscious disclosures and image construction, companies set themselves up to manage their reputations should finger pointing arise about their businesses' perpetration of racial inequality. Some companies successfully used race-conscious disclosures to squash criticisms, while in actuality discounting racial inequality and allowing it to persist. In this way, companies enjoyed the benefits of having a reputation of tackling racial inequality during a cycle of race-conscious image construction.[12]

Since late 2024, companies have begun the project of "race-conscious retraction," which is the modification or removal of race-conscious disclosures. Similar to race-conscious image construction, race-conscious retraction is designed to manage corporate reputation for financial gain.

This chapter establishes that race-conscious retraction is part of a cycle of disclosures and retraction whereby corporations shift from constructing race-conscious images to retracting race-conscious disclosures in an effort to manage their reputations for financial gain. Race-conscious retraction is a response to the polarization that has increased since Obama's presidency. Media coverage of corporate responses to political polarization has further entrenched polarization and fast-tracked race-conscious retraction.

LEGAL LANDSCAPE

Between 2020 and 2023, conservative groups mostly relied on the courts to push back against race-conscious disclosures and policies that were meant to address racial inequality, including policies mandating the disclosure of the racial composition of a firm, and state law requiring increases in corporate diversity.[13] Conservative groups have treated racial targets, for example, as indistinguishable from racial quotas because, in their view, both mechanisms can generate the hiring and promotion of people of color, even if one option is binding and the other is nonbinding.

In 2020, two conservative groups, the Alliance for Fair Board Recruitment (hereafter, the Alliance) and Judicial Watch, challenged California's "disclosure plus" law in Assembly Bill No. 979, requiring publicly traded companies in California to have and disclose at least one board director from an underrepresented minority group or from the LGBTQ+ community, on the basis that the law was discriminatory.[14] A California superior court judge struck down the rule as unconstitutional in 2022 in *Crest v. Padilla*.[15] The state court's ruling followed a similar ruling in federal court in the Eastern District of California, which held in *Alliance for Fair Board Recruitment v. Weber*,[16] that the rule violates the Equal Protection Clause of the US Constitution, the Fourteenth Amendment, and Section 1981 of the Civil Rights Act of 1866.[17]

In August 2022, the American Civil Rights Project, whose mission is "to assure that American law equally protects all Americans," filed a lawsuit on behalf of the National Center for Public Policy Research, a conservative think tank, against Starbucks, challenging seven of the company's policies as racially discriminatory under section 1981, Title VII, and various state antidiscrimination laws.[18] The case, *National Center for Public Policy Research v. Schultz*, was filed as a shareholder derivative lawsuit under Rule 23.1(a) of the federal rules of civil procedure. A shareholder in a derivative lawsuit seeks to enforce a corporation's rights and must fairly and adequately represent the interests of similarly situated shareholders.[19] The lawsuit came four years after Starbucks closed 8,000 stores nationwide to provide its 175,000 employees with four hours of racial bias training; this, in turn, followed a 2018 incident when an employee called the police on two Black men holding a meeting in a coffee shop in downtown Philadelphia.[20] The plaintiffs alleged that the company's policies required it to discriminate on the basis of race in employment decisions, in the compensation of its officers, and in contracting with suppliers. One of those policies involved a racial target, namely, Starbucks' goal of achieving BIPOC (Black, indigenous, and people of color) representation of at least 30% at all enterprise levels and at least 40% in all retail and manufacturing roles by 2025.[21]

Starbucks filed and won a motion to dismiss the case based on standing, arguing that the "[p]laintiff cannot proceed with [the] shareholder derivative lawsuit because it does not fairly and adequately represent the interests of shareholders, as required by Rule 23.1(a)."[22] A federal judge in Washington state dismissed the case in 2023 on those grounds, adding that the lawsuit centered on "political and public policy agendas" that are for "political branches" and "board[s] of directors of public corporations" to decide.[23] Motions to dismiss other similar conservative lawsuits have also rested on the procedural aspects of filing a lawsuit against or on behalf of a company.[24]

In a 2023 case, the Alliance challenged the nonbinding, nonmandatory SEC-approved diversity disclosure rule discussed in Chapters 2 and 6, in *Alliance for Fair Board Recruitment v. SEC*. The Alliance filed a petition in the US Court of Appeals for the Fifth Circuit asking the court to review the SEC-approved Nasdaq rule requiring Nasdaq-listed companies to disclose two diverse board members – one person of color and one woman – or explain why a company lacked two diverse board members.[25] The Alliance argued that the SEC's approval of the rules violated the constitutional right to equal protection by encouraging discrimination against potential board members and stigmatizing current board members based on race and sex. It also argued that the disclosure requirement violated the First Amendment and that the SEC's approval of the rules will lead to an uncompensated taking of property subject to the Fifth Amendment. The Nasdaq board diversity rule was neither binding nor mandatory because it merely required companies to either disclose or explain why their boards lack two diverse members.[26] Yet the Alliance and other conservative groups referred to it as a quota and it was fiercely contested by political leaders in southern and midwestern states.[27] As noted in Chapter 2, The United States Court of Appeals for the Fifth Circuit struck down the Nasdaq board diversity rule in December 2024. In 2025, Nasdaq formally asked the SEC to withdraw the rule to reflect the federal court's decision.[28] A formal withdrawal effectively removed the rule from Nasdaq's rulebook.

The legal decision that has had the greatest impact on providing support for conservative lawsuits and threats of lawsuits since 2023, and has accelerated race-conscious retraction is *Students for Fair Admissions v. Harvard*, the United States Supreme Court case that invalidated the use of race in college and university admissions.[29] The decision itself does not touch on the employment context but has been the source of authority for threats of litigation, actual litigation, and shareholder proposals by conservative groups against corporations. Those threats have worked to trigger the retraction of race-conscious disclosures. Conservative groups and the media were quick to extend the reach of the Harvard decision to the corporate setting, which has had a chilling effect on race-conscious disclosures and policies to combat racial inequality.

Race-conscious retraction is problematic because the need for racial diversity and inclusion in the employment context remains significant and directly impacts companies' bottom lines, workforce innovation, and the ability to represent diverse customer bases.[30] Hiring from a range of racial backgrounds opens up opportunities for ideas and leadership that are often suppressed by systems that perpetuate racial inequality.[31] That said, hiring is not enough. Corporations limit innovation and continuous improvement unless all employees are full participants in the enterprise.[32] They must be fully seen, heard, developed, engaged, and rewarded accordingly.[33]

MEDIA AND RACE-CONSCIOUS RETRACTION

In June 2023, the *Wall Street Journal* (WSJ) published an article declaring that companies had begun to keep quiet about diversity and sustainability issues amid political backlash that came swiftly after the murder of George Floyd.[34] The article based its findings on data from AlphaSense, a market intelligence platform, examining earnings calls from the first quarter of each year from 2018 to 2023. Earnings calls are

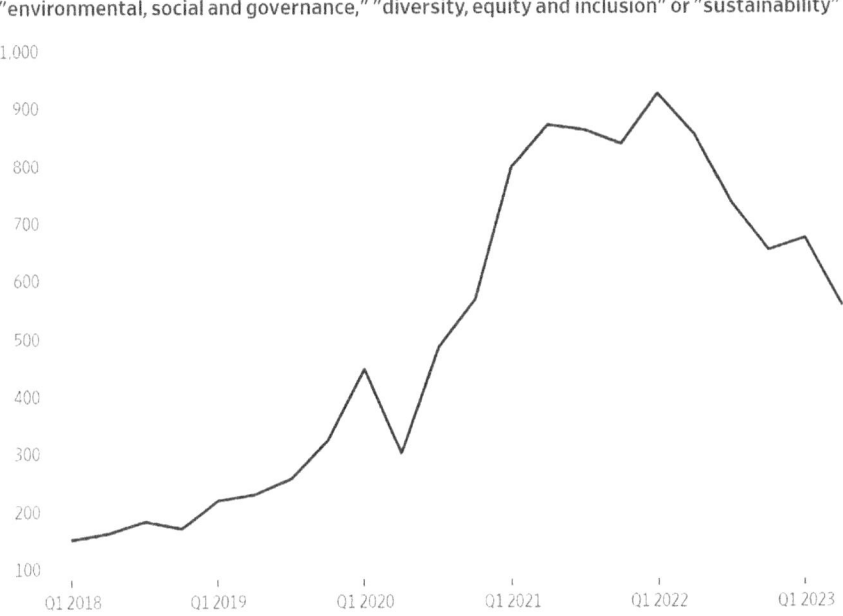

U.S.-listed company earnings calls where executives mentioned "ESG," "DEI,"
"environmental, social and governance," "diversity, equity and inclusion" or "sustainability"

Note: Q2 2023 is as of June 5.
Source: AlphaSense

FIGURE 5.1 *Wall Street Journal* use of terms in earnings calls, 2018–2023

usually conducted on a quarterly basis to help mitigate potential information asymmetries between managers and investors.[35] Unlike voluntary sustainability reports or other self-reported filings that provide an annual or even biannual view, earnings calls are conference calls that tend to occur more frequently – usually in each quarter – between the management of a public company, analysts, investors, and the media, to discuss the company's finances.[36]

As shown in Figure 5.1, the main thrust of the WSJ analysis was that companies had drastically reduced the use of specific terms – namely, "environmental, social, and governance," "ESG," "diversity, equity, and inclusion," "DEI," and "sustainability" – during earnings calls. A graph appeared to show a dramatic decline in the use of those five terms in earnings calls in the first quarter of 2023 – down 31 percent from the previous year.[37] The WSJ attributed this shift to the political backlash that developed in response to the "more boastful approach taken" by corporations after 2020.[38]

A year later, in April 2024, another media source, Axios, which claims to have over 3.3 million subscribers, also used data from AlphaSense to conclude that the backlash against DEI had resulted in a significant decline in the use of the terms DEI and diversity, equity, and inclusion in earnings calls, as shown in Figure 5.2.[39]

Mentions of "DEI" or "diversity, equity and inclusion" in quarterly earnings calls

Quarterly; Q1 2020 to Q1 2024

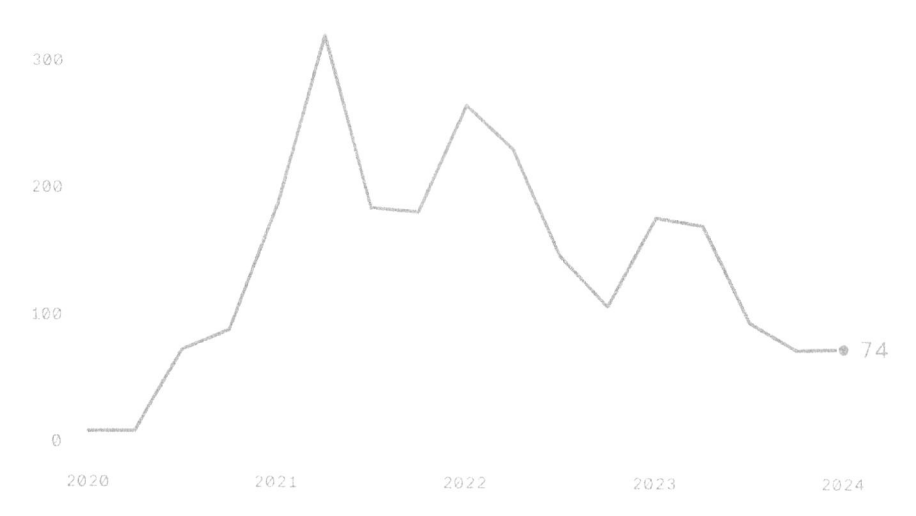

FIGURE 5.2 AlphaSense chart: Axios Visuals mentions of DEI in earnings calls, 2020–2024.

Axios apparently relied on a few hundred earnings calls. A few months after Axios published the article on its website, the WSJ published another article declaring that diversity goals are disappearing from companies' annual reports but without any systematic research or methodological analysis.[40]

These news articles and numerous media sources describing the death of DEI in 2023 and 2024 strongly suggested that the use of race-conscious disclosures was rapidly headed toward race-conscious retraction long before President Trump was elected to a second term in office. Alongside claims about the rolling back of race-conscious disclosures, numerous media outlets reported the rolling back of DEI programs and policies, including the shrinking of CDO positions and offices, and the threat of lawsuits against companies that retained DEI programs in southern and midwestern states.[41] News articles advised CDOs to tie their positions directly to the bottom line by saying things like, "we increased our market share by 5% through selling more Black-owned beauty brands," or "we increased our profit margin by 2% after instituting a supplier diversity program."[42] In other words, according to the media, it was reasonable to conclude that race-conscious disclosures generally no longer had a place in corporate America.[43]

However, despite what the media tends to portray and the negative impact the Trump administration has had on race relations in America, the true state of race-conscious disclosures in 2023, 2024 and today is a lot more nuanced and complex than we can glean from journalistic analyses of the state of DEI. For starters, studies on DEI do not necessarily capture useful information about race relations in companies. To be sure, many people, including politicians, job candidates, and even academics, tend to perceive and treat DEI as synonymous with race.[44] But DEI encompasses a lot of things, some of which are unrelated to racial equity concerns – one of the reasons that this book focuses on race and not DEI. Recognizing this important distinction might change the picture we see.

In addition, a look at a few hundred companies' earnings calls, or even a few companies' annual reports, is not sufficient to capture the story of race-conscious disclosures. My examination of over 2,000 companies' race-conscious disclosures from different sources tells a clearer story about race-conscious retraction. It is also important to note that not every company would engage in race-conscious retraction even in the face of reputational or litigation threat. The media hardly reports on those companies.

PARTIAL AND COMPLETE RACE-CONSCIOUS RETRACTION

There are two forms of race-conscious retraction. One form, which I refer to as "partial race-conscious retraction" involves the modification of language in race-conscious disclosures to effectively omit words and phrases that suggests that an organization is addressing racial inequality. The second form is "complete race-conscious retraction," which involves a total erasure of race-conscious disclosures that were previously made by an institution. Complete race-conscious retraction could revert a company to its disclosure regime prior to 2020 where its lumped race with other forms of "diversity," or result in a situation where the corporation no longer mentions anything related to race in its disclosures after the retraction. Complete race-conscious retraction can also involve the removal of the four major types of race-conscious disclosures discussed in Chapters 2–4: General statements, statistics on racial composition, racial targets, and CRP, from a company's disclosures.

Partial Race-Conscious Retraction

Partial race-conscious retraction is about the modification of language. With partial race-conscious retraction, companies would not be inclined to use the same type of language previously used in disclosures between 2020 and 2024, but rather, deliberately choose to replace terms that demonstrate a focus on addressing racial inequality.[45] In other words, companies continue to make disclosures without naming the problems of racial inequality and injustice. Companies shift the language in their race-conscious disclosures to seemingly more innocuous or mundane language. Replacing the language of racial oppression with mundane language constrains racial progress because it indicates a clear and measurable withdrawal of support for racial progress. Also, if the focus of race-conscious disclosures is not on injustice and the oppression of people of color, and there are no corporate disclosures about past racial inequality, then for conservative groups, it would seem like these words discriminate against white individuals because they would appear to seemingly have no factual basis or support. So, by not including words about injustice in their disclosures, corporations are directly limiting the extent of their responsibility.

Partial race-conscious retraction began in 2023 after the Harvard case. Media reporting between 2023 and 2024 suggested that race-conscious disclosures were a thing of the past. Based on the reporting, one would have expected to see an immediate and systematic retraction of race-conscious disclosures. In particular, 2024 signaled such dramatic shift. It was an election year with Donald Trump running for and winning a second term against the first Black and South Asian woman to ever run for president of the United States, a scenario that drew the ire of white Republicans, including Trump. The media was quick to report on companies that seemed to have ended their DEI programs.[46] The pace and magnitude of retraction in this predicted scenario would mirror that of the 2020 image-construction project: Companies would swiftly and dramatically resort to omitting any mention of race in their public disclosures, and companies that wanted to continue to address racial inequality would do so more stealthily. Race-conscious disclosures would be largely a thing of the past. Even as a researcher who studies the intersection between business, law, and society, I too expected this outcome. A full-blown race-conscious retraction means that companies would have pared back on communicating about race, regardless of whether they continued to internally maintain programs and policies geared toward any kind of racial progress.

However, recall that corporations engaged in race-conscious disclosures for reputational gain, which influences the extent to which they can choose to retract, and how they choose to retract. The stakeholders who pressured them to engage in race-conscious disclosures still expect them to tackle racial inequality.

As shown in Figure 5.3, my analysis indicates that in 2024, companies' use of race-conscious disclosures in voluntary sustainability reports was higher than ever.

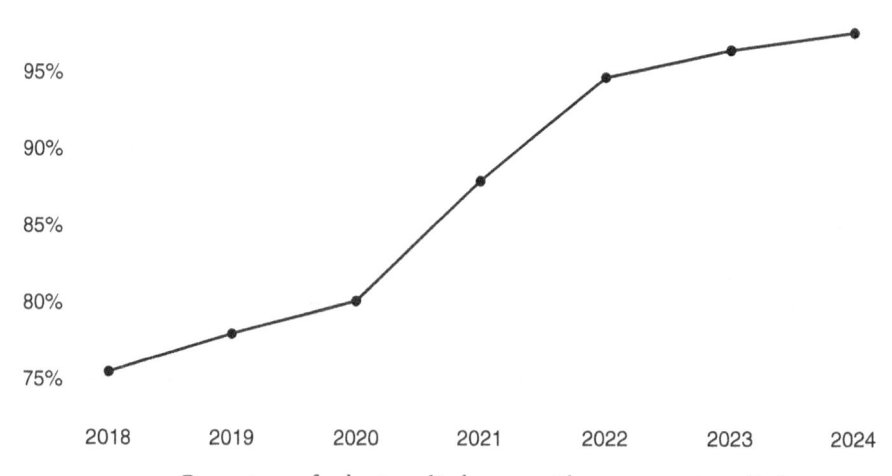

FIGURE 5.3 Percentage of voluntary disclosures with race-conscious disclosures

TABLE 5.1 *Average number of racial terms per voluntary report*

Year	Average
2018	10.39
2019	10.43
2020	11.61
2021	21.46
2022	29.12
2023	30.41
2024	31.52

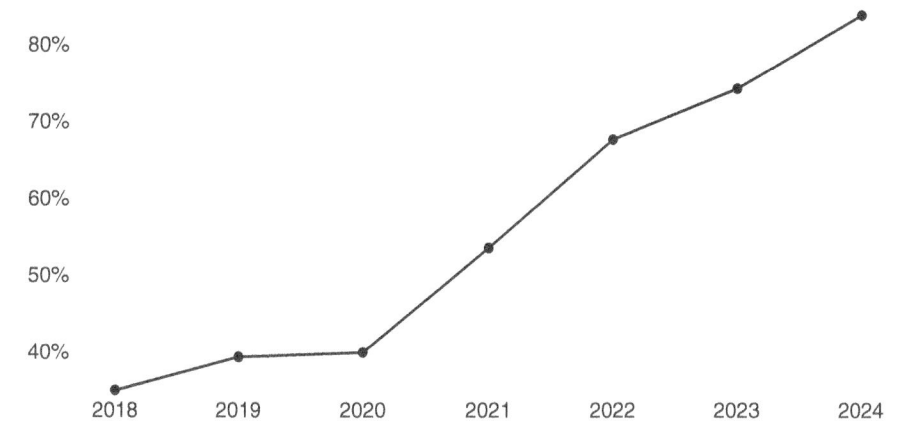

FIGURE 5.4 Percentage of companies making voluntary demographic disclosures with statistics

Indeed, 97.7% of the companies in my dataset made race-conscious disclosures in voluntary sustainability reports in 2024, up from 96.5% in 2023. So, while companies may have reduced their mentions of certain terms and subjects during meetings with investors and analysts, they continued to make systematic race-conscious disclosures in voluntary reports.

Companies also increased their disclosure of racial demographic statistics in voluntary sustainability reports. In 2024, 83.1% of the companies I examined disclosed some statistical information about the racial and ethnic makeup of their workforces, up from 73.9% in 2023, as shown in Figure 5.4.

In addition, as shown in Table 5.1 and Figure 5.5, the average number of race-related terms used per voluntary report increased from 30.4 terms per report in 2023 to 31.5 terms per report in 2024. This means that in 2024, companies talked more about race in their voluntary reports than in previous years. In fact, 2023–2024 was the second-highest jump, second only to 2020–2021. This was surprising, considering

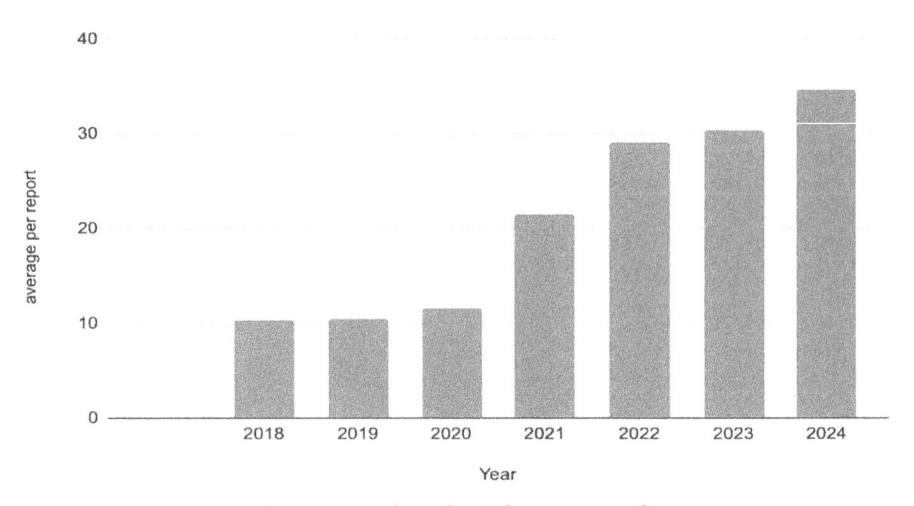

FIGURE 5.5 Average number of racial terms per voluntary report

how polarizing issues about race had become after the Harvard decision, a presidential election with Donald Trump running for and winning a second term, general political backlash at the time, and the media coverage of the decline of DEI, all of which would seem to suggest a shift in the opposite direction. My own conversations with companies' legal counsel revealed that many lawyers began to advise companies to backpedal on making race-conscious disclosures, yet these statistics suggest that corporations did not fully embrace that advice in 2024.

To the contrary, companies marched on with making race-conscious disclosures about Black people and other people of color and disclosing statistics about racial and ethnic demographic groups. This indicates that corporate race-conscious disclosures are actually a more complicated phenomenon than the media depicts. In 2024, while there was an increase in race-conscious disclosures, including both overall and in some specific types, there was also a decline in certain other types of race-conscious disclosures.

Specifically, in 2024, companies increased their use of the term "belonging" and drastically reduced the use of specific terms about race like "racism," "systemic racism," "structural racism," "racial justice," and "racial equity" that had entered the lexicon of corporate disclosures after 2020. Figures 5.6 and 5.7 show a decline in the use of these five terms in 2023 and a further decline in 2024.[47]

This change in the language used in race-conscious disclosures, in the context of an overall continued increase in race-conscious disclosures in 2024, amounts to partial race-conscious retraction. Similar to what I demonstrated earlier in the book, companies calibrated their use of race-conscious disclosures to optimize their own interests. Now, some companies are doing it in an increasingly nuanced and precise way in order to adapt to the complicated political landscape – attempting to appease the shareholders and stakeholders who originally

Partial and Complete Race-Conscious Retraction 123

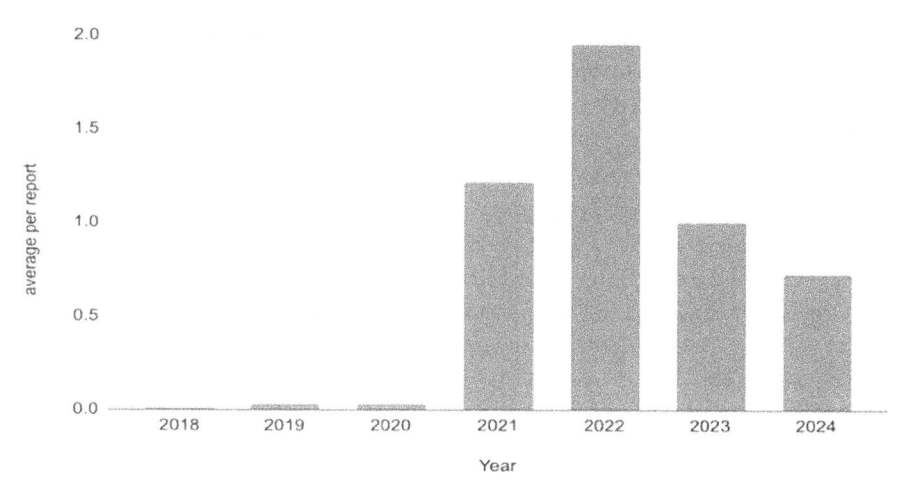

FIGURE 5.6 Average use of five specific terms per voluntary report

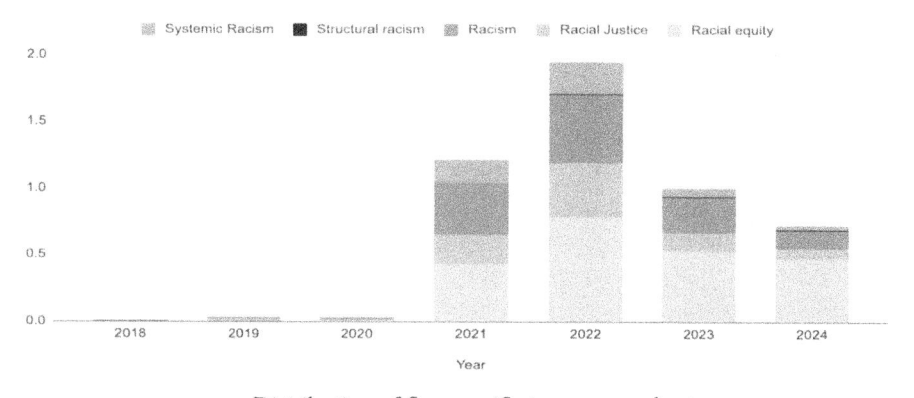

FIGURE 5.7 Distribution of five specific terms per voluntary report

wanted race-conscious disclosures while simultaneously pulling back on other types of content that are particularly inflammatory to conservative groups, thus posing a different set of reputational and litigation risks. Put simply, many companies are trying to have their cake and eat it too.

Complete Race-Conscious Retraction

Complete race-conscious retraction involves the erasure rather than modification or replacement of previously made race-conscious disclosures. Complete race-conscious retraction most vividly emerged in 2025 in response to President Trump's attacks on programs and policies that seem to address racial inequality in the federal government and other institutions, on the basis that addressing racial inequality discriminates against white individuals. Many firms began to erase race-conscious disclosures to protect their reputations, avoid possible litigation from conservative groups, or potentially being targeted by the Trump administration.

For some companies, complete race-conscious retraction would revert them back to their disclosure regime prior to 2020, in which case, their disclosures would be devoid of any mention of race, or most likely, the companies would lump race into a broad range of issues. This is precisely what Blackrock did in its proxy voting guidelines in 2025. In disclosures between 2020 and 2023, Blackrock disclosed a racial target to encourage corporations to diversify their boards by 30% with female directors, and directors who identify as members of underrepresented groups.[48] In 2025, Blackrock chose to lump its disclosures about race with a range of issues, by encouraging boards of directors to have diverse personal characteristics, including "gender; race/ethnicity; disability; veteran status; LGBTQ+; and national, Indigenous, religious, or cultural identity."[49]

When many companies made disclosures prior to 2020, like with Blackrock's 2025 move, race was often lumped together with other categories that companies categorized as part of diversity programs, including broad notions of viewpoint diversity, professional experience, education, skill, other individual qualities, and diversity of identity, including gender, LGBTQIA+, and disability. Lumping race together with other issues was an easy and ubiquitous way to address all the issues at once. Naming racial groups and racial discrimination explicitly was much more controversial than using a moniker like "diversity" that can mean so many different things, including geographical diversity, viewpoint diversity, and even cognitive diversity, which refers to the different ways in which people think, work, or learn.[50]

Further illustrating this trend, for example, W. W. Grainger, Inc.'s 2017 disclosure was a general statement of nondiscrimination that combined many identity groups, including age, gender, race, ethnicity, sexual orientation, veteran status, disabilities, or backgrounds: "Inclusion and diversity are integral to [W. W. Grainger, Inc.'s] business success, and the company is committed to fostering an inclusive environment where all team members feel safe, valued, and encouraged to voice their opinions, regardless of age, gender, race, ethnicity, sexual orientation, veteran status, disabilities or backgrounds."[51]

Prior to 2020, race-conscious disclosures that named specific racial or ethnic groups were also rare. When they did name specific groups, they were devoid of language about racial injustice or racism. For instance, Time Warner's 2017 racial philanthropy disclosure was a general statement about sponsoring Black media; the statement refers to Black content creators but does not invoke racism or racial injustice. "Time Warner is a leading sponsor of Blackhouse Foundation, which works to expand opportunities for Black multi-platform content creators by providing pathways into careers in film, television, digital and emerging platforms."[52]

The murder of George Floyd changed all of that. Race-conscious disclosures quickly became much more targeted and specific to racial and ethnic groups. With race-conscious image construction, disclosures about institutional racism and racial inequality became specific and impassioned. Companies talked about inequality and racism vis-à-vis a specific group – that is, Black/African Americans – and used the language of oppression, marginalization, injustice, and the importance of building community.[53] Consider, for example, the statements issued by Devon Energy, Lincoln Financial Group, Etsy, Red Venture, and Neiman Marcus Group in 2020 and 2021 (emphasis added).

> In 2020, business-as-usual has been declared obsolete. While a pandemic created disruption across the globe, acts of *racial injustice* against Black Americans came to the forefront after the killings of George Floyd, Ahmaud Arbery, Breonna Taylor, and others. Can Devon [Energy] do more to fight *institutional racism and racial inequality*? That's the question we're asking ourselves as a company.[54]
>
> We are supporting *racial justice and equity* by: Implementing sustainable, integrated practices in recruiting, retention, and development to increase Black populations at Lincoln [Financial Group] ... growing minority representation at the officer level ... with a special focus on the Black officer population. Combatting racism and bias by preserving the history of the Black experience and its relationship to American culture and progress, via a $1 million contribution to The History Makers over time. Leveraging the Lincoln Financial Foundation to further support *Black communities* by giving to nonprofits that advance Black communities and by engaging with philanthropic membership organizations that focus on equity-based grantmaking.[55]
>
> We featured and celebrated Black, Latino, and AAPI owned shops during a time when supporting small businesses was more important than ever before, and we created a Black-owned Business Etsy Community where sellers can opt-in, *build community*, and support one another.[56]
>
> Across [Red Venture's] largest race demographics, we saw year-over-year improvement in the D&I Index. While this is positive progress, we also see that other than Latino(a) or Hispanic employees, our BILAP (Black, Indigenous, Latino(a) or Hispanic, Asian, Pacific Islander) employees rate Red Venture between 3 and 8 percentage points *lower than white employees*.[57]
>
> In FY21, [Neiman Marcus Group] developed systems for managing supplier diversity across our retail and non-retail spend .... Through those efforts, we are working to promote and advance *Black, Hispanic, Asian, and LGBTQ-owned brands*.[58]

Complete race-conscious retraction gets rid of these post-George Floyd changes. Figure 5.8 shows the complex evolution of race-conscious disclosures and retraction from prior to 2020 until the present. As shown, before 2020, companies tended to not use terms about race or lumped race with other forms of diversity in disclosures. Between 2020 and 2024, companies engaged in race-conscious disclosures to develop their race-conscious images. 2023–2024 began the project of retraction, first with partial race-conscious retraction, which occurred simultaneously with race-conscious disclosures. And in 2025, complete race-conscious retraction emerged

Evolution of Race-Conscious Discourse and Refractive Balance 2020 Percent

Before 2020: No racial terms or lumping race with other forms of diversity	
2020–2024: Race-conscious disclosures	
2023–2024: Partial race-conscious retraction	
2025–Present: Partial and complete race-conscious retraction	

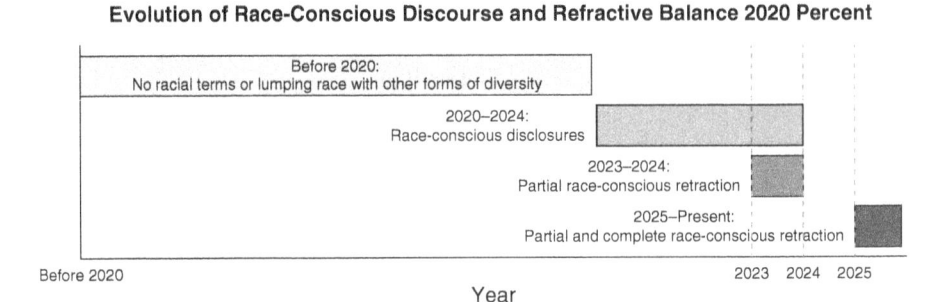

Year: Before 2020 ... 2023 2024 2025

FIGURE 5.8 Evolution of race-conscious disclosures and retraction

alongside partial race-conscious retraction. The problem is that both partial and complete race-conscious retraction contains racial progress.

CONSTRAINING RACIAL PROGRESS

With complete and partial race-conscious retraction, corporations constrain racial progress by taking active steps to remove indications that they are engaged in improving racial conditions. Race-conscious retraction is a signal that the problems companies highlighted in the process of race-conscious image construction are not important, or no longer important. Even partial race-conscious retraction, that seems like a mild modification, constrains racial progress and discounts the value of businesses publicly stating – however inaccurately or disingenuously – that they are taking steps to tackle racial inequality. By retracting such language, corporations limit the potential contribution they could make toward racial progress.

ALL ABOUT CORPORATE REPUTATION

Shareholders and stakeholders are unable to fully evaluate a firm's reputation without reliable information.[59] Companies engaged in race-conscious image construction using race-conscious disclosures to develop a reputation among shareholders and other stakeholders as seeking to address racial inequality; this image construction and reputation, in turn, generated goodwill toward improved financial conditions.[60]

The murder of George Floyd in 2020 prompted shareholders, employees, customers, and others to pressure companies to take steps toward addressing racial inequality, including by adopting and disclosing board and management diversity policies, adopting policies to prohibit inequality in employment, disclosing employment data, disclosing plans to achieve racial equity, supporting racial equity causes, and conducting racial equity or civil rights audits. Companies yielded to these pressures by taking steps that deviated from how most corporate executives have previously used disclosures. Corporate executives tend to be cautious in expanding voluntary disclosures in order to avoid setting a precedent that might be difficult to maintain in the future and that would be damaging to their reputation to retract in the future.[61] But the reputational risks and stakes for corporations of *not* making race-conscious disclosures transformed in 2020. Most corporations seemed to decide that reputational concerns outweighed the usual risks and thus found themselves disclosing much more than they ever had before about race.

Risks to a company's reputation can arise from outrage over both corporate decision-making and the lack thereof.[62] For example, employees and others expressed outrage when Disney failed to speak out against anti-LGBTQIA+ legislation in Florida, which impacted the company's reputation as an LGBTQIA+ friendly employer.[63] Disney quickly complied with external pressures to protect its reputation.[64] Similarly, public attention and potential backlash can arise from knowledge that a company's business practices perpetuate racial discrimination or have a disproportionate impact on minorities and it is not taking action to address it. To protect against this kind of negative reputational impact in 2020, companies made race-conscious disclosures to build race-conscious images. The initial surge of adopting race-conscious disclosures was to avoid a perception of inaction and the high reputational risks that such a perception posed at that particular point in time. Following Floyd's murder, shareholders, employees, prospective employees, customers, and others, desperately wanted companies to do something and to say something.

And when shareholders and stakeholders asserted that businesses could be sources of racial inequality even as they made race-conscious disclosures, companies sought to respond to those claims as potential threats to the reputations they had built with disclosures. They took steps to limit the parameters of those assertations and constrained racial progress in the process. One might have expected that companies that had engaged multiple departments and people, including the diversity, human resources, sustainability and philanthropy offices, and executive officers and managers, and expended resources to engage in race-conscious image construction would be willing to conduct racial equity audits, or take other steps suggested by shareholders and other stakeholders to ensure that they were not in fact perpetuating racism or racial inequality. Instead, they submitted no-action letter requests to the SEC, asked shareholders to vote against proposals about racial inequality, and used their constructed race-conscious public images as evidence that they were acting toward addressing racial inequality. Ultimately, these strategies undermined attempts to call attention to, or create avenues to address, racial inequality in business.

And, of course, conservative backlash against racial equity came swiftly and intensely with attacks on companies for engaging in progressive rhetoric on social and racial issues.[65] With accusations of "corporations that have gone woke,"[66] "woke capitalism,"[67] and "woke investing,"[68] public media discussions shifted to undoing race-conscious disclosures. Journalistic reporting focused on threatened and actual lawsuits against companies for their race-conscious disclosures.[69] By the end of 2023, the media began to report that companies were shifting away from making disclosures and toward addressing inequality through less visible methods. By 2025, corporations' risk calculus seemed to weigh being perceived as taking steps to address racial inequality on the one hand, against being targeted or potentially sued by conservative groups or the Trump administration for discriminating against white individuals and having media attention around that rhetoric, on the other hand.

My interviews with CSOs and CDOs reveal how companies perceived the magnitude of the risks. As one CDO explained in 2023, "one of the tools that the right and conservative movements are using, is [litigation and] the courts. And so, that changes everything." In response to a question about the impact of the political backlash on disclosures, in 2024, another CDO said, "Are [companies] now going to go out and be as loud about [statements about race] externally? Maybe not. They're still doing all the same things internally. That is my experience." The CSO of another company emphasized the impact of litigation risk on the trajectory of race-conscious retraction:

> Where industry is headed in general is very, very factual, very data-driven, take out all the marketing speak. And a lot of that is risk of litigation at this point because there is such a movement of greenwashing that happened, but that's also being brought to bear from a stakeholder point of view. That might be consumers and consumer lawsuits, or it could also be regulatory agencies investigating, et cetera. There's a lot more scrutiny of corporate disclosures right now as it relates to ESG.

Concern about litigation and litigation publicity surely increases pressure on organizations to change but does not by itself determine the types of changes they choose to adopt.[70] Companies can choose not to engage in race-conscious retraction – even the partial type – and some less risk adverse corporations will take this approach. However, considering the influence of legal counsel who advise companies on the risks associated with disclosures, most companies react to conservative threats of litigation, or potentially been targeted by conservative politicians by engaging in the project of race-conscious retraction.

I do not take the position that companies should ignore the risk of litigation or being targeted lightly. Those costs can be substantial and should be part of the larger consideration of how to respond to external pressures from conservative groups as well as shareholders and stakeholders.

However, race-conscious retraction is a *short-term* approach designed to appease individuals and groups who believe that corporations should not take steps to address racial inequality, without adequate consideration of the *long-term* financial and reputational impact of a corporation retracting what it has already pledged to do to address racial inequality.

I should emphasize here that although I am arguing that companies should refrain from race-conscious retraction because it poses problems for corporations and constrains racial progress, this does not take away from my earlier critiques of race-conscious disclosures and how companies have used them to advance their own interests. Even when companies are in a state of *construction*, they still constrain racial progress to gain reputational benefits.

CYCLES OF RACE-CONSCIOUS DISCLOSURES AND RETRACTION

It appears likely that, without regulation from a functioning future federal government, we will likely continue to have cycles of construction and retraction of race-conscious disclosures, like other cycles of engagement with race in America's history.

Recall the Plans for Progress program, which saw a number of large companies actively engage with racial justice concerns – some voluntarily, some less so – between 1961 and at least 1964. That program diffused then eventually dissolved. Other notable historical moments include when government institutions during FDR and Truman's presidencies engaged with race, specifically, with efforts to desegregate the military.

There will likely be another major event or moment in American history five, ten, twenty, or thirty years from now that could sway the political pressure back toward increased race-conscious disclosures, but then, as we saw after the murder of George Floyd, there will also be conservative pushback to swing the pendulum back to retraction – whether partially or completely – depending on the politics of the day.

Societal pressures of push and pull, the influence of social media, artificial intelligence, and other technological advances will likely dictate how companies respond. What is clear for now is that litigation and reputational risks – the particulars of which at given moments in time are shaped by social trends, politics, and power – drive race-conscious disclosures and retraction and how companies engage in them.

Finally, the very few companies that did not make race-conscious disclosures at all will, of course, not engage in retraction because they have nothing to retract. But those few corporations have stymied racial progress too by remaining silent, which likely means that they are also taking limited steps toward addressing racial inequality. And it is also likely that some of those companies will join one of the next cycles of race-conscious image construction in the future.

NOTES

1. Micheal Tesla, *Post-Racial or Most-Racial?: Race and Politics in the Obama Era* (Chicago: University of Chicago Press, 2016).
2. Eric Schickler, *Racial Realignment: The Transformation of American Liberalism, 1932–1965* (Princeton, NJ: Princeton University Press, 2018).
3. Ashley Jardina, *White Identity Politics* (Cambridge, UK: Cambridge University Press, 2019).
4. Ibid.

5. Ibid., 3.
6. Ibid.
7. Nathan P. Kalmoe and Lilliana Mason, *Radical American Partisanship: Mapping Extreme Hostility, Its Causes, and the Consequences for Democracy* (Chicago: University of Chicago Press, 2022).
8. Ibid.
9. Tesla, *Post-Racial*.
10. Kalmoe and Mason, *Radical American Partisanship*.
11. Project 2025 Presidential Transition Project, Mandate for Leadership the Conservative Promise, Heritage Foundation (Paul Dans and Steven Groves, eds., 2023).
12. Edelman Trust, *Special Report: Business and Racial Justice*, Edelman Trust Barometer website, 2024, www.edelman.com/trust/2024/trust-barometer/special-report-business-racial-justice.
13. Adediran, "Disclosing Corporate Diversity," 351.
14. "Judicial Watch Victories: California Court of Appeal Upholds Court Injunctions against Quotas for Corporate Boards," *Judicial Watch*, December 20, 2022, https://perma.cc/K5CR-CRXD; "Judicial Watch Victory: Court Declares Unconstitutional California's Racial, Ethnic, LGBT Quota for Corporate Boards," *Judicial Watch*, April 1, 2022, https://perma.cc/TFL3-L4RC; "'Director from an Underrepresented Community' means an individual who self-identifies as Black, African American, Hispanic, Latino, Asian, Pacific Islander, Native American, Native Hawaiian, or Alaska Native, or who self-identifies as gay, lesbian, bisexual, or transgender." California Corporations Code § 301.4(e)(1) (West 2021); Adediran, "Disclosing Corporate Diversity."
15. Crest v. Padilla, No. 19STCV27561, 2022 WL 1565613 (Cal. Super. Ct. May 13, 2022); Lauren Weber, "Judge Tosses California Law Mandating Diversity on Boards," *Wall Street Journal*, April 4, 2022, www.wsj.com/articles/judge-tosses-california-law-mandating-diversity-on-boards-11649078797 [https://perma.cc/M8VF-X435]; Patrick Temple-West, "California's Gender Diversity Board Mandate Struck Down in Court," *Financial Times*, May 16, 2022, www.ft.com/content/d89c0adc-52f5-4151-a344-fa25ab4b4178 [https://perma.cc/6NFV-N5GV]; Ellen Meyers, "Investors Keep Up Diversity Pressure after California Law Tossed," *Roll Call*, April 7, 2022, https://perma.cc/MRX8-YS8A. Despite these decisions, institutional investors maintain that they will keep pressure on companies to diversify their boards by race and gender.
16. Alliance for Fair Board Recruitment v. SEC, 85 F.4th 226 (5th Cir. 2023).
17. 42 U.S.C. § 1981.
18. American Civil Rights Project, "Our Mission," April 11, 2021, www.americancivilrightsproject.org/our-mission/ [https://perma.cc/SQC8-34R4]; National Center for Public Policy Research. v. Schultz (*The Starbucks Case*), No. 2:22-cv-00267-SAB, 2023 WL 5945958 (E.D. Wash. Sept. 11, 2023). Based on the language of Section 1981, it is surprising that racial targets are being challenged under the statute. The Civil Rights Act of 1866, and Section 1981 therein, targeted "Black Codes," which were "passed in several southern states immediately after ratification of the Thirteenth Amendment." According to scholar George Rutherglen, "[t]hese codes imposed severe legal disabilities on the newly freed slaves and sought to return them to a legal status practically equivalent to slavery, but formally in conformity with the Thirteenth Amendment"; see George Rutherglen, "The Improbable History of Section 1981: Clio Still Bemused and Confused," *Supreme Court Review* (2003), 308. An article in the *Wall Street Journal* reported that conservatives had turned Section 1981 on its head "by gathering several white, male business

owners as plaintiffs"; see Theo Francis, "The Legal Assault on Corporate Diversity Efforts Has Begun," *Wall Street Journal*, August 8, 2023, www.wsj.com/articles/diversity-equity-dei-companies-blum-2040b173 [https://perma.cc/D5F6-U66P].
19. Fed. R. Civ. P. 23.1(a) (2023).
20. *The Starbucks Case*, 2023 WL 5945958, at *2; *Bolduc v. Amazon*, No. 4:22-cv-00615 (E.D. Tex. July 20, 2022); Do No Harm v. Pfizer, Inc., 646 F. Supp. 3d 490 (S.D.N.Y. 2022); Siegel and Horton, "Starbucks to Close 8,000 Stores; Stevens, "Starbucks C.E.O. Apologizes."
21. Starbucks, 2020 *Global Environmental & Social Impact Report*, 8.
22. Defendant Starbucks Corp.'s Motion to Dismiss Complaint, *The Starbucks Case*, No. 2:22-cv-00267-SAB (E.D. Wash. May 19, 2023), 2023 WL 6962044, at *3.
23. *The Starbucks Case*, 2023 WL 5945958, at *3–5; Jody Godoy, "Conservative Starbucks Investor Loses Diversity Challenge," *Reuters*, August 14, 2023, https://perma.cc/9FYM-8G3G.
24. For example, Do No Harm v. Pfizer Inc., 646 F. Supp. 3d 490 (S.D.N.Y. 2022); Moses v. Comcast Cable Commc'ns Mgmt., LLC, No. 1:22-cv-00665-JPH-MJD, 2022 U.S. Dist. LEXIS 101312 (S.D. Ind. June 7, 2022).
25. Alliance for Fair Board Recruitment, 85 F.4th; Notice of Filing of Proposed Rule Change to Adopt Listing Rules Related to Board Diversity, Exchange Act Release No. 90547, 2020 WL 7226158 (Dec. 4, 2020).
26. Adediran, "Disclosing Corporate Diversity," 348.
27. John A. Zecca, Letter from John A. Zecca, Executive Vice President, Chief Legal & Regulation Officer, Nasdaq, to Vanessa A. Countryman, Secretary, SEC, February 26, 2021, www.sec.gov/comments/sr-nasdaq-2020-081/srnasdaq2020081-8425992-229601.pdf [https://perma.cc/X9JE-SH8K]. In October 2024, the Attorneys General of Iowa, Alabama, Arkansas, Florida, Georgia, Kansas, Idaho, Indiana, Louisiana, Mississippi, Missouri, Montana, Nebraska, New Hampshire, Ohio, Oklahoma, South Carolina, Texas, Utah, Virginia, West Virginia, and Wyoming wrote a joint letter to Nasdaq to express their strong view that the Nasdaq rule is a quota. Letter to Adena T. Friedman, Chair and Chief Executive, Nasdaq, October 2024, https://perma.cc/UU4Z-VR2E.
28. US Securities and Exchange Commission (SEC), Form 19b-4, January 16, 2025, https://listingcenter.nasdaq.com/assets/rulebook/nasdaq/filings/SR-NASDAQ-2025-007.pdf.
29. Students for Fair Admissions, Inc., v. President & Fellows of Harvard College, 143 S. Ct. 2141, 2116 (2023).
30. Dame Vivian Hunt, Dennis Layton, and Sara Prince, "Why Diversity Matters," *McKinsey & Co.*, January 1, 2015, www.mckinsey.com/capabilities/people-and-organizational-performance/our-insights/why-diversity-matters [https://perma.cc/LUF3-S3KM]. This company explained in its voluntary diversity report that disclosures about race are "material to [its] business, helpful to [its] stakeholders, and increasingly expected by investors." Moody's, *Diversity, Equity and Inclusion Report*.
31. Robin J. Ely and David A. Thomas. "Getting Serious about Diversity: Enough Already with the Business Case," *Harvard Business Review* (November–December 2020), https://hbr.org/2020/11/getting-serious-about-diversity-enough-already-with-the-business-case.
32. Ibid.
33. Ibid.
34. Mark Maurer, "Companies Quiet Diversity and Sustainability Talk amid Culture War Boycotts," *Wall Street Journal*, June 12, 2023, www.wsj.com/articles/executives-quiet-their-sustainability-talk-on-earnings-calls-amid-growing-culture-war-3a358c1f.
35. Andrew Baker, David F. Larcker, Charles McClure, Durgesh Saraph, and Edward Watts, "Diversity Washing," *Journal of Accounting Research* (2024).

36. James Chen, "Earnings Calls," *Investopedia*, last updated June 20, 2021, www.investopedia.com/terms/e/earnings-call.asp.
37. Maurer, "Companies Quiet."
38. Ibid.
39. Emily Peck, "'The Backlash Is Real': Behind DEI's Rise and Fall," *Axios*, April 2, 2024, www.axios.com/2024/04/02/dei-backlash-diversity. Axios touted its large number of subscribers in an article: "Axios Named Winner of Adweek's Hottest in News Award," *Axios*, March 12, 2024, www.axios.com/press-past-releases/axios-named-winner-of-adweeks-hottest-in-news-award.
40. Ben Glickman and Lauren Weber, "Diversity Goals Are Disappearing from Companies' Annual Reports," *Wall Street Journal*, April 21, 2024, www.wsj.com/business/diversity-goals-are-disappearing-from-companies-annual-reports-459d1ef3.
41. Te-Ping Chen and Lauren Weber, "The Rise and Fall of the Chief Diversity Officer," *Wall Street Journal*, July 21, 2023, www.wsj.com/business/c-suite/chief-diversity-officer-cdo-business-corporations-e110a82f; Gibson Dunn, "Attorneys General of 13 States Issue Warning to Fortune 100 Companies Regarding Their Diversity and Inclusion Programs in Wake of Supreme Court's Decision Overturning Affirmative Action in Higher Education," Gibson Dunn website, July 18, 2023, www.gibsondunn.com/attorneys-general-of-13-states-warning-to-fortune-100-companies-regarding-their-diversity-and-inclusion-programs-in-wake-of-supreme-court-decision/; Hunter Gilmore, "Microsoft Says Bye-Bye DEI, Joins Growing List of Corporations Dismantling Diversity Teams," *Atlanta Daily World*, July 19, 2024; Temple-West, "Companies Drop DEI Targets."
42. Barbara Frankel, "Making DEI Matter: From the Business Case to a Business Driver," Seramount website, October 16, 2023, https://seramount.com/articles/making-dei-matter-from-the-business-case-to-a-business-driver/.
43. Sarah Kessler, "D.E.I. Goes Quiet," *New York Times*, January 13, 2024; Taylor Telford, "As DEI Gets More Divisive, Companies Are Ditching Their Teams," *Washington Post*, February 18, 2024.
44. Matt Gonzales, "Elon Musk Calls DEI 'Another Word for Racism'. Workplace Experts Say He's Wrong," *SHRM*, January 16, 2024, www.shrm.org/topics-tools/news/inclusion-equity-diversity/elon-musk-dei-racist; Abigail M. Folberg, Laura Brooks Dueland, Matthew Swanson, Sarah Stepanek, Mikki Hebl, and Carey S. Ryan, "Racism Underlies Seemingly Race-neutral Conservative Criticisms of DEI Statements among Black and White People in the United States," *Journal of Occupational and Organizational Psychology* 97, no. 23 (2024): 719–816; Donald T. Tomaskovic-Devey, Jorge Quesada Velazco, and Kevin L. Young, "We Analysed Racial Justice Statements from the 500 Largest US Companies and Found That DEI Officials Really Did Have an Influence," *The Conversation*, March 28, 2025.
45. Jeff Green and Simone Foxman, "Uber and Citi Cut 'Anti-Racist' from Corporate Vocabulary Following DEI Backlash," *Bloomberg*, March 1, 2024, www.bloomberg.com/news/articles/2024-03-01/uber-citi-among-us-companies-dropping-anti-racist-tag-with-dei-backlash?embedded-checkout=true.
46. Robert Klara, "The Real Reasons Why So Many Brands Have Broken Their DEI Promises," *Adweek*, October 3, 2024, www.adweek.com/brand-marketing/why-brands-have-broken-dei-promises/.
47. Industry research in 2024 also indicates that terms and phrases like "belonging culture," "building a diverse talent pipeline," and "promoting ERGs" are beginning to replace race in disclosures. Umesh Chandra Tiwari, "DEI Metrics in Executive Compensation," Harvard Law School Forum on Corporate Governance, June 26, 2024, https://corpgov.law.harvard.edu/2024/06/26/dei-metrics-in-executive-compensation/.

48. Daniel Chang, "BlackRock Updated 2023 U.S. Proxy Voting Guidelines," Georgeson, January 11, 2023, www.georgeson.com/us/insights/proxy/blackrock-updated-2023-us-voting-guidelines.
49. BlackRock Investment Stewardship, Proxy Voting Guidelines for Benchmark Policies – U.S. Securities (January 2025).
50. Bárí A. Williams, "How Companies Use 'Cognitive Diversity' as an Excuse to Keep Hiring White Men, Fast Company," *Fast Company*, May 16, 2024, www.fastcompany.com/90856183/30-ai-tools-you-can-try-for-free.
51. W. W. Grainger, *CSR Report*, 2017; Vyacheslav Fos, Wei Jiang, and Huasheng Nie, "A Diverse View on Board Diversity," SSRN website, December 20, 2023, https://papers.ssrn.com/sol3/papers.cfm?abstract_id=4667857.
52. Time Warner, *CSR Report*, 2017.
53. Iris Marion Young, "Five Faces of Oppression," in *Justice and the Politics of Difference* (Princeton, NJ: Princeton University Press, 2011).
54. Devon Energy, *Sustainability Report*, 2020; emphasis added.
55. Lincoln Financial Group, *CSR Report*, 2020; emphasis added.
56. Etsy, *Annual 10-K Report*, 2021; emphasis added.
57. Red Ventures, 2020–2021 *Annual Diversity, Equity, and Inclusion Progress Report*; emphasis added.
58. Neiman Marcus Group, *Our Journey to Revolutionize Impact, 2021 ESG Report*; emphasis added.
59. Kim T. Baumgartner, Carolin A. Ernst, and Thomas M. Fischer, "How Corporate Reputation Disclosures Affect Stakeholders' Behavioral Intentions: Mediating Mechanisms of Perceived Organizational Performance and Corporate Reputation," *Journal of Business Ethics* 175 (2022): 361–89.
60. Li Cai, Jinhua Cui, and Hoje Jo, "Corporate Environmental Responsibility and Firm Risk," *Journal of Business Ethics* 139 (2016): 563–664.
61. John R. Graham, Campbell R. Harvey, and Shiva Rajgopal, "The Economic Implications of Corporate Financial Reporting," *Journal of Accounting and Economics* 40, no. 1–3 (2005): 3–73.
62. Gadinis and Miazad, "Corporate Law and Social Risk," 1410.
63. Brooks Barnes, "Disney C.E.O. Says Company Is 'Opposed' to Florida's 'Don't Say Gay' Bill," *New York Times*, March 9, 2022, www.nytimes.com/2022/03/09/business/disney-ceo-florida-lgbtq-bill.html.
64. Elizabeth Blair, "After Protests, Disney CEO Speaks Out against Florida's 'Don't Say Gay' Bill," *NPR*, March 10, 2022, www.npr.org/2022/03/08/1085130633/disney-response-florida-bill-dont-say-gay.
65. Jamelle Bouie, "Republicans' Fake War against 'Woke Capital,'" *New York Times*, April 9, 2021, www.nytimes.com/2021/04/09/opinion/republicans-fake-war-against-woke-capital.html.
66. Jessica Guynn, "GOP Wins House Majority, Sends a Message to 'Woke' Businesses: Get Out of Politics," *USA Today*, November 16, 2022, www.usatoday.com/story/money/2022/11/16/republican-house-warning-woke-business/10711866002/.
67. Jamelle Bouie, "Before He Takes On 'Woke Capitalism,' Ron DeSantis Should Read His Karl Marx," *New York Times*, December 2, 2022, www.nytimes.com/2022/12/02/opinion/mccarthy-desantis-capitalism.html.
68. Andrew Ramonas and Clara Hudson, "ESG Foes in States, Congress Ready Attacks on 'Woke' Investing," *Bloomberg Law*, November 21, 2022, https://news.bloomberglaw.com/securities-law/esg-foes-in-states-congress-ready-attacks-on-woke-investing.

69. Jody Godoy and Disha Raychaudhuri, "Some Companies Alter Diversity after Conservatives' Lawsuit Threat," *Reuters*, December 18, 2023, www.reuters.com/business/some-companies-alter-diversity-policies-after-conservatives-lawsuit-threat-2023-12-18/.
70. Kishanthi Parella, "Reputational Regulation," *Duke Law Journal* 67, no. 5 (February 2018): 907–80.

6

Regulating Race-Conscious Disclosures and Retraction

Legal scholars Dorothy Lund and Elizabeth Pollman have argued that corporate governance functions as a system composed of laws, institutions, and culture that orients decision-making toward shareholders.[1] They call this structure the "corporate governance machine."[2] The participants in this machine drive the focus on shareholders in companies rather than the consideration of the interests of stakeholders like employees and communities.[3] Since this multifaceted corporate governance machine shapes how companies function, I take the approach that a single institutional player cannot be expected to regulate companies in a world characterized by advanced technologies, a growing need for transparency, and a shift in political pressures and institutional expectations about how companies should respond to societal changes.

The norms of engagement for corporate governance actors and institutions have changed. Employees and prospective employees are no longer passive onlookers in companies. They have taken on a vocal role in shaping the companies they work for and are discerning in their choice of employers. Shareholders make demands that go beyond the traditional notion of profit maximization and are drivers of social change by exerting pressure on corporate managers. As discussed in Chapter 2, shareholders have become crucial catalysts in the quest to address racial inequality. The goal then is to harness this landscape in a new framework for regulating businesses, drawing on the newfound roles and powers of various constituencies in a multi-institutional approach.

Because these constituents are limited in the information available to them, this chapter conceives of the role of a functioning federal government as an "information enforcer," serving as the conduit for essential information and enforcing rules that govern the use of voluntary race-conscious disclosures. Other constituents would then use the information the government makes available to regulate race-conscious disclosures. "Regulation" here refers to the process of monitoring, overseeing, and helping to improve voluntary disclosures about race. This is an intentionally broad definition that is consistent with the sociology of regulation and is meant to extend the power to guide what companies say and do to a multiplicity of actors, institutions, and stakeholders.[4] To be sure, the extent to which nongovernmental institutions and agents can regulate companies varies in practice. But limitations imposed by law, politics, incentive structures, and resources, make a multi-institutional approach much more desirable than reliance on the federal government alone.

But we are currently in a state of "ungoverning" as described by political scientists Russell Muirhead and Nancy Rosenblum in their book *Ungoverning: The Attack on the Administrative State and the Politics of Chaos*. Muirhead and Rosenblum define ungoverning as a state in which leaders intentionally weaken the state in which they govern.[5] Since Trump came into office a second time in 2025, his administration has taken unprecedented steps to intentionally weaken the ability of federal government agencies to function through tactics like disparaging federal workers as illegitimate, major cuts to civilian employment, and the closure or shrinkage of whole federal agencies. By the time the Trump administration is done weakening the administrative state, typical agency functions, such as "collecting information and data, consulting with affected groups, harnessing expert knowledge, and implementing policies"[6] to address significant societal concerns, including climate and environmental hazards, racial and gender discrimination, human rights violations, and corporate corruption, will likely be significantly decreased.

This chapter stands on the premise that the forces of ungoverning will be defeated and we will one day return to a functioning federal government that works to protect vulnerable citizens. That citizens themselves will appreciate the legitimacy of the administrative state, understanding that no private entity can do what the federal government does.

In this chapter, I make normative suggestions for a pathway toward ensuring that corporations are accountable to the government, their stakeholders, and the public when that time comes. Unlike the Plans for Progress program in the 1960s, discussed in Chapter 1, in which the government took a hands-off approach to regulating businesses, I argue that the government should be central to any future regulatory regime that seeks to collect, disseminate, and guide the use of race-conscious disclosures.

Before delving into the federal government's information-enforcing role, I first discuss how the federal government regulated social and environmental matters mostly through mandatory disclosures, before Trump's second term in office.

FEDERAL GOVERNMENT MANDATES

The federal government has attempted to regulate racial and other forms of diversity, and climate risks, mostly by mandating corporate disclosures. While this book is not about mandatory disclosures, it is worth noting what steps the government has taken to address social and environmental concerns.

Mandatory Diversity Disclosures

In 2009, the SEC required companies to disclose whether and how they consider diversity in their board nominations.[7] Under the provision, companies could define diversity as broadly as they liked.

In 2020, the SEC amended Item 101(c) of Regulation S-K to mandate "human capital disclosures" to the extent that the information is material to an understanding of their business.[8] The SEC noted that it did not define human capital disclosures because it wanted individual companies to determine the meaning for themselves. The regulation came on the heels of the murder of George Floyd, so not surprisingly, lots of companies included discussions about diversity, equity, and inclusion in that definition between November 2020 and July 2021.[9] In September 2023, the SEC's Investor Advisory Committee made recommendations for providing investors with full information for accurate valuation of human capital, including workforce demographic data.[10]

As discussed in Chapters 2 and 5, in 2021, Nasdaq established a rule, which the SEC approved, and which conservatives furiously opposed, requiring companies listed on the Nasdaq stock exchange to disclose at least one board director who is a person of color, or explain why their board lacks diversity. I have previously discussed the pitfalls of the Nasdaq rule, particularly the "disclose or explain" provision in Rule 5605(f), for lacking the power to make significant progress toward board and management diversity because companies needed only to explain why they lacked diversity on their boards, and there were no other regulatory bodies mandating the rules.[11] The rule also expressly eschewed any enforcement by the SEC.[12] The rule also likely helped Nasdaq-listed companies to construct race-conscious public images by disclosing their racial compositions. The United States Court of Appeals for the Fifth Circuit struck down the rule in December 2024.

The SEC raised the specter of direct regulation of racial diversity after the murder of Floyd. In 2020, then Acting SEC Commissioner Allison Herren Lee released a statement heralding the human capital disclosure rule while also expressing regret that the rule is silent on "diversity in the face of profound racial injustice."[13] And in June 2021, SEC Chair Gary Gensler noted in a speech, which the Trump administration removed in 2025 from the SEC's website, that human capital could include diversity metrics.[14] There was some speculation in 2023 that the SEC would establish its own rules that would require the disclosure of more board diversity information, similar in scope to the Nasdaq board diversity rule.[15] No such SEC rule has come to fruition.

Congress has also attempted to mandate ESG disclosures. In June 2021, the House of Representatives passed the Corporate Governance Improvement and Investor Protection Act (hereafter, "Investor Protection Act"), which the Senate did not pass. The Investor Protection Act would have required the SEC to enact rules requiring companies to make climate risk, workforce diversity, and board diversity disclosures.[16]

Outside of the United States, it is informative to compare other regimes of disclosure and regulation of race and gender in corporations. Canada, South Africa, and Scandinavian countries such as Norway have used disclosures or in some cases, "disclosure plus" additional regulation to address racial inequality in business and markets. In 2020, Canada began to require publicly traded companies established under the Canada Business Corporations Act to disclose the racial compositions of their boards and senior management, among other identity factors.[17] While, in general, mandating disclosures is unlikely to move the needle on addressing bias and discrimination within corporations after people of color have been hired, it has resulted in some successes in representation and hiring. Canadian companies have seen some progress from disclosures with the percentage of companies with at least one member of a minority group on their boards increasing from 23% in 2022 to 27% in 2023.[18] Similar to California's "disclosure plus" model, in 2003, Norway amended its Companies Act to require 40 percent of board members of public companies to be women and has been successful in that regard.[19]

Even if the United States continues to use a disclosure regime to regulate corporations, it is important to note that mandatory disclosures do not regulate voluntary disclosures, nor are mandatory disclosures likely to have as significant an impact as the "disclosure plus" regimes adopted then eventually struck down in California as discussed in Chapter 5, or that have been used more successfully in Norway. If the goal is to ensure that corporations do not constrain racial progress with their words, simply requiring more words is insufficient, although mandating certain disclosures about race can create uniformity and allow the government to set the limits of what corporations do with regards to race-conscious disclosures.

Mandatory Climate Disclosures

In 2022, the SEC proposed rules for the "Enhancement and Standardization of Climate-Related Disclosures for Investors."[20] A watered-down version of the rules was adopted in 2024, which the SEC under the Trump administration chose not to pursue.[21] The rules would have required companies to disclose climate-related financial impact, assumptions, and expenditure metrics.[22] If the rules ever become revived in the future, they will apply to public companies, as well as some private companies. However, even these rules are focused largely on mandatory disclosures rather than voluntary disclosures about climate and the environment and the impact of corporations on climate change and the environment.

The European Union (EU), a jurisdiction whose laws affect thousands of American companies, has been an exemplar in not only mandating nonfinancial corporate disclosures but also in its regulation and holding of corporations accountable for climate and social issues. In 2023, the EU established the Corporate Sustainability Reporting Directive, or CSRD, to take effect between 2025 and 2028 (depending on the type of company), in a regulatory effort to boost visibility on greenhouse gas emissions, gender pay gaps, human rights violations, and working conditions.[23] The CSRD also requires disclosures from companies that are registered in the EU as well as non-EU firms with significant activity in the EU, defined as having more than 450€ million or about $490 million in annual revenue and at least one subsidiary or branch with net revenue of more than €40 million in the EU.[24] Each EU member state will establish the penalties for noncompliance, ranging from fines of €25,000 or imprisonment for individual directors, to fines imposed on the company that could equal the higher of €10 million or 5 percent of the company's global annual turnover.[25]

In addition to disclosures, the EU established accountability measures through its Corporate Sustainability Due Diligence Directive (CSDDD or CS3D).[26] CS3D applies to American companies with a net revenue of more than €450 million in the EU.[27] Thousands of American companies fall into this category.[28] CS3D requires companies to identify actual and potential adverse environmental and human rights impacts arising from their operations, their subsidiaries' operations, and their value chains.[29] Firms would also need to take measures to end, prevent, or mitigate any such identified impacts and can be sued for wrongdoing by those who are affected by their operations, as well as by advocacy groups and trade unions on behalf of those affected. The CS3D also mandates the adoption of a climate transition plan.[30] Failure to act will result in regulatory liability from member states, as well as potential civil litigation from those who are impacted.[31]

The EU's regulatory regime on climate change suggests that the US federal government could and should be doing more to regulate corporations' race-conscious disclosures as well as their approaches to climate and other social inequality issues, beyond mandating disclosures alone.

PROPOSAL FOR A GOVERNMENT INFORMATION-ENFORCING ROLE

The US Congress and the executive branch have explicit authority to regulate private and public companies on a national scale. However, all national governmental entities are hamstrung by a number of political, legal, and practical limits. Political polarization makes it challenging for federal agencies to act because of concerns that partisan decision-making would impact agency function. Administrative agencies are limited by the Administrative Procedure Act, which requires courts, rather than federal agencies, to exercise their independent judgment in deciding whether an agency has acted within its statutory authority.[32] Federal administrative agencies are also limited by the "nondelegation doctrine," a legal standard that prevents Congress from assigning its lawmaking powers to agencies.[33] As I have written in previous work, there are also limitations arising from the authority granted to each agency to implement government interests. For example, the securities laws and the SEC were constituted primarily to provide transparency to investors in making investment decisions, and not to address inequality.[34] There are also potential limitations from the White House, depending on who the president is, that can severely weaken federal agencies. As evidenced during Trump's second term in office, which is characterized by closures of whole federal agencies and offices, indiscriminate firings of federal civil servants, recrimination and blaming agencies for economic and social problems, and so on. There are also resource allocation limitations that can make regulation challenging.

Finally, while the First Amendment to the US Constitution might appear to limit government regulation of corporate communication in this regard, there is a strong argument that race-conscious disclosures are commercial speech. Legal scholars Amanda Shanor and Sarah Light have argued that because people are dependent for information on commercial speakers, like corporations, regulation of such speech for truthfulness is consistent with the First Amendment and is subject to the laxer review of the commercial speech doctrine because society must have accurate information for market participation.[35]

What the Federal Government Should Do

Despite the government's limited ability to intervene in the actions of private actors, federal government agencies like the Federal Trade Commission (FTC) and Securities and Exchange Commission (SEC) were situated until 2024, to serve as information enforcers that other constituents can rely on to regulate race-conscious disclosures. In terms of enforcement, the FTC protects consumers against deceptive and unfair business practices and can be an information-enforcing agent.[36] For example, in 2014, the FTC sent warning letters to more than sixty companies for not making adequate disclosures in their television and print ads.[37] In 2021, the FTC sent a notice to over 1,000 companies that pitch money-making ventures, warning that if said companies deceive or mislead consumers about potential earnings, the FTC would not hesitate to use its authority to target them with large civil penalties.[38] These enforcement strategies can effectively put corporations on alert for possible penalties and deter behavior.

The SEC protects investors from fraud and undisclosed risks and fosters market access.[39] The SEC has taken enforcement action against corporations for making false environmental disclosures. For example, in 2022, the SEC commenced action against a Brazilian mining company for making misleading statements about environmental responsibility in its sustainability report, and against an investment advisor for misrepresenting or implying in various statements that all investments in the funds it managed had undergone an ESG quality review, resulting in $55.9 and $1.5 million settlements, respectively.[40] In 2023, the SEC issued a fine against a subsidiary of Deutsche Bank for making misleading statements about its controls for incorporating ESG factors into research and investment recommendations, while marketing itself as being a leader in ESG.[41] In 2024, the SEC charged Keurig

Dr Pepper Inc. with making inaccurate statements regarding the recyclability of its K-Cup single-use beverage pods, requiring it to pay a $1.5 million civil penalty.[42] Though few in number, such enforcement actions can deter future "bad" corporate behavior. And these agencies can do more.

Specifically, I argue that, in its information-enforcing role for race-conscious disclosures, the federal government should: (1) *track* race-conscious disclosures, (2) *monitor* how companies use them, (3) *share* the disclosures publicly, and (4) *set up accountability* mechanisms. Given limited government resources, the focus should be on companies with revenues of at least $1 billion because they are more likely to make race-conscious disclosures.[43] These large companies also hire the most employees and use the most resources with impact on ordinary people's day-to-day lives.

Tracking is the foundational step before regulation can occur. Advancements in Natural Language Processing and Machine Learning make this a feasible role for the federal government. The federal government should track where and when corporations use race-conscious disclosures. Companies tend to use race-conscious disclosures in shareholder proposals, no-action letter requests, or in media sources. Government staff should also be able to track the types of disclosures corporations are making, whether they are more general statements, statistics, racial targets, and/or philanthropy, the ebbs and flows of race-conscious disclosures, and seek further explanation when changes appear to be motivated solely by corporate profit or reputational risk.

Such a monitoring role would give the government a sense of what corporations are saying, how they are saying it, to whom they are saying it, and with what frequency. Federal government staff should be trained to identify instances when companies refer to prior disclosures and conduct further assessment to determine whether they are being used to limit formal or informal claims of racial bias and discrimination in business activities. Staff should monitor when corporations expand on race-conscious disclosures or engage in retraction. Companies should not be able to make race-conscious disclosures in one year and engage in race-conscious retraction of those same disclosures the next year without bona fide reasons for needing to do so. In those cases, the government should determine why a company backtracked or reneged on a commitment. Companies should have appropriate reasons for choosing not to pursue a program they previously said they would. And when such a good reason is lacking, the government should provide warnings the first time and sanctions for repeated backtracking. This would help to ensure that race-conscious disclosures are not used only for corporate strategic interests.

The federal government should also share the disclosures it tracks and monitors publicly so that stakeholders and other constituents can use the information to regulate race-conscious disclosures themselves, to some extent. Indeed, this would be one of the major benefits of a multi-institutional approach, namely, that it would allow other sources of regulation to occur alongside government regulation.

Finally, the federal government should set up accountability measures to hold companies accountable. It could do this by publishing a list of companies who use race-conscious disclosures as evidence of addressing racial inequality without taking actual steps, or taking only minimal steps to address racial inequality, and companies that consistently engage in race-conscious retraction. In cases where companies consistently engage in retraction, the federal government can impose fines or other sanctions. When made public, these accountability measures can deter other uses of race-conscious disclosures and provide additional information for stakeholder regulators of race-conscious disclosures. Federal agencies could also establish rules prohibiting corporations from making disclosures with no intention to follow through with them, or from engaging in misrepresentation of race-conscious disclosures in ways that confuse investors and the public, such as engaging in race-conscious construction and retraction without notice or reasons to support the decision.[44] This kind of rulemaking would be consistent with First Amendment principles and, combined with accountability measures, could make a difference in the use of race-conscious disclosures.

To be sure, government oversight is extremely unlikely under the Trump administration. However, future administrations would be poised to begin the accountability process for race-conscious disclosures and retraction.

Is There a Role for State Governments?

While the federal government through agencies such as the FTC, SEC, and EEOC regulates corporations, corporate law in the United States is governed by state law.[45] However, outside of the context of employment discrimination and bias, state intervention to address race relations in corporations has focused almost exclusively on diversifying boards of directors.

In comparison to other US states, the state of California is an exemplar in terms of regulating race, as well as climate concerns. California has regulated both gender and racial diversity on corporate boards of directors, as well as climate risk. Regarding the latter, California has relied largely on mandating disclosures through SB (Senate Bill) 261, which as discussed in Chapter 5, required any public or private company "doing business" in California with an annual revenue of at least $500 million, to disclose climate-related risks and measures adopted to reduce those risks.[46]

California went beyond mandating disclosures alone to also require diversity on corporate boards through its AB (Assembly Bill) 979, requiring corporations with principal executive offices in the state to have a minimum of one director from an underrepresented racial or ethnic community or of LGBTQ+ status.[47] The law also required corporations with more than four but fewer than nine directors to have a minimum of two such directors, and corporations with nine or more directors to have a minimum of three such directors.[48] AB 979 was not California's first law requiring diversity on corporate boards. In 2018, California became the first state in the United States to mandate gender diversity on boards, through SB 826.[49] After that, other states began to enact similar laws. But unlike those in California, most of the laws in other states were nonbinding, goal-like rules that only encouraged corporations to increase gender diversity on their boards. Colorado, Illinois, Maryland, and Massachusetts all passed nonbinding resolutions on gender diversity on boards. New York passed a law requiring companies doing business in the state to merely disclose the number of women on their boards. Washington state went a little father with Revised Code of Washington (RCW) 23.08.120, requiring boards to comprise of at least 25 percent women.[50] But unlike California, violators face no fiscal penalties and are only required to publicly disclose the criteria they use to choose board members.[51] This alternative makes the rule similar to the Nasdaq rule discussed in Chapters 2 and 5, requiring Nasdaq-listed companies to either disclose diverse board members or explain why they lack board diversity.

In 2022, a California Superior Court judge struck down California's board diversity rules for gender, sexual orientation, and race, ruling in favor of Judicial Watch, a conservative organization claiming that the rules violated equal protection.[52] As of this writing, Washington remains the only state with a rule mandating board diversity.

Therefore, state regulation in this area has been limited to board diversity and has largely been nonmandatory or invalidated by courts. So, there is not much strong precedent for state regulation of race. The question is whether states *can* regulate race-conscious disclosures to minimize constraints on racial progress. Could there be a state equivalent of the federal government proposal to regulate race-conscious disclosures? The simple answer is yes, although regulation would be limited to corporations that are incorporated or headquartered in, or at a minimum, doing business in a state.

Companies can choose to incorporate in any of the fifty states, regardless of the location of their headquarters or where they primarily conduct their business.[53] A large majority, 68.2 percent, of all Fortune 500 corporations and many Russell 3000 companies are incorporated in the state of Delaware as of this writing.[54] Consequently, if Delaware were to establish what I have proposed here for the federal government, many US public companies would be regulated by state corporate law. However, it is unlikely that Delaware's legislative body would be inclined to regulate race relations in corporations.[55] The legislative culture in Delaware is centered around the notion that change should not be made unless it is apparent that there will be a significant benefit from it to corporations, and typically not this kind of benefit, without any countervailing disruption.[56] Legal scholar Lawrence Hamermesh has referred to Delaware's culture as a "first do no harm conservatism."[57] No wonder Delaware has never encouraged or mandated companies to even make disclosures related to gender, race, or other social issues. Moreover, even if the Delaware legislature were to legislate along these lines, thousands of public companies incorporated elsewhere, as well as many private companies, would still be left out, unless other states – such as those where a company has its headquarters, its principal place of business, or a significant number of employees or consumers – were also to pass similar legislation to regulate corporations.

Nonetheless, with this blueprint, a state that wishes to innovate around regulating race-conscious disclosures can do so within the limits of their regulatory authorities and resources.

MULTI-INSTITUTIONAL APPROACH

In this multi-institutional approach, government regulation facilitates action by other parties. A range of constituents and stakeholders can use information drawn from the federal government and elsewhere, to regulate race-conscious disclosures, including corporate boards of directors and managers, stock exchanges like Nasdaq, and the New York Stock Exchange (NYSE), which collectively command 48.9 percent of the global market capitalization,[58] shareholders, consumers, employees, prospective employees, advocacy groups, and others. In this part of the chapter, I make suggestions regarding how some of these constituents could approach their regulatory roles, using the government's information-enforcing role as a starting point. The list of constituents is not meant to be exhaustive, nor are the suggestions here complete. They are instead a starting point for how corporate constituents and stakeholders might conceive of regulating race-conscious disclosures.

Boards of Directors and Managers

The supervisory role of a company lies in its board of directors, so boards (and executives) have a vital role to play in regulating race-conscious disclosures.[59] Delaware corporate law, for example, mandates boards of directors to manage the business and affairs of their corporations.[60] In their book, *Breaking Through: The Making of Minority Executives in Corporate America*, management scholar and former president of Morehouse College David Thomas and management scholar John Gabarro, explained that executives have a vital role in the success of racial diversity and inclusion in corporate leadership ranks.[61] Legal scholar Tom C. W. Lin similarly argues that executives are "uniquely situated ... because they control so many critical financial and economic levers."[62]

Boards of directors can hold executives and managers accountable for what they say, when they say it, how they say it, as well as whether they follow through on promises made in these statements, and whether or how they use these statements later to deflect criticism of possible racial disparities in their operations. Boards of directors and executives have access to data internal to their corporations and should ensure that the company has steps in place to do the things it claims it will do, and that the company will not simply pull back on commitments it previously made in the face of potential threats, without fulfilling them or at least making clear why they were not fulfilled. They should also keep in mind that taking those actions does not mean that the company has achieved the highest level of racial progress, but rather that race-conscious disclosures are an invitation toward doing better.

Aided by internal data and information tracked and collected by the federal government on other firms, boards and managers should monitor the use of general race-conscious disclosures, racial targets, and CRP, and ensure, in particular, that corporations do not use race-conscious disclosures as leverage to get out of addressing racial inequality issues. When shareholders or other constituents ask companies to do more, by, for example, conducting internal audits, evaluating themselves on racial equity, disclosing data on pay equity, or increasing diversity, boards and managers should ensure that previously made race-conscious disclosures are not used as tools to foreclose or reject such measures or inquiries. If anything, inquiries should serve as starting points on the quest for how to do better. Similarly, boards and managers should ensure that their actions around race-conscious disclosures take into account the implications and long-term financial risks of race-conscious retraction, as discussed in Chapter 5.

Stock Exchanges

Notwithstanding what happened with the Nasdaq board diversity rule, in the future, stock exchanges could condition good standing and being listed as compliant with federal government regulation, on how a company uses race-conscious disclosures. They can also establish their own rules to encourage corporations to refrain from using race-conscious disclosures as evidence of doing something about racial inequality, except when the disclosure is used to address compliance or concerns related specifically to the particular issue raised. For example, if a company's shareholders were to ask to examine pay gap concerns by race and ethnicity, a stock exchange's rules could prohibit the company from proffering other race-conscious disclosures *unrelated* to pay gaps when addressing the pay gap issue in public disclosures.

Shareholder Activists

Far from the mostly powerless shareholders depicted in legal scholar Adolf A. Berle, Jr. and economist Gardiner C. Means's classic book, *The Modern Corporation and Private Property*, shareholders now have considerable influence.[63] This is largely because financial institutions, particularly large asset managers, now dominate the investment landscape in public companies, constituting about 78 percent of all shareholders in Russell 3000 companies, and an even larger share of those in the S&P 1500 index.[64] The growth in institutional shareholders has raised the profile of shareholders in regulating corporations. Institutional shareholders differ from individual shareholders in their incentives and behavior.[65] Institutional shareholders can form alliances and make demands on corporations because they control large assets.[66] Changes in law following a wave of corporate scandals in the early 2000s, including the well-publicized one involving Enron Corporation, also fueled shareholder engagement in corporate governance.[67]

Shareholder activists raise awareness about issues, and challenge corporations to change.[68] These shareholders regulate the modern corporation by monitoring corporate action through activism. Shareholder activists can use information provided and enforcement strategies taken by the federal government for their own strategies through shareholder proposals or other means. As discussed in Chapter 2, submitting a shareholder proposal can trigger a range of responses from a company, from agreement to address an issue, to challenging the proposal by requesting a no-action letter from the SEC, to opposing it. Part of the regulatory role of shareholders in this regard is that a proposal alerts other shareholders to an issue, allowing them to communicate their support for or against the proposal if the company does not settle it.

Activity around proposals can also extend to other stakeholders.[69] Current and potential employees may identify with a proposal and use it as a starting point for internal employee activism.[70] Government actors, including regulatory agencies and Congress, may become alerted to issues through activist investors' proposals and consider them in rulemaking or legislation.[71] Customers may become aware of issues through proposals, which can impact their perception of a company and their willingness to buy goods from the company, or they too can use the subject of a proposal for their own activism.[72] Chapter 2 described in detail how shareholders have used proposals to push for change. Most companies have not been supportive of these proposals but have had to respond to them, nonetheless.

Barring limitations, such as SEC staff guidelines put forward during Trump's second term that restrict informal communication between large institutional shareholders and corporate representatives, shareholder activists should first engage in behind-the-scenes negotiations with corporations.[73] Small shareholder activist groups can partner with more prominent institutional investors, if feasible, to raise their profiles. If shareholder proposals are still necessary despite shareholders' best efforts, activists should consider wording their requests carefully so as not to impede their goals. For example, suppose the federal government finds that a company failed to meet its closed-ended racial target of the type discussed in Chapter 3, or omitted its previous racial targets from subsequent disclosures; a shareholder activist can use that information to request details about these concerns from the company. In this case, the proposal should explicitly ask the company not to include prior disclosures unrelated to the issues on which the request was based as proof that it has addressed those issues. This can disrupt the pattern of corporations claiming that prior disclosures have addressed unresolved issues. Recall from discussion in Chapter 2 that many companies have used this method to halt requests for racial equity audits. Explicit language to this effect – a sort of "we're on to you" message – in shareholder proposals may minimize this strategy.

If the company includes prior nonrelevant disclosures despite the request not to do so, an activist should continue to pursue the original goal rather than accept the company's submission of prior disclosures as resolution. Disclosures do not amount to action, and disclosures about unrelated matters certainly do not amount to relevant change.

Shareholder activism is limited to publicly traded corporations and may be infrequent during cycles of retraction. Nevertheless, shareholder activism can be a powerful regulatory tool for publicly traded corporations.

Consumers

For consumer-facing companies, consumers are some of the most important stakeholders. In interviews, CSOs and CDOs elaborately described their consumers as essential. One CDO said that the company's "relevance is only measured in terms of customers' feelings about the company, and customers from underrepresented groups want to feel invited." While they are outsiders and may not see themselves as regulating companies, consumers have the influence to regulate corporate behavior. Political scientist Caroline Heldman classifies consumer activism into non-purchasing actions, social media actions, and direct consumer activism.[74] Non-purchasing actions are boycotts and buycotts. Boycotting is refraining from buying products from companies.[75] "Buycotting," or reverse boycotting, is purchasing products to reward companies for favorable practices or products.[76] Boycotts and buycotts are the most popular mechanisms consumers use to regulate corporate behavior.[77] Boycotts targeting racial discrimination have negatively impacted companies like Coca-Cola, Proctor & Gamble, Starbucks, and Target.[78]

Consumers can regulate corporate use of race-conscious disclosures in discrete instances. Consider, for example, a scenario in which a company is asked to conduct a racial pay gap analysis, and it claims that its previous general race-conscious disclosures should suffice as evidence of addressing racial inequality, or the case of a company that points to its previous disclosures to oppose a proposal to increase racial diversity on its board. Consumers can use social media to shame such companies for using their previous disclosures for profit and to stymie racial diversity, and potentially deploy other kinds of tools, including boycotts, buycotts, and individual activism to convey their values in a meaningful way.

The main limitation of consumer regulation is that consumers are unlikely to stay motivated to continuously pressure companies to change, and they generally lack information about what companies are saying and doing. If the federal government assumes an information-enforcing role, consumers would have access to more information about corporate use of race-conscious disclosures. Sustained advocacy group campaigns through social media could also help keep consumers informed and maintain their motivation to regulate race-conscious disclosures.

Employees and Prospective Employees

When Amazon made general race-conscious disclosures after the murder of George Floyd, some of its employees shot back on the social media platform Twitter (now X), criticizing the company for actions they saw as antithetical to those statements, including holding police contracts for its Ring doorbell and facial recognition software, and limited advancement for Black workers.[79]

Employees and prospective employees are important stakeholders who influence management and change organizational structures, norms, practices, and culture.[80] Most employees are invested in the long-term success of companies they work for, possess firm-specific skills, and make contributions to the ongoing value of the business.[81] Employees and prospective employees are also interested in what companies are doing regarding racial inequality. Today's employees believe in the power to drive societal change in companies.[82] One industry study of 1,000 participants found that four in ten employees had spoken up to support or criticize their employers' actions over an issue that affects society.[83] In a survey published in the *MIT Sloan Management Review*, over half of the surveyed 1,500 employees said they usually or always speak up to influence organizational action on wider societal or environmental issues.[84] According to an Edelman survey, many employees and prospective employees, especially in younger generations, are "belief driven" because they are more concerned about a company's values around matters like inclusion and the environment than the amount they receive in compensation.[85]

In recent years, employee activism has been organized at a number of companies to protest a range of social issues; for example, at Activision Blizzard for sexism and sexual harassment, Amazon for climate and environmental impact, Facebook (now Meta) for then-President Trump's rhetoric advocating violence against Black protesters, Uber for better working conditions and pay equity, and Wayfair for sales to migrant detention camps, among other examples.[86] Research suggests that the effect of employee activism can be limited to incremental change in the workplace, but that employee activists' processes and tactics can result in significant change over time.[87] And managers are not always opponents of employee activism.[88] Indeed, in some cases, they can also be important allies and leverage their power to support certain causes.[89] However, like consumer activism, employee activism also tends to fluctuate.[90] It is often at its highest during opportunistic moments when, for example, racial injustice has become particularly visible or high-profile within a company, or when employees can point to apparent hypocrisy or inconsistencies.

Information provided by the federal government could be critical for employee activism because it would provide prospective or present employees with information to call out companies that obtain financial gain from race-conscious disclosures or that choose to disregard the importance of addressing racial inequality solely because of risk mitigation concerns.

Advocacy Groups

Advocacy groups engage consumers, employees, prospective employees, shareholders, traditional media, and social media to regulate corporate action and pressure companies to act. There are different kinds of advocacy groups, including those that focus on socially and politically conservative goals.[91] For the purposes of this discussion, I am primarily concerned with advocacy organizations whose goals include making society more equitable by addressing economic and social inequality, and the outcomes and experiences of people of color.

There are many such advocacy groups, including organizations such as As You Sow, Ceres, Color of Change, and Open to All, that engage a range of tactics to draw attention to their concerns and call for changes in corporate behavior. The tactics include organizing protests and boycotts, engaging in litigation, conducting research, and producing reports and petitions.

In response to the killing of Trayvon Martin in 2012, Black Lives Matter and Color of Change – both organizations whose goals include addressing racial bias and discrimination – called for a boycott of the American Legislative Exchange Council (ALEC), a conservative group of state legislators funded by companies that promoted the "stand your ground" gun laws in many states that likely emboldened Martin's killer, George Zimmerman.[92] Over $10,000 people signed a petition, and this along with social media pressure led to more than thirty companies withdrawing their support from ALEC, including Amazon, Coca-Cola Company, General Motors, Intuit, Kraft, and Walmart.[93] Through this and other forms of engagement, advocacy groups regulate corporate behavior. As corporate outsiders, however, advocacy groups require information from corporate members, or government regulators, to effectively regulate race-conscious disclosures.

The federal government should take measures to make information readily available to advocacy groups who can support "regulatory networks" as they partner with corporate stakeholders like shareholders, consumers, employees, and prospective employees in their own activism efforts.[94] Many advocacy organizations also have the motivation and capacity to use available information to create and publish easily digestible reports that would outline companies' true conduct with regard to race issues – including whether they actually follow through on their race-conscious disclosures and whether they have employed disclosures to deny discriminatory practices, or those that disproportionately impact racial and ethnic minorities.

Media and Social Media as a Regulatory Tool

The media has a great influence on corporate behavior. Perceived negative media attention can threaten a company's reputation.[95] Research in management has shown, for example, that boycotters are more likely to exert influence on corporate behavior when the boycott receives a great deal of media attention.[96] Because of the influence the media possesses, journalists should make their coverage of race-conscious disclosures deeper and more nuanced – not just flagging things like an alleged retraction in disclosures, but looking more deeply for hidden phenomena like companies using race-conscious disclosures to evade claims that they are engaging in racially discriminatory conduct, or that their operations may disproportionately negatively affect people of color.

But even more than traditional media – newspaper, television, and the like – social media, including video-sharing sites, have facilitated the transmission of persuasive information about social issues, as well as information implicating organizations or their leaders in relation to social issues.[97] Social media has had a profound impact on collective action, enabling users to mobilize and swiftly communicate information to other users.[98]

Social media tools are a cheap and easy way for shareholders, consumers, employees, and advocacy groups to communicate and build regulatory networks for race-conscious disclosures. Shareholders use social media to discuss the market with other shareholders.[99] Consumers use social media to broadcast their experiences, shame companies, and organize boycotts or buycotts. Employees and prospective employees use social media to communicate their preferences and values.[100] As companies embraced making race-conscious disclosures and expressed their views on social issues, employees have been empowered to raise their voices about workplace inequality on social media despite the risk of loss of employment.[101] Advocacy groups also use social media for their campaigns. As such, companies now hire social media professionals to manage their online reputations on social issues.[102]

Social media has also fueled race-conscious disclosures as companies have responded to advocacy groups and influencers calling for corporate response. This has resulted in public statements and commitments in response to pressure on social media.[103] Social media can also be a platform for regulating those same race-conscious disclosures. It is important for stakeholders who use social media for corporate accountability to understand how companies can turn around to use their responses for corporate financial gain. Understanding the intricacies of social media as a tool for social change would allow it to be channeled more appropriately for good.

When communicating via social media, stakeholders should make more specific and targeted demands of companies. Stakeholders can push companies to go beyond making mundane disclosures and instead request disclosures about past behavior, or action plans for specific issues. Going back to how Chevron's operations have harmed residents of Richmond, California, as discussed in Chapter 2, stakeholders could target an issue like that and push companies to respond to it publicly on social media rather than making vague demands that simply prompt companies to make general race-conscious disclosures – particularly because such disclosures alone, as I have shown, are unlikely to resolve the issue and further help companies to construct their race-conscious public images.

In sum, a multi-institutional approach with a functioning federal government as information enforcer, would mobilize and assist other institutions and groups to also regulate race-conscious disclosures. This approach would demand corporate accountability through individual institutional regulation, or through regulatory networks involving a range of institutions rallying around the same or similar issues.

NOTES

1. Dorothy S. Lund and Elizabeth Pollman, "The Corporate Governance Machine," *Columbia Law Review* 121, no. 8 (December 2021): 2563–634.
2. Ibid.
3. Ibid.
4. Bettina Lange, "Sociology of Regulation," in *Research Handbook on the Sociology of Law*, ed. Jiří Přibáň (Cheltenham: Edward Elgar, 2020).
5. Russell Muirhead and Nancy L. Rosenblum, *Ungoverning: The Attack on the Administrative State and the Politics of Chaos* (Princeton, NJ: Princeton University Press, 2024).
6. Ibid., 27.
7. 17 C.F.R. § 229.407(c)(2)(vi); Dhir, *Challenging Boardroom Homogeneity*.
8. 17 C.F.R. § 229.101(b)(2)(ii).
9. Gibson Dunn, "Discussing Human Capital."
10. The Investor Advisory Committee was established under Section 911 of the Dodd-Frank Act, Public Law 203, U.S. Statutes at Large 124 (2010): 1376–2223. SEC Investor Advisory Committee, "Recommendation of the SEC Investor Advisory Committee's Investor-as-Owner Subcommittee regarding Human Capital Management Disclosure," *United States Securities Exchange Commission*, September 21, 2023, www.sec.gov/files/spotlight/iac/20230921-recommendation-regarding-hcm.pdf.
11. Adediran, "Disclosing Corporate Diversity." The rule has come under scrutiny from conservative organizations, the Alliance for Fair Board Recruitment ("AFBR") and the National Center for Public Policy Research ("NCPPR"), who filed petitions for review of the SEC order approving the rule in 2021. The groups claim that the rule is unconstitutional under the Fifth Amendment's Equal Protection Clause and the First Amendment's Freedom of Expression clause, and that the SEC exceeded its authority in approving the rule. On October 18, 2023, a three-judge panel for the US Court of Appeals for the Fifth Circuit denied those petitions. *Alliance for Fair Board Recruitment*, 85 F.4th. The rule was necessary because there remains a racial diversity problem among corporate executives.
12. Adediran, "Disclosing Corporate Diversity."
13. Allison Herren Lee, "Regulation S-K and ESG Disclosures: An Unsustainable Silence," SEC Press Release, August 26, 2020, https://perma.cc/4FDH-8LGT.
14. Gary Gensler, "Prepared Remarks at London City Week," *United States Securities Exchange Commission Press Release*, June 23, 2021, www.sec.gov/news/speech/gensler-speechlondon-city-week-062321 [https://perma.cc/A4W8-C5JH].
15. David A. Bell, Dawn Belt, and Ron C. Llewellyn, "Diversifying the Boardroom: 2022 Disclosures," Harvard Law School Forum on Corporate Governance, May 11, 2023, https://corpgov.law.harvard.edu/2023/05/11/diversifying-the-boardroom-2022-disclosures/.
16. U.S. Congress, House, *Corporate Governance Improvement and Investor Protection Act*, HR 1187, 117th Cong., passed by House June 16, 2021.

17. Canada Business Corporation Act amendment, R.S.C., 1985, c. C-44 (2020).
18. Government of Canada, "Diversity of Boards of Directors and Senior Management of Federal Distributing Corporations," Annual Report, 2023; Diana Nakka, "An Update on Corporations Canada Reporting Requirements and 2023 Review Outcomes," *Dentons*, May 15, 2024, www.dentons.com/en/insights/alerts/2024/may/15/an-update-on-corporations-canada-reporting-requirements-and-2023-review-outcomes.
19. Dhir, *Challenging Boardroom Homogeneity*.
20. SEC, Final Stage Rule, *Enhanced Disclosures by Certain Investment Advisers and Investment Companies about Environmental, Social, and Governance Investment Practices* (May 25, 2022), RIN: 3235-AM96, SEC Release No. 33-11068; SEC, Final Stage Rule, *The Enhancement and Standardization of Climate-Related Disclosures for Investors* (March 21, 2022), RIN 3235-AM87, SEC Release Nos. 33-11042, 34-94478.
21. "SEC Votes to End Defense of Climate Disclosure Rules," Press Release, March 27, 2025, www.sec.gov/newsroom/press-releases/2025-58.
22. SEC, *The Enhancement and Standardization of Climate-Related Disclosures for Investors*.
23. European Parliament and the Council, "Directive (EU) 2022/2464," *Official Journal of the European Union*, December 14, 2022.
24. Dieter Holger, "At Least 10,000 Foreign Companies to Be Hit by EU Sustainability Rules," *Wall Street Journal Pro*, April 5, 2023, www.wsj.com/articles/at-least-10-000-foreign-companies-to-be-hit-by-eu-sustainability-rules-307a1406; Deloitte, "European Commission Proposes Reduction in Sustainability Reporting and Due Diligence Requirements – Considerations for U.S. Entities," *Deloitte*, March 7, 2025, https://dart.deloitte.com/USDART/home/publications/deloitte/heads-up/2025/eu-commission-omnibus-proposal-sustainability-reporting-reduction-csrd.
25. Greg Norman, Simon Toms, Adam M. Howard, and Kathryn Gamble, "Q&A: The EU Corporate Sustainability Reporting Directive – to Whom Does It Apply and What Should EU and Non-EU Companies Consider?," *Skadden*, October 9, 2023, www.skadden.com/insights/publications/2023/10/qa-the-eu-corporate-sustainability-reporting-directive.
26. European Commission. "Corporate Sustainability Due Diligence." European Commission website, July 25, 2024. https://commission.europa.eu/business-economy-euro/doing-business-eu/corporate-sustainability-due-diligence_en.
27. European Counsel of the European Union, "Corporate Sustainability Due Diligence: Council Gives Its Final Approval," Press Release, May 24, 2024, www.consilium.europa.eu/en/press/press-releases/2024/05/24/corporate-sustainability-due-diligence-council-gives-its-final-approval/.
28. "CSRD: A Guide to the Corporate Sustainability Reporting Directive," *Persefoni*, July 2023, www.persefoni.com/blog/what-is-csrd.
29. The value chain covers activities related to the production of a good or provision of services by a company. *Corporate Sustainability Due Diligence* (2023), preamble, para. 18.
30. A plan that ensures their business models and strategies are aligned with limiting global warming to 1.5C, in turn forcing them to devise and implement key changes to the way they operate. Sophie Flores, Ruth Kilsby, and Magda Puzniak-Holford, "What Is the European Corporate Sustainability Due Diligence Directive?" Deloitte website, September 12, 2023, www.deloitte.com/uk/en/services/legal/blogs/what-is-the-european-corporate-sustainability-due-diligence-directive.html.
31. Jon McGowan, "EU Corporate Sustainability Due Diligence Law Most Likely Dead, For Now," *Forbes*, February 15, 2024, www.forbes.com/sites/jonmcgowan/2024/02/16/eu-corporate-sustainability-due-diligence-law-most-likely-dead-for-now/?sh=4b39f3c2453c.

32. Loper Bright Enterprises v. Raimondo, 144 S. Ct. 2244 (2024); Corner Post, Inc. v. Board of Governors of the Federal Reserve System, 144 S. Ct. 2440 (2024).
33. SEC v. Jarkesy, 144 S. Ct. 2117 (2024).
34. Adediran, "Disclosing Corporate Diversity."
35. Shanor and Light, "Greenwashing." On the other hand, because the United States Supreme Court has yet to decide whether corporate communication in things like press releases and sustainability reports rather, than advertisement is commercial speech, some corporations can argue that the proposals in this chapter regulate political speech. Nike made this argument in Nike, Inc. v. Kasky, 539 U.S. 654 (2003), where Nike was accused of producing its shoes in sweatshops. Nike responded in myriad ways, including by making statements about its labor practices to customers, the media, university officials, and athletic directors, which the plaintiff claimed was false and violated California's laws. Nike contended that the statements were made within a larger public debate about the labor practices of multinational companies abroad, and were therefore protected political speech, such that even if the statements were false, they were constitutionally shielded from suit. The California Supreme Court decided that Nike's speech was commercial.
36. Federal Trade Commission, www.ftc.gov/about-ftc/mission; Rohit Chopra and Samuel A. A. Levine, "The Case for Resurrecting the FTC Act's Penalty Offense Authority," *University of Pennsylvania Law Review* 170, no. 1 (2021): 71–124.
37. Federal Trade Commission, "Operation 'Full Disclosure' Targets More than 60 National Advertisers: FTC Initiative Aims to Improve Disclosures in Advertising," FTC Press Release, September 23, 2014, www.ftc.gov/news-events/news/press-releases/2014/09/operation-full-disclosure-targets-more-60-national-advertisers.
38. Federal Trade Commission, "FTC Puts Businesses on Notice that False Money-Making Claims Could Lead to Big Penalties," FTC Press Release, October 26, 2021, www.ftc.gov/news-events/news/press-releases/2021/10/ftc-puts-businesses-notice-false-money-making-claims-could-lead-big-penalties.
39. In addition to publicly traded companies, the SEC regulates private fund advisors by requiring disclosures to investors. 17 C.F.R. § 275, File No. S7-03-22, November 13, 2023. The SEC also regulates issuers who can be private or public companies. Rule 506 of Regulation D, 17 CFR § 230.506.
40. United States Securities and Exchange Commission, "SEC Charges Brazilian Mining Company with Misleading Investors about Safety Prior to Deadly Dam Collapse," SEC Press Release, April 28, 2022, www.sec.gov/news/press-release/2022-72; United States Securities and Exchange Commission, "SEC Charges BNY Mellon Investment Adviser for Misstatements and Omissions Concerning ESG Considerations," SEC Press Release, May 23, 2022, www.sec.gov/news/press-release/2022-86.
41. Mark Segal, "SEC Fines Deutsche Bank Subsidiary DWS $19 Million Following Greenwashing Investigation," *ESG Today*, September 26, 2023, www.esgtoday.com/sec-fines-deutsche-bank-subsidiary-dws-19-million-following-greenwashing-investigation/.
42. United States Securities and Exchange Commission, "SEC Charges Keurig with Making Inaccurate Statements Regarding Recyclability of K-Cup Beverage Pod," SEC Press Release, September 10, 2024, www.sec.gov/newsroom/press-releases/2024-122.
43. Some include that large corporations are more visible to consumers and the public, and employ many workers, which may pressure them to publicly respond to social concerns, even when they are privately held. With higher revenues and broader operations, these companies also often have a more extensive and diverse group of stakeholders, including investors, customers, employees, and communities. These stakeholders demand transparency on social issues. Also because of their size, they are also more likely to operate

in multiple jurisdictions, which may require or encourage them to make disclosures on social issues.
44. Wendy Gerwick Couture, "The Collision between the First Amendment and Securities Fraud," *Alabama Law Review* 65, no. 4 (2014): 903–74.
45. Robert IV Anderson and Jeffrey Manns, "The Delaware Delusion," *North Carolina Law Review* 93 (May 2015): 1049–105.
46. Senate Bill 261, Chapter 383 (Cal 2023).
47. California Corporations Code § 301.4(a) (West 2021). By underrepresented community, the statute included individuals who self-identified as Black, African American, Hispanic, Latino, Asian, Pacific Islander, Native American, Native Hawaiian, or Alaska Native, or as gay, lesbian, bisexual, or transgender.
48. Ibid.
49. Ibid. § 301.3(a)–(b) (West 2021).
50. RCW 23B.08.120 (2020).
51. Ibid.
52. Crest v. Padilla, No. 19STCV27561 (Cal. Super. Ct. May 13, 2022); Weber, "Judge Tosses California Law."
53. Lucian Arye Bebchuk and Alma Cohen. "Firms' Decisions Where to Incorporate," *Journal of Law & Economics* 46 (2003): 383–425.
54. Delaware Division of Corporations: 2022 Annual Report. The Russell 3000 Index comprises 98 percent of the U.S. equity market.
55. While the Delaware General Assembly is the state's legislative body, because of the large number of Delaware public corporations, the Council of the Corporation Law Section of the State Bar Association has identified and crafted legislative initiatives in the field of corporate law for decades. Noteworthy is the fact that fourteen of the twenty-one members who craft legislation are members of commercial law firms in Delaware. Lawrence A. Hamermesh, "The Policy Foundations of Delaware Corporate Law," *Columbia Law Review* 106 (November 2006): 1749–92.
56. Ibid.
57. Ibid., 1772.
58. Statista, "Largest Stock Exchange Operators Worldwide as of December 2023, by Market Capitalization of Listed Companies (in Trillion U.S. Dollars)," Statista website, February 1, 2024, www.statista.com/statistics/270126/largest-stock-exchange-operators-by-market-capitalization-of-listed-companies/.
59. Lynne L. Dallas, "The Multiple Roles of Corporate Boards of Directors," *San Diego Law Review* 40, no. 3 (August–September 2003): 781–820.
60. Del. Code Ann. tit. 8, § 141(a) (2014); Model Bus. Corp. Act Ann. § 8.01 annot. (2013).
61. Thomas and Gabarro, *Breaking Through*; Woodson, *Black Ceiling*.
62. Tom C. W. Lin, *The Capitalist and the Activist: Corporate Social Activism and the New Business of Change* (California: Berrett-Koehler, 2022), 92.
63. Adolf A. Berle Jr. and Gardiner C. Means, *The Modern Corporation and Private Property* (New York: Macmillan, 1933).
64. "80% of Equity Market Cap Held by Institutions," *Pensions & Investments*, June 30, 2024, www.pionline.com/article/20170425/INTERACTIVE/170429926/80-of-equity-market-cap-held-by-institutions; Jennifer G. Hill, "Images of the Shareholder – Shareholder Power and Shareholder Powerlessness," in *Research Handbook on Shareholder Power*, eds., Jennifer G. Hill and Randall S. Thomas (Cheltenham: Edward Elgar, 2015), 53–74.
65. Hill, "Images of the Shareholder."
66. Ibid.

67. Francis J. Aquila and Lauren S. Boehmke, "United States," in *The Shareholder Rights and Activism Review*, ed. Francis J. Aquila, 8th ed. (New York: Sullivan & Cromwell, 2023).
68. Mary Ann Cloyd, "Shareholder Activism: Who, What, When, and How?," Harvard Law School Forum on Corporate Governance, April 7, 2015, https://corpgov.law.harvard.edu/2015/04/07/shareholder-activism-who-what-when-and-how/.
69. Parthiban et al., "Investor Activism," 91–100.
70. Ibid.
71. Ibid.
72. Ibid.
73. Behind-the-scenes process, while significant, has been limited under the Trump administration's SEC staff guidelines of Regulations 13D and 13G. The guidelines limit the ability for institutional shareholders with 5 percent or more in shares to inform a corporation's board of its voting direction because that kind of shareholder engagement may constitute "attempts to influence control" over management. Cooley alert, "SEC Staff Adopts Significant New Guidance Affecting Shareholder Proposals and Engagement," February 14, 2025, www.cooley.com/news/insight/2025/2025-02-14-sec-staff-adopts-significant-new-guidance-affecting-shareholder-proposals-and-engagement.
74. Heldman includes investment actions of shareholders as a fourth category. I subsume that category in shareholder regulation. Caroline Heldman, *Protest Politics in the Marketplace: Consumer Activism in the Corporate Age* (Ithaca: Cornell University Press, 2017).
75. Ibid.
76. Ibid.
77. Monroe Friedman, *Consumer Boycotts: Effecting Change through the Marketplace and Media* (New York: Routledge, 1999); Heldman, *Protest Politics*.
78. Kasaundra M. Tomlin, "Assessing the Efficacy of Consumer Boycotts of U.S. Target Firms: A Shareholder Wealth Analysis," *Southern Economic Journal* 86, no. 2 (2019): 503–29.
79. Isobel Asher Hamilton, "Amazon Workers Slammed the Company for Supporting the George Floyd Protesters While Still Flogging Surveillance Tech to Police," *Business Insider*, June 3, 2020, www.businessinsider.com/amazon-workers-accuse-company-hypocrisy-george-floyd-statement-2020-6.
80. Maureen Scully and Amy Segal, *Passion with an Umbrella: Grassroots Activists in the Workplace*, vol. 19, Research in the Sociology of Organizations (Stamford, CT: JAI Press, 2002).
81. Grant M. Hayden and Matthew T. Bodie, *Reconstructing the Corporation: From Shareholder Primacy to Shared Governance* (Cambridge: Cambridge University Press, 2021).
82. "Employee Activism in the Age of Purpose: Employee (Up)Rising," Weber Shandwick report, May 2019, https://cms.webershandwick.com/wp-content/uploads/2023/02/Employee-Activism-in-the-Age-of-Purpose-FINAL.pdf; Gerald F. Davis and Christopher J. White, "The New Face of Corporate Activism," *Stanford Social Innovation Review* (Fall 2015), https://ssir.org/articles/entry/the_new_face_of_corporate_activism.
83. "Employee Activism."
84. Megan Reitz and John Higgins, "Leading in an Age of Employee Activism," *MIT Sloan Management Review*, January 19, 2022, https://sloanreview.mit.edu/article/leading-in-an-age-of-employee-activism/.
85. Edelman Trust, *Special Report: The Belief-Driven Employee*, Edelman Trust Barometer website, 2021, www.edelman.com/trust/2021-trust-barometer/belief-driven-employee.

86. Angela Reddock-Wright, "Welcome to the New Age of Employee Activism," *Bloomberg Law*, August 18, 2021, https://news.bloomberglaw.com/daily-labor-report/welcome-to-the-new-age-of-employee-activism.
87. Scully and Segal, *Passion with an Umbrella*.
88. Ibid.
89. Ibid.
90. Ibid.
91. Ann Southworth, *Lawyers of the Right: Professionalizing the Conservative Coalition* (Chicago: University of Chicago Press, 2008).
92. Mary-Hunter McDonnell and Brayden King, "Keeping up Appearances: Reputational Threat and Impression Management after Social Movement Boycotts," *Administrative Science Quarterly* 58, no. 3 (2013): 387–419.
93. Heldman, *Protest Politics*.
94. Christopher J. Koliba, Jack W. Meek, Asim Zia, and Russell W. Mills, *Governance Networks in Public Administration and Public Policy* (Oxford: Taylor & Francis, 2018). State governments may also have information that could potentially be helpful to advocacy groups that are regulating corporations.
95. Brayden G. King, "A Political Mediation Model of Corporate Response to Social Movement Activism," *Administrative Science Quarterly* 53, no. 3 (2008): 395–421.
96. Ibid.
97. Forrest Briscoe and Abhinav Gupta, "Social Activism in and around Organizations," *Academy of Management Annals* 10, no. 1 (2016): 671–727.
98. Seth C. Oranburg, "Social Media Activism," in *A History of Financial Technology and Regulation: From American Incorporation to Cryptocurrency and Crowdfunding*, 96–111 (Cambridge: Cambridge University Press, 2022).
99. SEC, "Investor Alerts and Bulletins, Updated Investor Alert: Social Media and Investing – Stock Rumors," November 5, 2015, www.sec.gov/oiea/investor-alerts-bulletins/ia-rumors.
100. "Employees Rising: Seizing the Opportunity in Employee Activism," Weber Shandwick website, April 2, 2014, https://webershandwick.com/news/employees-rising-seizing-the-opportunity-in-employee-activism.
101. Zulekha Nathoo, "How Can Employees Also Be Social-Media Activists?," BBC website, www.bbc.com/worklife/article/20201118-how-can-employees-also-be-social-media-activists.
102. Briscoe and Gupta, *Social Activism*.
103. Tiffany Hsu, "Corporate Voices Get behind 'Black Lives Matter' Cause," *New York Times*, May 31, 2020, www.nytimes.com/2020/05/31/business/media/companies-marketing-black-lives-matter-george-floyd.html.

Conclusion

Founded in 2019 in Atlanta, Georgia, by three Black women, the Fearless Fund is a venture capital (VC) firm – a private equity firm that invests in startups and early-stage businesses. Fearless Fund was established to address disparities in VC funding for Black, Latina, and Asian women entrepreneurs, groups that have historically received significantly less VC funding than white entrepreneurs. The private equity industry has been a major source of wealth creation for its owners and the economy, yet racial minorities have struggled to break into the market in part because of investor bias against minority-owned funds.[1] Fearless Fund was able to do this, probably buoyed by the occurrences of 2020, as research has shown that the fundraising success of minority-owned private equity firms increases sharply during periods of high racial awareness that impacts minority groups, like that after George Floyd was murdered.[2]

In addition to its business arm, the Fund also established a private foundation, a nonprofit organization that operates exclusively for charitable purposes. In February 2023, the Fearless Foundation established a $20,000 grant for its Fearless Strivers Grant contest, with eligibility limited to Black-owned businesses. In addition to receiving $20,000, four contest winners were also offered access to mentorship and digital tools to help them grow their businesses online.

In August 2023, relying on the Harvard decision, the American Alliance for Equal Rights (AAER), a conservative group founded by Edward Blum – the same white man who spearheaded the lawsuits against Harvard University and the University of North Carolina for using race in admissions – filed a lawsuit asking a federal court to stop the Fearless Foundation from awarding funds to Black women entrepreneurs.[3] AAER claimed that the grant violated 42 U.S.C. § 1981, which prohibits discriminating based on race in contracting because three white business owners were "ready and able" to apply for the grant but were barred from doing so by the eligibility criterion that focused on Black founders.[4]

The case generated significant media attention and support from progressive corporations, lawyers, and others.[5] In September 2023, the federal district court denied AAER's request to stop the grant awards process, on the basis that it qualifies as charitable giving, a form of protected speech under the First Amendment.[6] AAER appealed the decision to a three-person panel on the US Court of Appeals for the 11th Circuit. The 11th Circuit blocked the grant program on the basis that it was exclusionary and unlikely to enjoy First Amendment protection in violation of § 1981.[7] And in June 2024, the 11th Circuit upheld the injunction against the grant. With so many defeats in the courts, in September 2024, the Fearless Fund decided to settle the case by permanently closing the program. Precisely because the grant was designed to address a racial wealth gap in business, it was fiercely opposed and ultimately defeated by conservatives who do not want racial progress.

* * *

Corporate capitalism is here to stay. The problem of racial inequality also remains. There are many more examples of programs and policies established to redress historical and contemporary racial inequality that have shut down, particularly since Trump returned to office for a second term in 2025.

Disclosureland offers academic and practical tools for thinking about the relationship between racial inequality, race-conscious disclosures, race-conscious retraction, and racial progress.

We are currently in a high tide of conservative pushbacks, which among other things, drives race-conscious retraction and outcomes that repress racial progress. Like other points in history, at some point it, we will likely return to another cycle of race-conscious image construction, during which corporations will again firmly declare their fight against racial injustices.

The struggle for corporations should be pushing back against backlash while moving forward toward racial progress. To paraphrase John Lewis, one of the greatest civil rights leaders that have fought for social change: We are not in the struggle of one presidential term. America's race relations is a struggle of a lifetime. Each one of us in every generation must do our part.

Corporations *should* tackle racial inequality, contributing – through words and actions – toward achieving true racial progress. True racial progress, as I define it in this book, is the kind that ultimately breaks cycles of racial subordination. It is not enough to hire people of color. True racial progress requires taking steps to facilitate progress for the next generation. Corporations should think expansively, rather than in ways that constrain racial progress. Instead of prioritizing the disclosure of demographical statistics, loans to minority-owned businesses, supplier diversity programs, and hiring for entry-level positions (rather than leadership development and growth), corporations should use their words and actions to make clear their past contributions to racial inequality, take actionable steps to develop future leaders of color, ensure equity in compensation, and make grants to close the still significant racial wealth gap (rather than focusing on income inequality alone) between racial minorities, especially Black communities and white communities.[8] Instead of recoiling and taking back previously made public commitments to racial equity, and shutting down programs set up to redress inequality, corporations should prioritize racial progress.

To be sure, focusing on racial progress in this way will likely open more corporations to the risk of litigation from conservative groups or being targeted by a conservative administration. But corporations and society will be better off in the long run if corporations use their words to support true racial progress rather than limiting it or withdrawing from words that are more likely to generate racial progress.

In her book, *Words Matter: Meaning and Power*, linguist Sally McConnell-Ginet explains that words are powerful as dominating weapons of oppression but also as effective tools to resist oppression.[9] Words also shape how people respond to social inequality.[10] *Disclosureland* shows that even though corporate words might seem anodyne, they have the power to change societal views of what should be done regarding racial inequality in hiring, promotion, philanthropy, and even outside of the corporate context. Corporate words can also inadvertently delimit society's view of how far we need to go to address racial inequality.

How corporations deploy disclosures – making them or taking them back – matter because the words set the tone and define corporations' roles in tackling racial inequality and can limit the expectations for corporations to act. Regulation by a functioning future government, as well as engagement by corporate shareholders and stakeholders, can help to mitigate how corporate words constrain racial progress.

NOTES

1. Johan Cassel, Josh Lerner, and Emmanuel Yimfor, "Racial Diversity in Private Capital Fundraising," Working Paper 30500, National Bureau of Economic Research website, September 2022, www.nber.org/papers/w30500.
2. Ibid.
3. Complaint, *American Alliance for Equal Rights v. Fearless Fund* (N.D. Ga. Aug. 2, 2023).
4. Ibid.
5. Janell Ross, "The Fearless Fund Is Investing in Women of Color – and Fighting in Court," *Time Magazine*, February 1, 2024, https://time.com/collection/closers/6564920/arian-simone-ayana-parsons/.
6. American Alliance for Equal Rights v. Fearless Fund, No. 1:23 CV 3424-TWT (N.D. Ga. 2023).
7. Appeal from the United States District Court for the Northern District of Georgia, American Alliance for Equal Rights v. Fearless Fund, No. 23-13138 (11th Circuit, Sep. 30, 2023).
8. Board of Governors of the Federal Reserve System, "Greater Wealth, Greater Uncertainty: Changes in Racial Inequality in the Survey of Consumer Finances," 2023, www.federalreserve.gov/econres/notes/feds-notes/greater-wealth-greater-uncertainty-changes-in-racial-inequality-in-the-survey-of-consumer-finances-accessible-20231018.htm#fig1; Andre M. Perry, Hannah Stephens, and Manann Donoghoe, "Black Wealth Is Increasing, But So Is the Racial Wealth Gap," Brookings website, January 9, 2024, www.brookings.edu/articles/black-wealth-is-increasing-but-so-is-the-racial-wealth-gap/.

9. Sally McConnell-Ginet, *Words Matter: Meaning and Power* (Cambridge: Cambridge University Press, 2020).
10. Sora Jun, Rosalind M. Chow, A. Maurits van der Veen, and Erik Bleich, "Chronic Frames of Social Inequality: How Mainstream Media Frame Race, Gender, and Wealth Inequality," *PNAS Proceedings of the National Academy of Sciences of the United States of America* 119, no. 21 (2022): 1–9.

Methodology Appendix: Data and Methods

This book relies on a wide range of empirical data and methodologies. These data come from voluntary nonfinancial reports, mandatory Securities and Exchange Commission (SEC) reports – Form 10-K annual reports and Form 8-K reports (used for major events reporting) – shareholder proposals, proxy statements, SEC no-action letter requests, news articles, historical documents, and interviews with twenty-two chief sustainability officers (CSOs) and chief diversity officers (CDOs). My data span an eight-year period from 2018 to 2025. For all reports (voluntary and mandatory), I use the year of disclosure, rather than the reporting year, for analysis. For example, a company's 2017 sustainability report was almost always disclosed in 2018, so I analyze it for 2018. The most recent data are from 2025.

DATA COLLECTION

Voluntary Nonfinancial Reports

I obtained most of the voluntary reports in my analysis from Corporate Register, the most comprehensive repository of nonfinancial corporate reports.[1] Since the 1990s, companies have submitted voluntary nonfinancial reports to Corporate Register, and in some cases Corporate Register harvests reports directly from companies' websites. Voluntary reports have varied titles as illustrated in Table A.1. Most reports fall in the ESG, Sustainability, Corporate Responsibility, and Diversity and Inclusion categories.

I restricted data collection to companies headquartered in the United States and listed on the New York Stock Exchange (NYSE) and Nasdaq, Inc., because these stock exchanges are the world's largest by market capitalization. As of March 2023, the NYSE had a combined total of 2,385 listed companies, of which 75.8 percent were American companies. Similarly, 76.6 percent of Nasdaq's 3,611 listings belonged to American companies.[2]

Scholars often focus on the largest 500 corporations in research on nonfinancial aspects of companies.[3] The data I retrieved from Corporate Register

TABLE A.1 *Titles of voluntary reports*

Bond Impact Report
Bond Impact Review
Climate
Communication on Progress
Community
Community Review
Corporate Responsibility (EHS/Community/Social)
Corporate Responsibility Review
Diversity & Inclusion
Diversity & Inclusion Review
Environment
Environment & Social
Environment, Health & Safety & Social/Community
Environmental Review
ESG (Environmental, Social, and Governance)
ESG Review (Environmental, Social, and Governance)
Framework Report
Health & Safety
Human Rights
Human Rights Review
Non-Financial Statement
Philanthropy
Responsible Business
Site Corporate Responsibility
Site Environment
Social
Social Review
Specific Issue Report
Sustainable (Environment/Social/Economic)
Sustainable (Environment/Social/Economic) & EMAS
Sustainable Review (Environment/Social/Economic)
Tax Transparency
Tax Transparency Review
Transparency

included reports for 460 of those companies. I employed data managers from Pareto, a talent firm, to manually collect reports for the remaining forty companies. Pareto's data managers also manually collected voluntary reports directly from websites for the largest 200 private companies in America based on Forbes's rankings.[4]

In total, I collected 10,460 voluntary reports for 2,104 public companies, 600 voluntary reports for 215 private companies, or a total of 11,060 voluntary reports for 2,319 public and private companies combined. These reports contained hundreds of thousands of pages of text. Before analyzing the data, I excluded reports that could not be converted to TXT files for analysis in Python. My analysis thereafter included a total of 10,729 voluntary reports for 2,292 public and private companies (2,093 public and 199 private). The data includes very large multinational and well-known companies, as well as medium and smaller publicly traded companies. Including large-, medium-, and small-cap companies ensured the sample was not limited to companies facing significant external pressures to make disclosures; this provided a fuller picture of race-conscious disclosures regardless of a company's public visibility or the perception of visibility.

All public companies in my study are either currently Russell 3000 Index companies or part of the Russell 3000 between 2020 and 2024. The Russell 3000 Index comprises 98 percent of the US equity market, covering a substantial portion of the economy. The Russell 3000 therefore has a large reach in terms of not only financial power but also the ability to influence national discourse on race and other social issues.

SEC Reports

To collect SEC Form 10-K annual reports and Form 8-K reports, my data scientist used Python to extract reports from EDGAR, the electronic data gathering and retrieval system that collects and indexes company filings directly from the SEC for the same companies already included in my research.[5] EDGAR has a complete set of annual reports, including Form 10-Ks, but also 10-Qs, 8-Ks, and others.[6] Although there are other sources for filings, EDGAR is a first-source repository for the information.[7]

After direct data collection through Python, I manually reviewed the data for completeness. In some cases, law student research assistants manually collected additional reports to supplement the initial direct retrieval from EDGAR.

My data scientist also assisted with the collection of Form DEF 14A proxy statements from EDGAR for the same companies. There were initially 9,035 proxy statements for 1,809 companies. I excluded proxy statements that Python could not analyze, resulting in a total of 5,511 proxy statements for 1,560 corporations.

I manually collected shareholder proposals for the years 2018 to 2022 from ISS's Shareholder Proposal database. My analysis included proposals related to race and racial diversity. I omitted proposals purely related to gender diversity.

Law student research assistants assisted with manually collecting SEC no-action letters from Intelligize.[8] To obtain no-action letter requests, I searched for all no-action letters submitted to the SEC with any mention of the word "race" between January 2020 and June 2023 in Intelligize's database. My search yielded 345 no-action letters. Law school research assistants then manually downloaded each letter from the database and assisted in coding them.

DATA ANALYSIS

Voluntary and SEC Reports

To analyze voluntary reports and SEC reports, I first created a dictionary of terms associated with race, ethnicity, and people of color using inductive and deductive methods.

The inductive process involved reading 100 voluntary reports and 10-Ks to determine how companies describe race and people of color in those reports. Deductively, I relied on academic articles and generally accepted terms used to describe race, people of color, and racial diversity in companies. The combination of these two processes generated forty-eight terms, as shown in Table A.2.

In addition to inductive and deductive methods, my data scientist used natural language processing (NLP) techniques to extend the dictionary to make it more robust. The extension allowed me to capture alternative expressions, such as "Native American" and "American Indian." We used Python's library spaCy to extract words and phrases from each sentence of each report that functions as a subject, object, or prepositional object.[9] These words and phrases are called "noun phrases." Noun phrases are based on parts-of-speech (POS) tags and syntactic dependencies of each word in that sentence. SpaCy defines a noun phrase as a noun and the words describing the noun. SpaCy uses its pretrained statistical models to make predictions of which tag or label most likely applies to each word in a sentence in its context.[10]

We used the Universal Sentence Encoder provided through Tensor Flow Hub to convert each noun phrase to a fixed length numeric vector that represents the semantic meaning of the phrase (embedding vector). Universal Sentence Encoder is a publicly available pretrained model that allows for the representation of words, sentences, and texts as a collection of numbers (numeric vectors) that machines can analyze and mathematical models can use.[11] Universal Sentence Encoder works well with this research because it was trained on general collections of texts that cover most English language words available online through Wikipedia, web news, web question–answer pages, and discussion forums. Terms that connote race are part of those sources. A possible limitation of the model is that when it encounters a noun phrase it does not recognize, it converts it to a numeric vector that means "out-of-vocabulary" and discards the phrase. However, because most terms in the dictionary are common English language words found in ordinary text the model was trained on, it was unlikely to encounter this issue. Universal Sentence Encoder also works with two-word phrases rather than single words or long texts, and a deep averaging network (DAN) encoder that allows the model to represent the meaning of a noun phrase as a precise numeric vector.

To locate synonyms in the data, we compared each noun phrase embedding vector with each dictionary term using cosign similarity measure. Cosign similarity measure ($\cos(\theta)$) is a measure of similarity between two sequences of numbers

TABLE A.2 *Dictionary of racial terms*

Asian
Pacific Islander
Black
African American
Black owned
black-owned
black-led
Black led
Blacklatino
Latino
Hispanic
American Indian
Native American
Race
Ethnic
Racial Diversity
Ethnic Diversity
Board Racial Diversity
Board Ethnic Diversity
People of Color
Underrepresented Communities
Underrepresented Minorities
urm
Indigenous
Tribe
Tribal
Communities of Color
Minority
Minorities
Minority owned
Underrepresented
Under represented
Under-represented
Marginalized
Racial Equity
Racism
Structural Racism
Racial Justice
POC
Systemic Racism
White Privilege
Black Lives Matter
Cultural appropriation
White Fragility
Black Empowerment
BIPOC
Racial
Racial Equity

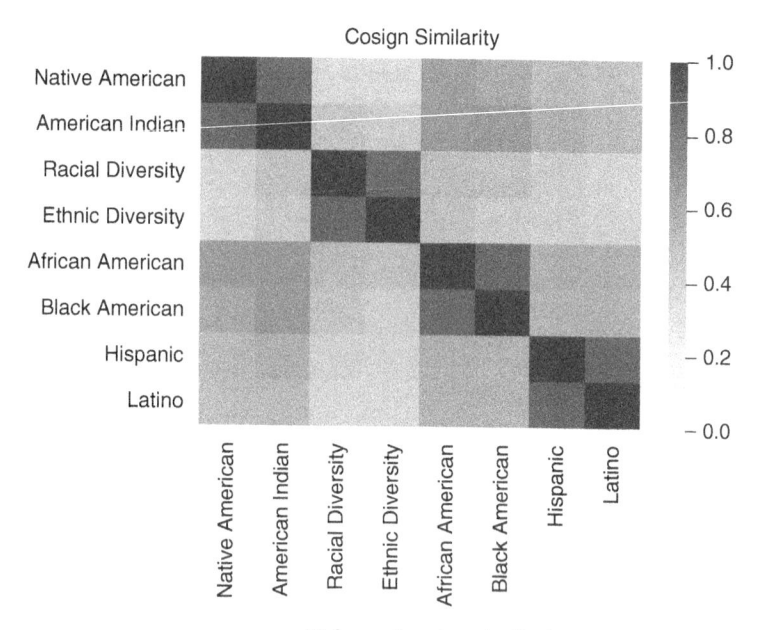

FIGURE A.1 Values of cosign similarity

(two numeric vectors A and B in the following formula). This measure represents how similar noun phrases A and B are in the semantic meaning.

$$\cos(\theta) = \frac{\mathbf{A} \cdot \mathbf{B}}{\|\mathbf{A}\|\|\mathbf{B}\|} = \frac{\sum_{i=1}^{n} A_i B_i}{\sqrt{\sum_{i-1}^{n} A_i^2} \sqrt{\sum_{i-1}^{n} B_i^2}}$$

Here, 1s are synonyms and 0s represent unrelated terms. Figure A.1 represents the values of cosign similarity between pairs of some racial terms in my dictionary. Each row and column correspond to a selected dictionary term. Each cell of the figure is colored according to the value of the cosign similarity between the terms in rows and columns. The darkest hue represents the most similar terms (values close to 1), and the lightest represents unrelated terms (values close to 0). For example, the words Hispanic and Latino have similar meaning and are represented by dark colors. I selected noun phrases that have cosign similarities higher than 0.80, which generated hundreds of phrases.

I manually checked the noun phrase list for accuracy and removed phrases that were either already in the dictionary or that did not meet the definition of a terms about race, such as "board diversity." We added sixty-two noun phrases to the dictionary of racial terms, including "Black American" and "Hispanic descent." We collapsed noun phrases into the dictionary.

Twelve of the terms in the dictionary of racial terms have meanings beyond the context of racial equity, so we restricted them in the analysis. For example, the term

"Black" can generate words like Blackrock, Blackhawk, Blacksmith, and "Jetblack," "race" can generate discussions about "terrace," "embrace," and "Horace," and the word "Asian" can generate words that include "Caucasian" and "pan-Asian." We restricted those terms by omitting them when they appear three sentences away from the other words in the dictionary or the following words: "diversity," "equity," and "inclusion" or their noun phrases. This provided confidence that when the word "Black" is counted, it is only in the context of racial and ethnic minorities.

Methodologically, we measured the number, percentage, and frequency to which dictionary terms appear in the data. Because the dictionary was curated specifically for the data, this methodology allowed me to capture the prevalence of race-conscious disclosures over time.[12]

No-Action Letter Request

I created a code book to analyze the 345 no-action letters law student research assistants manually downloaded from Intelligize. Two law school research assistants then manually and individually coded each no-action letter request using numbers 0, 1, 2, and so on to denote shareholder type (individual or institutional), proposal subject (race, racial equity audit, etc.), reasons for requesting a no-action letter (vague, micromanagement, etc.), the SEC's decision, and whether there was a prior similar shareholder proposal discussed in the letter. I served as the tie breaker in cases where research assistants disagreed on how to code requests.

Content Analysis

In addition to quantitative analysis, I engaged in extensive qualitative analysis of voluntary and 10-K reports. I trained six law student research assistants and a PhD student research assistant to manually code text into themes such as race general, current and future statistics, and racial philanthropy using Atlas.ti software.[13]

INTERVIEWS

Data Collection

Interviews were helpful for exploring why companies make race-conscious disclosures, including the role of the aftermath of the murder of Floyd on that decision, who determines what is disclosed, the emergence of internal programs and policies since 2020, the role of stakeholders in transparency, how companies meet their racial targets, the relationship between racial equity and philanthropy, the role of law and regulation in race-conscious disclosures, and the process of race-conscious retraction starting from 2024.

In previous research, I have conducted hundreds of interviews and gained significant expertise and experience in recruiting professionals who work in institutions for research. However, I encountered immense challenges in recruiting CDOs, while I had an easier time recruiting (CSOs) who sometimes responded to my cold contacts via email.

I relied on convenience sampling, recruiting any CSO and CDO willing to speak to me. I also relied on snowball sampling, whereby current participants helped to recruit other potential participants. This was not an unusual recruiting strategy as convenience and snowball sampling are the most common sampling methods used in qualitative research.[14]

For CDOs, I also relied on sponsorship from a nonprofit organization. The nonprofit invited me to attend gatherings where I had one-to-one conversations and group meetings with potential research participants. Those meetings were invaluable and instrumental in recruiting many CDOs as I gained their trust, and I am exceedingly grateful to the nonprofit for letting me in.

Perhaps it is surprising that recruiting CDOs was challenging for me even as a Black professor conducting this research. Most CDOs are people of color, women, and others from marginalized groups, including members of the LGBTQ+ community. However, considering how politically charged race has become and how CDOs face career-threatening situations in certain circumstances, personal recruitment methods, including snowballing were needed to make participants more comfortable.[15]

I personally conducted sixty-minute confidential interviews with twenty-two CSOs and CDOs via Zoom between March 2022 and February 2025. I recorded each interview on a portable device for later transcription as approved by my institution's Institutional Review Board.

CDOs describe themselves as leaders in inclusion and belonging strategies and implementation in companies. Some are members of the C-Suite, while others are not. Some are part of the human resources department, while others are part of the department that manages people on a broader scale.

Like CDOs, CSOs also wear many different hats, but in general, lead their companies' foundations, sustainability departments, community engagement initiatives, and philanthropy.

My research and analysis benefited immensely from insights from CDOs and CSOs, and I am deeply grateful for their generosity (Table A.3).

Data Analysis

I coded interview data using the grounded theory method. Grounded theory is a systematic method for constructing theoretical analysis from data into distinct units of meaning.[16] Themes are initially clustered into descriptive categories and then reevaluated for their interrelationships through a series of analytical steps that

TABLE A.3 *List of interviewees*

ID	Title	Industry	Classification
1	CDO	Financial services	Publicly traded
2	CDO	Retail	Private
3	CDO	Financial services	Publicly traded
4	CDO	Retail	Publicly traded
5	CDO	Food and beverage	Publicly traded
6	CDO	Retail	Publicly traded
7	CDO	E-commerce	Publicly traded
8	CDO	Retail	Publicly traded
9	CDO	Retail	Private
10	CDO	Financial services	Private
11	CSO	Financial services	Private
12	CSO	Financial services	Publicly traded
13	CSO	Financial services	Publicly traded
14	CSO	Technology	Publicly traded
15	CSO	Financial services	Publicly traded
16	CSO	Technology	Private
17	CSO	Retail	Private
18	CSO	Technology	Private
19	CSO	E-commerce	Publicly traded
20	CSO	E-commerce	Publicly traded
21	CSO	Food and beverage	Publicly traded

involve gradually subsuming themes into higher order concepts.[17] As is typical for grounded theory, analysis begins at the same time as data is being collected rather than after all the information has been gathered.[18] To achieve this, I wrote extensive memos immediately after each interview, describing the interview experience, my impressions, and information that stood out to me. I then read each interviewee's memo before beginning the formal coding process in Atlas.ti. Formal coding involved reading each interview line by line to identify key words and phrases that connect interviewees' accounts to the topic under study. I used Atlas.ti software to organize codes as I moved from the descriptive level of words and phrases to theory development borne from making connections between concepts. This was an ongoing process that involved coding and re-coding until themes were fully realized.

NOTES

1. Corporate Register, https://corporateregister.com/.
2. Statista, "Comparison of the Number of Listed Companies on the New York Stock Exchange (NYSE) and Nasdaq From 2018 to 1st Quarter 2023, by Domicile," Statista website, May 1, 2023, www.statista.com/statistics/1277216/nyse-nasdaq-comparison-number-listed-companies/.
3. Dhir, *Challenging Boardroom Homogeneity*.
4. Murphy, "America's Largest Private Companies."

5. United States Securities Exchange Commission, "Search Filings," www.sec.gov/edgar/search-and-access.
6. Tim Loughran and Bill McDonald, "The Use of EDGAR Filings by Investors," *Journal of Behavioral Finance* 18 (2017): 231–48.
7. Ibid.
8. Intelligize pulls together and links a broad set of SEC disclosure documents. Intelligize website, www.intelligize.com/.
9. Duygu Altinok, *Mastering SpaCy: An End-to-End Practical Guide to Implementing NLP Applications Using the Python Ecosystem* (United Kingdom: Packt Publishing, 2021).
10. Ibid.
11. Daniel Cer et al., "Universal Sentence Encoder," arXiv website, Cornell University, last modified March 28, 2018, https://arxiv.org/abs/1803.11175.
12. For discussions on the dictionary method see Justin Grimmer, Margaret E. Roberts, and Brandon Stewart, *Text as Data: A New Framework for Machine Learning and the Social Sciences* (Princeton: Princeton University Press, 2022).
13. Atlas.ti is a computer-assisted qualitative data analysis software that facilitates analysis of qualitative data. "ATLAS.ti: The Qualitative Data Analysis & Research Software," ATLAS.ti website, https://atlasti.com/.
14. Robert S. Weiss, *Learning from Strangers: The Art and Method of Qualitative Interview Studies*, 1st Free Press paperback ed. (New York: Free Press, 1995).
15. For discussions about interviewing Black professionals in other settings, see Woodson, *The Black Ceiling*.
16. Kathy Charmaz, "Qualitative Interviewing and Grounded Theory Analysis," in *The SAGE Handbook of Interview Research: The Complexity of the Craft*, eds. Jaber F. Gubrium, James A. Holstein, Amir B. Marvasti, and Karyn D. McKinney, 2nd ed. (Thousand Oaks, CA: SAGE, 2012); Christina Goulding, *Grounded Theory: A Practical Guide for Management, Business, and Market Researchers* (Thousand Oaks, CA: SAGE, 2002).
17. Goulding, *Grounded Theory*.
18. Ibid.

Bibliography

ARTICLES, BOOKS, AND REPORTS

Adediran, Atinuke O. "Disclosures for Equity." *Columbia Law Review* 122, no. 4 (2022): 865–922.
Adediran, Atinuke O. "Nonprofit Board Composition." *Ohio State Law Journal* 83 (2022): 357–421.
Adediran, Atinuke O. "Disclosing Corporate Diversity." *Virginia Law Review* 109, no. 2 (April 2023): 307–72.
Adediran, Atinuke O. "Racial Targets." *Northwestern University Law Review* 118, no. 6 (2024): 1455–502.
Alexander, Richard D., and Georges F. Doriot. *The Management of Racial Integration in Business: Special Report to Management.* New York: McGraw-Hill, 1964.
Altinok, Duygu. *Mastering SpaCy: An End-to-End Practical Guide to Implementing NLP Applications Using the Python Ecosystem.* United Kingdom: Packt Publishing, 2021.
Amazon. "Diversity, Equity and Inclusion at Amazon." *Amazon website.* April 18, 2018. www.aboutamazon.co.uk/news/working-at-amazon/diversity-equity-and-inclusion-at-amazon.
Amazon. "Amazon Closing AmazonSmile to Focus Its Philanthropic Giving to Programs with Greater Impact." *Amazon website*, January 18, 2023. www.aboutamazon.com/news/company-news/amazon-closing-amazonsmile-to-focus-its-philanthropic-giving-to-programs-with-greater-impact.
Amazon. *NYCRF Amazon Shareholder Proposal.* Office of the New York State Comptroller website. 2021. www.osc.state.ny.us/files/press/pdf/nycrf-amazon-shareholder-proposal.pdf; www.osc.ny.gov/files/press/pdf/nycrf-amazon-shareholder-proposal.pdf.
Amazon. "Our Positions." https://perma.cc/D35H-T6T2.
Amazon Employees for Climate Justice. "How Amazon's Emissions Are Hurting Communities of Color." Medium, May 26, 2020. https://amazonemployees4climatejustice.medium.com/environmental-justice-and-amazons-carbon-footprint-9e10fab21138.
American Bar Association. "What Is an Executive Order?" American Bar Association website, January 25, 2021. www.americanbar.org/groups/public_education/publications/teaching-legal-docs/what-is-an-executive-order-/.
Amorelli, María-Florencia, and Isabel-María García-Sánchez. "Trends in the Dynamic Evolution of Board Gender Diversity and Corporate Social Responsibility." *Corporate Social Responsibility and Environmental Management* 28 (2021): 537–54.
Anderson, Bernard E. *The Negro in the Public Utility Industries, Report No. 10.* Philadelphia: University of Pennsylvania Press, 1970.

Anderson, Robert IV, and Jeffrey Manns. "The Delaware Delusion." *North Carolina Law Review* 93 (May 2015): 1049–105.

Andrews, F. Emerson. *Corporation Giving*. New York: Russell Sage Foundation, 1952.

Aquila, Francis J., and Lauren S. Boehmke. "United States." In *The Shareholder Rights and Activism Review*, edited by Francis J. Aquila, 179–90. 8th ed. New York: Sullivan & Cromwell, 2023.

Aras, Guler, and David Crowther. "Governance and Sustainability: An Investigation into the Relationship between Corporate Governance and Corporate Sustainability." *Management Decision* 46 (2008): 433–38.

Armstrong, Megan, Eathyn Edwards, and Duwain Pinder. "Corporate Commitments to Racial Justice: An Update." McKinsey Institute for Black Economic Mobility website, February 21, 2023. www.mckinsey.com/bem/our-insights/corporate-commitments-to-racial-justice-an-update#/.

Ayas, Reyhan, Paulina Tilly, and Devan Rawlings. "Cutting Costs at the Expense of Diversity." *Revelio Labs website*, February 7, 2023. www.reveliolabs.com/news/social/cutting-costs-at-the-expense-of-diversity/.

Azmat, Fara, and Ruth Rentschler. "Gender and Ethnic Diversity on Boards and Corporate Responsibility: The Case of the Arts Sector." *Journal of Business Ethics* 141 (2017): 317–36.

Bainbridge, Stephen M. *Corporate Law and Economics*. New York: Foundation Press, 2022.

Baker, Andrew, David F. Larcker, Charles McClure, Durgesh Saraph, and Edward Watts. "Diversity Washing." Forthcoming in the *Journal of Accounting Research*, Chicago Booth Research Paper No. 22-18, SSRN website, last updated April 18, 2024. https://ssrn.com/abstract=4298626.

Baker, Philip. "The New Business Mandate." University of Chicago Professional Education website, June 12, 2024. https://professional.uchicago.edu/stories/inclusive-business-and-supplier-diversity-strategies/new-business-mandate?language_content_entity=en.

Balakrishnan, Maya, Jimin Nam, and Ryan W. Buell. "Differentiating on Diversity: How Disclosing Workforce Diversity Influences Consumer Choice." *Production and Operations Management* 34, no. 3 (2025): 457–74.

Banks, Patricia A. *Black Culture, Inc.: How Ethnic Community Support Pays for Corporate America*. Stanford: Stanford University Press, 2022.

Barman, Eugene. "The Social Bases of Philanthropy." *Annual Review of Sociology* 43, no. 1 (2017): 271–90.

Barnett, Michael L., John M. Jermier, and Barbara A. Lafferty. "Corporate Reputation: The Definitional Landscape." *Corporate Reputation Review* 9, no. 1 (2006): 26–38.

Barron, Milton Leon. *Minorities in a Changing World*. New York: Knopf, 1967.

Baumgartner, Kim T., Carolin A. Ernst, and Thomas M. Fischer. "How Corporate Reputation Disclosures Affect Stakeholders' Behavioral Intentions: Mediating Mechanisms of Perceived Organizational Performance and Corporate Reputation." *Journal of Business Ethics* 175 (2022): 361–89.

Bebchuk, Lucian A., and Assaf Hamdani. "Independent Directors and Controlling Shareholders." *University of Pennsylvania Law Review* 165, no. 6 (2017): 1271–316.

Bebchuk, Lucian Arye, and Alma Cohen. "Firms' Decisions Where to Incorporate." *Journal of Law & Economics* 46 (2003): 383–425.

Bebchuk, Lucian A., and Roberto Tallarita. "Will Corporations Deliver Value to All Stakeholders?" *Vanderbilt Law Review* 75, no. 4 (2022): 1031–91.

Bell, David A., Dawn Belt, and Ron C. Llewellyn. "Diversifying the Boardroom: 2022 Disclosures." Harvard Law School Forum on Corporate Governance, May 11, 2023. https://corpgov.law.harvard.edu/2023/05/11/diversifying-the-boardroom-2022-disclosures/.

Bennington, Allison, Anne Sheehan, and John C. Coates, IV. "Recommendation from the Investor-as-Owner Subcommittee of the SEC Investor Advisory Committee Relating to ESG Disclosure." Harvard Law School Forum on Corporate Governance, May 28, 2020. https://corpgov.law.harvard.edu/2020/05/28/recommendation-from-the-investor-as-owner-subcommittee-of-the-sec-investor-advisory-committee-relating-to-esg-disclosure/.

Berenblat, Ron S., and Elizabeth R. Gonzalez-Sussman. "Racial Equity Audits: A New ESG Initiative." Harvard Law School Forum on Corporate Governance, October 30, 2021. https://corpgov.law.harvard.edu/2021/10/30/racial-equity-audits-a-new-esg-initiative/.

Berle, Adolf A., Jr. "Corporate Powers as Powers in Trust." *Harvard Law Review* 44 (1931): 1049–74.

Berle, Adolf A., Jr., and Gardiner C. Means. *The Modern Corporation and Private Property*. New York: Macmillan, 1933.

Berrey, Ellen. *The Enigma of Diversity: The Language of Race and the Limits of Racial Justice*. Chicago: University of Chicago Press, 2015.

BlackRock Investment Stewardship. Proxy Voting Guidelines for Benchmark Policies – U.S. Securities (January 2025).

Board of Governors of the Federal Reserve System. "Greater Wealth, Greater Uncertainty: Changes in Racial Inequality in the Survey of Consumer Finances." Federal Reserve website, last updated October 23, 2023. www.federalreserve.gov/econres/notes/feds-notes/greater-wealth-greater-uncertainty-changes-in-racial-inequality-in-the-survey-of-consumer-finances-accessible-20231018.htm#fig1.

Boesso, Giacomo, Francesco Favotto, and Giovanna Michelon. "Corporate Social Responsibility and Environmental Management." *Corporate Social Responsibility and Environmental Management* 22 (2015): 424–40.

Bohnet, Iris. *What Works: Gender Equality by Design*. Cambridge, MA: Harvard University Press, 2018.

Brakman Reiser, Dana. "Corporate Philanthropy: Development Tool or Profitable Strategy?" In *The Handbook on Philanthrocapitalism*, edited by Steph Haydon, Tobias Jung, and Shona Russell. Cheltenham: Edward Elgar, 2025.

Brakman Reiser, Dana, and Steven A. Dean. *For-Profit Philanthropy: Elite Power & the Threat of Limited Liability Companies, Donor-Advised Funds, & Strategic Corporate Giving*. New York: Oxford University Press, 2023.

Briscoe, Forrest, and Abhinav Gupta. "Social Activism in and Around Organizations." *Academy of Management Annals* 10 (2016): 671–727.

Brown, Pamela, Tiffany Burns, Tyler Harris, Charlotte Lucas, and Israe Zizaoui. "The Rise of the Inclusive Consumer." McKinsey & Company website, February 8, 2022. www.mckinsey.com/industries/retail/our-insights/the-rise-of-the-inclusive-consumer#/.

Brudney, Victor, and Allen Ferrell. "Corporate Charitable Giving." *University of Chicago Law Review* 69 (2002): 1191–218.

Brummer, Chris. "Stock Exchanges and the New Markets for Securities Laws." *University of Chicago Law Review* 75, no. 4 (2008): 1435–92.

Burk, Robert Frederick. *The Eisenhower Administration and Black Civil Rights*. Knoxville: University of Tennessee Press, 1984.

Cai, Li, Jinhua Cui, and Hoje Jo. "Corporate Environmental Responsibility and Firm Risk." *Journal of Business Ethics* 139 (2016): 563–94.

Cai, Wei, Yue Chen, Shiva Rajgopal, and Li Azinovic-Yang. "Diversity Targets." *Review of Accounting Studies* 29 (2024): 1–52.

Carnahan, Seth, David Kryscynski, and Daniel Olson. "When Does Corporate Social Responsibility Reduce Employee Turnover? Evidence from Attorneys before and after 9/11." *Academy of Management Journal* 60, no. 5 (2017): 1932–62.

Cassel, Johan, Josh Lerner, and Emmanuel Yimfor. "Racial Diversity in Private Capital Fundraising." Working Paper 30500, National Bureau of Economic Research, September 2022. www.nber.org/papers/w30500.

Caughey, Devin, James Dunham, and Christopher Warshaw. "The Ideological Nationalization of Partisan Subconstituencies in the American States." *Public Choice* 176 (2018): 133–51.

Cavaco, Sandra, and Patricia Crifo. "CSR and Financial Performance: Complementarity between Environmental, Social and Business Behaviours." *Applied Economics* 46 (2014): 3323–38.

Cer, Daniel, Yinfei Yang, Sheng-yi Kong, Nan Hua, Nicole Limtiaco, Rhomni St. John, Noah Constant, Mario Guajardo-Cespedes, Steve Yuan, Chris Tar, Yun-Hsuan Sung, Brian Strope, Ray Kurzweil. "Universal Sentence Encoder." arXiv website, Cornell University, last modified March 28, 2018. https://arxiv.org/abs/1803.11175.

Ceres. "Record Number of Negotiated Agreements between Investors and Companies in 2022 Proxy Season." Ceres website, August 1, 2022. www.ceres.org/news-center/press-releases/record-number-negotiated-agreements-between-investors-and-companies-2022.

Chafe, William Henry. *Civilities and Civil Rights: Greensboro, North Carolina, and the Black Struggle for Freedom*. Oxford: Oxford University Press, 1980.

Chang, Daniel. "BlackRock Updated 2023 U.S. Proxy Voting Guidelines." Georgeson, January 11, 2023. www.georgeson.com/us/insights/proxy/blackrock-updated-2023-us-voting-guidelines.

Charmaz, Kathy, and Linda Liska Belgrave. "Qualitative Interviewing and Grounded Theory Analysis." In *The SAGE Handbook of Interview Research: The Complexity of the Craft*, edited by Jaber F. Gubrium, James A. Holstein, Amir B. Marvasti, and Karyn D. McKinney, 347–56. 2nd ed. Thousand Oaks, CA: SAGE, 2012.

Christensen, Hans B., Luzi Hail, and Christian Leuz. "Mandatory CSR and Sustainability Reporting: Economic Analysis and Literature Review." *Review of Accounting Studies* 26 (2021): 1176–248.

Cloyd, Mary Ann. "Shareholder Activism: Who, What, When, and How?" Harvard Law School Forum on Corporate Governance, April 7, 2015. https://corpgov.law.harvard.edu/2015/04/07/shareholder-activism-who-what-when-and-how/.

Colmer, Jonathan M., Suvy Qin, John L. Voorheis, and Reed Walker. "Income, Wealth, and Environmental Inequality in the United States." National Bureau of Economic Research, Working Paper 33050, October 2024.

Cooley Alert. "SEC Staff Adopts Significant New Guidance Affecting Shareholder Proposals and Engagement." February 14, 2025. www.cooley.com/news/insight/2025/2025-02-14-sec-staff-adopts-significant-new-guidance-affecting-shareholder-proposals-and-engagement.

Corrington, Abby, Naomi M. Fa-Kaji, Mikki R. Hebl, Eden B. King, Dillon Stewart, and Temi Alao. "The Impact of Organizational Statements of Support for the Black Community in the Wake of a Racial Mega-Threat on Organizational Attraction and Revenue." *Human Resource Management* (2022): 699–722.

Costley, Drew. "Once Again, a Chevron Oil Spill Is Impacting a Community of Color." Medium, February 12, 2021. https://medium.com/future-human/once-again-a-chevron-oil-spill-is-impacting-a-community-of-color-1f55f09a0694.

Couture, Wendy Gerwick. "The Collision between the First Amendment and Securities Fraud." *Alabama Law Review* 65, no. 4 (2014): 903–74.

Cross, Theodore L. *Black Capitalism: Strategy for Business in the Ghetto*. New York: Atheneum, 1974.

"CSRD: A Guide to the Corporate Sustainability Reporting Directive." Persefoni.com blog, July 2023. www.persefoni.com/blog/what-is-csrd.

Curzan, Myron P., and Mark L. Pelesh. "Revitalizing Corporate Democracy: Control of Investment Managers' Voting on Social Responsibility Proxy Issues." *Harvard Law Review* 93 (1980): 670–700.
Cutlip, Scott M. *Fundraising in the United States: Its Role in America's Philanthropy*. New Brunswick, NJ: Rutgers University Press, 1965.
Cuttino, Nakita Q. "Private Debt for Public Good." *Florida Law Review* 76 (2024): 637–722.
Cyril, Malkia Devich, Lyle Matthew Kan, Ben Francisco Maulbeck, and Lori Villarosa. *Mismatched: Philanthropy's Response to the Call for Racial Justice*. Philanthropic Initiative for Racial Equity website, 2021. https://racialequity.org/mismatched/.
Cziraki, Peter, Luc Renneboog, and Peter G. Szilagyi. "Shareholder Activism through Proxy Proposals: The European Perspective." *European Financial Management* 16, no. 5 (2010): 738–77.
Dahlsrud, Alexander. "How Corporate Social Responsibility Is Defined: An Analysis of 37 Definitions." *Corporate Social Responsibility and Environmental Management* 15 (2008): 1–13.
Dalfiume, Richard M. "The Fahy Committee and Desegregation of the Armed Forces." *The Historian* 31, no. 1 (1968): 1–20.
Dallas, Lynne L. "The Multiple Roles of Corporate Boards of Directors." *San Diego Law Review* 40, no. 3 (2003): 781–820.
Davis, Gerald F., and Christopher J. White. "The New Face of Corporate Activism." *Stanford Social Innovation Review* (Fall 2015). https://ssir.org/articles/entry/the_new_face_of_corporate_activism.
Deloitte CFO Insights. "Activist Shareholders: How Will You Respond?" Deloitte website, 2015. www2.deloitte.com/content/dam/Deloitte/us/Documents/finance/wallace-cfo-insight-activist-shareholder.pdf.
Deloitte. "European Commission Proposes Reduction in Sustainability Reporting and Due Diligence Requirements – Considerations for U.S. Entities." *Deloitte*, March 7, 2025. https://dart.deloitte.com/USDART/home/publications/deloitte/heads-up/2025/eu-commission-omnibus-proposal-sustainability-reporting-reduction-csrd.
Delton, Jennifer. *Racial Integration in Corporate America, 1940–1990*. Cambridge: Cambridge University Press, 2009.
Dhir, Aaron A. *Challenging Boardroom Homogeneity: Corporate Law, Governance and Diversity*. Cambridge: Cambridge University Press, 2015.
DiMaggio, Paul J., and Walter W. Powell. "The Iron Cage Revisited: Institutional Isomorphism and Collective Rationality in Organizational Fields." *American Sociological Review* 48 (1983): 147–60.
Dobbin, Frank. *Inventing Equal Opportunity*. Princeton, NJ: Princeton University Press, 2009.
Dobbin, Frank, and Alexandra Kalev. *Getting to Diversity: What Works and What Doesn't*. Cambridge, MA: Harvard University Press, 2022.
Dodd, E. Merrick, Jr. "For Whom Are Corporate Managers Trustees?" *Harvard Law Review* 45 (1932): 1145–63.
Donaldson, Gordon. "Financial Goals and Strategic Consequences." *Harvard Business Review* (1985): 1–26. https://hbr.org/1985/05/financial-goals-and-strategic-consequences.
Dorsey, Cheryl, Jeff Bradach, and Peter Kim. "Racial Equity and Philanthropy: Disparities in Funding for Leaders of Color Leave Impact on the Table." Report by Echoing Green and the Bridgespan Group, 2020. www.bridgespan.org/insights/disparities-nonprofit-funding-for-leaders-of-color.
Dorsey, Cheryl, Peter Kim, Cora Daniels, Lyell Sakaue, and Britt Savage. "Overcoming the Racial Bias in Philanthropic Funding." *Stanford Social Innovation Review*, May 4, 2020. https://ssir.org/articles/entry/overcoming_the_racial_bias_in_philanthropic_funding.

Ealy, Lenore T., and Steven D. Ealy. "Progressivism and Philanthropy." *The Good Society* 15, no. 1 (2006): 35–42.

Eccles, Robert G., and Svetlana Klimenko. "The Investor Revolution." *Harvard Business Review* 97 (2019): 106–16.

Edelman, Lauren B. *Working Law: Courts, Corporations, and Symbolic Civil Rights.* Chicago: University of Chicago Press, 2016.

Ekwueme, C. M., C. F. Egbunike, and C. I. Onyali. "Benefits of Triple Bottom Line Disclosures on Corporate Performance: An Exploratory Study of Corporate Stakeholders." *Journal of Management and Sustainability* 3, no. 2 (2013): 79–91.

Ely, Robin J. and David A. Thomas. "Getting Serious about Diversity: Enough Already with the Business Case." *Harvard Business Review* 98, no. 6 (2020): 114–22.

"Employee Activism in the Age of Purpose: Employee (Up)Rising." Weber Shandwick website, May 2019. https://cms.webershandwick.com/wp-content/uploads/2023/02/Employee-Activism-in-the-Age-of-Purpose-FINAL.pdf.

"Employees Rising: Seizing the Opportunity in Employee Activism." Weber Shandwick website, April 2, 2014. https://webershandwick.com/news/employees-rising-seizing-the-opportunity-in-employee-activism.

Ertimur, Yonca, Fabrizio Ferri, and Stephen R. Stubben. "Board of Directors' Responsiveness to Shareholders: Evidence from Shareholder Proposals." *Journal of Corporate Finance* 16, no. 1 (2010): 53–72.

European Commission. "Corporate Sustainability Due Diligence." European Commission website, July 25, 2024. https://commission.europa.eu/business-economy-euro/doing-business-eu/corporate-sustainability-due-diligence_en.

European Counsel of the European Union. "Corporate Sustainability Due Diligence: Council Gives Its Final Approval." Press Release, May 24, 2024. www.consilium.europa.eu/en/press/press-releases/2024/05/24/corporate-sustainability-due-diligence-council-gives-its-final-approval/.

European Parliament and the Council. "Directive (EU) 2022/2464." EUR-Lex website, December 14, 2022. https://eur-lex.europa.eu/legal-content/EN/TXT/?uri=CELEX%3A32022L2464.

Fairfax, Lisa M. "Breaking Down Bias: Legal Mandates vs. Corporate Interests." *Washington Law Review* 92 (2017): 1473–506.

Fairfax, Lisa M. "Dynamic Disclosure: An Expose on the Mythical Divide between Voluntary and Mandatory ESG Disclosure." *Texas Law Review* 101, no. 2 (2022): 273–337.

Fairfax, Lisa M. "Radical Rhetoric or Reality? Cautious Optimism on the Link between Corporate #BLM Speech and Behavior." *Columbia Business Law Review* 118 (2022): 118–205.

Fairfax, Lisa M. "Stakeholderism, Corporate Purpose, and Credible Commitment." *Virginia Law Review* 108, no. 5 (2022): 1163–242.

Fairfax, Lisa M. "ESG Hypocrisy and Voluntary Disclosure." *New York University Journal of Legislation and Public Policy* 26, no. 1 (2024): 127–71.

Finkelman, Paul, "The American Suppression of the African Slave Trade: Lessons on Legal Change, Social Policy, and Legislation." *Akron Law Review* 42, no. 2 (2009): 431–68.

Fletcher, Gina-Gail S., and H. Timothy Lovelace, Jr. "Corporate Racial Responsibility." *Columbia Law Review* 124, no. 2 (2024): 361–430.

Flores, Sophie, Ruth Kilsby, and Magda Puzniak-Holford. "What Is the European Corporate Sustainability Due Diligence Directive?" *Deloitte*, September 12, 2023. www.deloitte.com/uk/en/services/legal/blogs/what-is-the-european-corporate-sustainability-due-diligence-directive.html.

Folberg, Abigail M., Laura Brooks Dueland, Matthew Swanson, Sarah Stepanek, Mikki Hebl, and Carey S. Ryan. "Racism Underlies Seemingly Race-Neutral Conservative Criticisms of DEI Statements among Black and White People in the United States." *Journal of Occupational and Organizational Psychology* 97, no. 3 (2024): 791–816.

Fombrun, Charles J. *Reputation: Realizing Value from the Corporate Image*. Boston: Harvard Business School Press, 1996.

Fos, Vyacheslav, Wei Jiang, and Huasheng Nie. "A Diverse View on Board Diversity." SSRN website, December 20, 2023. https://papers.ssrn.com/sol3/papers.cfm?abstract_id=4667857.

Fox, Merritt B., Lawrence R. Glosten, and Gabriel V. Rauterberg. *The New Stock Market: Law, Economics, and Policy*. New York: Columbia University Press, 2019.

Frankel, Barbara. "Making DEI Matter: From the Business Case to a Business Driver." Seramount website, October 16, 2023. https://seramount.com/articles/making-dei-matter-from-the-business-case-to-a-business-driver/.

Fraser, Nancy. *Cannibal Capitalism: How Our System Is Devouring Democracy, Care, and the Planet, and What We Can Do about It*. London: Verso, 2023.

Friedman, Monroe. *Consumer Boycotts: Effecting Change through the Marketplace and Media*. New York: Routledge, 1999.

Furman, David M. "The Development of Corporate Image: A Historiographic Approach to a Marketing Concept." *Corporate Reputation Review* 13, no. 1 (2010): 63–75.

Gadinis, Stavros, and Chris Havasy. "The Quest for Legitimacy: A Public Law Blueprint for Corporate Governance." *U.C. Davis Law Review* 57 (2024): 1581–657.

Gadinis, Stavros, and Amelia Miazad. "Corporate Law & Social Risk." *Vanderbilt Law Review* 73, no. 5 (2020): 1401–77.

Gasman, Marybeth, and Noah Drezner. "White Corporate Philanthropy and Its Support of Private Black Colleges in the 1960s and 1970s." *International Journal of Educational Advancement* 8 (2008): 79–92.

Gautier, Arthur, and Anne-Claire Pache. "Research on Corporate Philanthropy: A Review and Assessment." *Journal of Business Ethics* 126, no. 3 (2015): 343–69.

Gensler, Gary. "Prepared Remarks at London City Week." SEC Press Release, June 23, 2021. www.sec.gov/news/speech/gensler-speechlondon-city-week-062321.

Gibson Dunn. "Attorneys General of 13 States Issue Warning to Fortune 100 Companies Regarding Their Diversity and Inclusion Programs in Wake of Supreme Court's Decision Overturning Affirmative Action in Higher Education." Gibson Dunn website, July 18, 2023. www.gibsondunn.com/attorneys-general-of-13-states-warning-to-fortune-100-companies-regarding-their-diversity-and-inclusion-programs-in-wake-of-supreme-court-decision/.

Gibson Dunn. "Discussing Human Capital: A Survey of the S&P 500's Compliance with the New SEC Disclosure Requirement One Year after Adoption." Gibson Dunn website, November 10, 2021. www.gibsondunn.com/discussing-human-capital-survey-of-sp-500-compliance-with-new-sec-disclosure-requirement-one-year-after-adoption/.

Goldman Sachs. "Fund for Racial Equity." Goldman Sachs website. 2020. https://perma.cc/7JAN-PVN9.

Golob, Urša, and Klement Podnar. "Corporate Marketing and the Role of Internal CSR in Employees' Life Satisfaction: Exploring the Relationship between Work and Non-work Domains." *Journal of Business Research* 131 (2021): 664–72.

Gonzales, Matt. "Elon Musk Calls DEI 'Another Word for Racism'. Workplace Experts Say He's Wrong." SHRM website, January 16, 2024. www.shrm.org/topics-tools/news/inclusion-equity-diversity/elon-musk-dei-racist.

Goulding, Christina. *Grounded Theory: A Practical Guide for Management, Business, and Market Researchers*. Thousand Oaks, CA: SAGE, 2002.

Graham, Hugh Davis. *The Civil Rights Era: Origins and Development of National Policy*. Oxford: Oxford University Press, 1990.

Graham, John R., Campbell R. Harvey, and Shiva Rajgopal. "The Economic Implications of Corporate Financial Reporting." *Journal of Accounting and Economics* 40, nos. 1–3 (2005): 3–73.

Grasso, Wendy. "The Future of DEI Shareholder Proposals." Harvard Law School Forum on Corporate Governance, June 13, 2024. https://corpgov.law.harvard.edu/2024/06/13/the-future-of-dei-shareholder-proposals/.

Green, Jeff, and Simone Foxman. "Uber and Citi Cut 'Anti-Racist' from Corporate Vocabulary Following DEI Backlash." *Bloomberg*, March 1, 2024. www.bloomberg.com/news/articles/2024-03-01/uber-citi-among-us-companies-dropping-anti-racist-tag-with-dei-backlash?embedded-checkout=true.

Grimmer, Justin, Margaret E. Roberts, and Brandon Stewart. *Text as Data: A New Framework for Machine Learning and the Social Sciences*. Princeton: Princeton University Press, 2022.

Haines, Herbert H. "Black Radicalization and the Funding of Civil Rights: 1957–1970." *Social Problems* 32, no. 1 (1984): 31–43.

Hamermesh, Lawrence A. "The Policy Foundations of Delaware Corporate Law." *Columbia Law Review* 106 (2006): 1749–92.

Hampton, Henry, and Steve Fayer. *Voices of Freedom: An Oral History of the Civil Rights Movement from the 1950s through the 1980s*. New York: Bantam Books, 1990.

Hanlon, Gail, and Peter P. Fleming. "Updating the Critical Perspective on Corporate Social Responsibility." *Sociology Compass* 3 (2009): 937–48.

Hayden, Grant M., and Matthew T. Bodie. *Reconstructing the Corporation: From Shareholder Primacy to Shared Governance*. Cambridge: Cambridge University Press, 2021.

Heldman, Caroline. *Protest Politics in the Marketplace: Consumer Activism in the Corporate Age*. Ithaca: Cornell University Press, 2017.

Hill, Jennifer G. "Images of the Shareholder – Shareholder Power and Shareholder Powerlessness." In *Research Handbook on Shareholder Power*, edited by Jennifer G. Hill and Randall S. Thomas, 53–73. Cheltenham: Edward Elgar, 2015.

Hunt, Dame Vivian, Dennis Layton, and Sara Prince. "Why Diversity Matters." McKinsey & Company website, January 1, 2015. www.mckinsey.com/capabilities/people-and-organizational-performance/our-insights/why-diversity-matters.

Immergluck, Dan. *Red Hot City: Housing, Race, and Exclusion in Twenty-First-Century Atlanta*. Berkeley: University of California Press, 2022.

Indiana University Lilly Family School of Philanthropy. *Giving USA: The Annual Report on Philanthropy for the Year 2021*. Giving USA Foundation website, 2022. https://store.givingusa.org/products/2021-annual-report?variant=39329211613263.

Jackson, Kevin T. *Building Reputational Capital: Strategies for Integrity and Fair Play That Improve the Bottom Line*. Oxford: Oxford University Press, 2004.

Jardina, Ashley. *White Identity Politics*. Cambridge: Cambridge University Press, 2019.

Judicial Watch. "Judicial Watch Victory: Court Declares Unconstitutional California's Racial, Ethnic, LGBT Quota for Corporate Boards." Judicial Watch website, April 1, 2022. www.judicialwatch.org/quota-for-corporate-boards.

Judicial Watch. "Judicial Watch Victories: California Court of Appeal Upholds Court Injunctions against Quotas for Corporate Boards." Judicial Watch website, December 20, 2022. www.judicialwatch.org/judicial-watch-victories-2/.

Jun, Sora, Rosalind M. Chow, A. Maurits van der Veen, and Erik Bleich. 2022. "Chronic Frames of Social Inequality: How Mainstream Media Frame Race, Gender, and Wealth Inequality." *PNAS Proceedings of the National Academy of Sciences of the United States of America* 119 (21): 1–9.

Kahan, Marcel. "Some Problems with Stock Exchange-Based Securities Regulation—Commentary." *Virginia Law Review* 83, no. 7 (1997): 1509–20.

Bibliography

Kalmoe, Nathan P., and Lilliana Mason. *Radical American Partisanship: Mapping Extreme Hostility, Its Causes, and the Consequences for Democracy*. Chicago: University of Chicago Press, 2022.

Kamalnath, Akshaya. *The Corporate Diversity Jigsaw*. Cambridge: Cambridge University Press, 2022.

Keller, Elisabeth, and Gregory A. Gehlmann. "Introductory Comment: A Historical Introduction to the Securities Act of 1933 and the Securities Exchange Act of 1934." *Ohio State Law Journal* 49 (1988): 329–52.

Kersten, Andrew Edmund. *Race, Jobs, and the War: The FEPC in the Midwest, 1941–46*. Urbana: University of Illinois Press, 2007.

King, Brayden G. "A Political Mediation Model of Corporate Response to Social Movement Activism." *Administrative Science Quarterly* 53, no. 3 (2008): 395–421.

Kinsley, Michael E. *Creative Capitalism: A Conversation with Bill Gates, Warren Buffett, and Other Economic Leaders*. New York: Simon & Schuster, 2010.

Klarman, Michael J. 1994. "How Brown Changed Race Relations: The Backlash Thesis." *Journal of American History* 81 (1): 81–118.

Koehn, Nancy. "The Time Is Right for Creative Capitalism." Harvard Business School, Working Knowledge website, August 20, 2008. https://hbswk.hbs.edu/item/the-time-is-right-for-creative-capitalism.

Koliba, Christopher J., Jack W. Meek, Asim Zia, and Russell W. Mills. *Governance Networks in Public Administration and Public Policy*. Oxford: Taylor & Francis Group, 2018.

Kovvali, Aneil. "Countercyclical Corporate Governance." *North Carolina Law Review* 101, no. 1 (2022): 141–206.

Lange, Bettina. "Sociology of Regulation." In *Research Handbook on the Sociology of Law*, edited by Jiří Přibáň, 93–108. Cheltenham: Edward Elgar, 2020.

Lange, Donald, Peggy Lee, and Ye Dai, "Organizational Reputation: A Review." *Journal of Management* 37, no. 1 (2011): 1347–59.

Larcker, David F., Brian Tayan, and Stephen A. Miles. "Protests from Within: Engaging with Employee Activists." Harvard Law School Forum on Corporate Governance, March 24, 2021. https://corpgov.law.harvard.edu/2021/03/24/protests-from-within-engaging-with-employee-activists/.

Lee, Allison Herren. "Regulation S-K and ESG Disclosures: An Unsustainable Silence." SEC Press Release, August 26, 2020. www.sec.gov/news/public-statement/lee-regulation-s-k-2020-08-26.

Lewis, Marianna O., ed. *The Foundation Directory*. 3rd ed. New York: Russell Sage Foundation, 1967.

Li, Fei, Chris K. Y. Lo, and Christopher S. Tang. "Will Diversity Equity and Inclusion Commitment Improve Manufacturing Firms' Performance? A Signaling Theory Perspective on DEI Announcements." SSRN website, December 15, 2022. https://ssrn.com/abstract=4318187.

Lien, Ann. "An Oil Giant Is No Match for Resistance and Resilience in Richmond, California." NRDC website, May 7, 2021. www.nrdc.org/stories/oil-giant-no-match-resistance-and-resilience-richmond-california.

Liket, Kellie, and Karen Maas. "Strategic Philanthropy: Corporate Measurement of Philanthropic Impacts as a Requirement for a 'Happy Marriage' of Business and Society." *Business & Society* 55, no. 6 (2016): 889–921.

Lim, Terence. *Measuring the Value of Corporate Philanthropy: Social Impact, Business Benefits, and Investor Returns*. New York: Committee Encouraging Corporate Philanthropy, 2010.

Lin, Tom C. W. *The Capitalist and the Activist: Corporate Social Activism and the New Business of Change*. California: Berrett-Koehler, 2022.

Logan, Nneka. "Corporate Personhood and the Corporate Responsibility to Race." *Journal of Business Ethics* 154, no. 4 (2019): 977–88.

Logsdon, J. M., M. Reiner, and L. Burke. "Corporate Philanthropy: Strategic Responses to the Firm's Stakeholders." *Nonprofit and Voluntary Sector Quarterly* 19, no. 2 (1990): 93–109.

Loughran, Tim, and Bill McDonald. "The Use of EDGAR Filings by Investors." *Journal of Behavioral Finance* 18 (2017): 231–48.

Love, Geoffrey E., and Matthew Kraatz. "Character, Conformity, or the Bottom Line? How and Why Downsizing Affected Corporate Reputation." *Academy of Management Journal* 52 (2009): 314–35.

Love, Katy, and Jody Myrum. "Practicing Participatory Philanthropy: Five Key Findings" *Nonprofit Quarterly*, October 10, 2023. https://nonprofitquarterly.org/practicing-participatory-philanthropy-five-key-findings/.

Lund, Dorothy S., and Elizabeth Pollman. "The Corporate Governance Machine." *Columbia Law Review* 121, no. 8 (2021): 2563–634.

Lyon, Thomas P., and William Mandelkorn. "Measuring Corporate Political Responsibility." In *Corporate Political Responsibility*, edited by Thomas P. Lyon, 62–97. Cambridge: Cambridge University Press, 2023.

MacKinnon, Catharine A. *Only Words*. Cambridge, MA: Harvard University Press, 1993.

MacLaury, Judson. "President Kennedy's E.O. 10925: Seedbed of Affirmative Action." *Federal History* 48 (2010): 42–57.

MacLean, Nancy. *Freedom is Not Enough: The Opening of the American Workplace*. Cambridge, MA: Harvard University Press, 2008.

Mahoney, Paul G. "The Exchange as Regulator." *Virginia Law Review* 83, no. 7 (1997): 1453–500.

Martinez, Veronica Root, and Gina-Gail S. Fletcher. "Equality Metrics." *Yale Law Journal Forum* 130 (2021): 869–98.

Mattison, E. G. *Implementing Plans for Progress: A Selection of Resumes of Experiences of Plans for Progress Companies in Implementing Their Programs – Intended for Use by Other Interested Plans for Progress Companies*. Advisory Council on Plans for Progress, and President's Committee on Equal Opportunity Employment. Washington, DC: Advisory Council on Plans for Progress, 1964.

Matusow, Allen J. *The Unraveling of America: A History of Liberalism in the 1960s*. Athens: University of Georgia Press, 1984.

McConnell-Ginet, Sally. *Words Matter: Meaning and Power*. Cambridge: Cambridge University Press, 2020.

McDonnell, Mary-Hunter, and Brayden King. "Keeping up Appearances: Reputational Threat and Impression Management after Social Movement Boycotts." *Administrative Science Quarterly* 58, no. 3 (2013): 387–419.

Mikati, Ihab, Adam F. Benson, Thomas J. Luben, Jason D. Sacks, and Jennifer Richmond-Bryant. "Disparities in Distribution of Particulate Matter Emission Sources by Race and Poverty Status." *American Journal of Public Health* 108 (2018): 480–85.

Milkis, Sidney, and Katherine Rader. "The March on Washington Movement, the Fair Employment Practices Committee, and the Long Quest for Racial Justice." *Studies in American Political Development* 38, no. 1 (2023): 16–35.

Miller, Toyah, and Triana María Del Carmen. "Demographic Diversity in the Boardroom: Mediators of the Board Diversity–Firm Performance Relationship." *Journal of Management Studies* 46 (2009): 755–86.

Moote, Kilian, and Amanda Buthe. "Early Season Review: 2024 US AGM." Harvard Law School Forum on Corporate Governance, June 13, 2024. https://corpgov.law.harvard.edu/2024/06/16/early-season-review-2024-us-agm/.

Morris, Aldon D. *The Origins of the Civil Rights Movement: Black Communities Organizing for Change*. New York: Free Press, 1984.

Muirhead, Russell, and Nancy L. Rosenblum. *Ungoverning: The Attack on the Administrative State and the Politics of Chaos*. Princeton, NJ: Princeton University Press, 2024.

Murray, Conor, and Molly Bohannon. "MLB Removes References to Diversity from Careers Website: Here Are All the Companies Rolling Back DEI Programs," *Forbes*, March 22, 2025. www.forbes.com/sites/conormurray/2025/03/22/mlb-removes-references-to-diversity-from-careers-website-here-are-all-the-companies-rolling-back-dei-programs/.

Naciti, Valeria, Fabrizio Cesaroni, and Luisa Pulejo. "Corporate Governance and Sustainability: A Review of the Existing Literature." *Journal of Management and Governance* 1 (2021): 1–20.

Nasdaq. "Nasdaq to Advance Diversity through New Proposed Listing Requirements." Nasdaq website, December 1, 2020. www.nasdaq.com/press-release/nasdaq-to-advance-diversity-through-new-proposed-listing-requirements-2020-12-01.

Nathan, Richard P. *Jobs & Civil Rights: The Role of the Federal Government in Promoting Equal Opportunity in Employment and Training*. Brookings Institute, Clearinghouse Publication No. 16, April 1969. https://files.eric.ed.gov/fulltext/ED039338.pdf.

National Industrial Conference Board. *Company Experience with Negro Employment*. Vol. 1. New York: National Industrial Conference Board, 1966.

Nelson, Ralph L. "Company-Sponsored Foundations." In *Economic Factors in the Growth of Corporation Giving*. New York: National Bureau of Economic Research, 1970.

Nelson, Ralph L. "Economic Analysis of Corporate Giving." In *Economic Factors in the Growth of Corporation Giving*. New York: National Bureau of Economic Research, 1970.

Nevin-Gattle, Kim. "Predicting the Philanthropic Response of Corporations: Lessons from History." *Business Horizons* 39, no. 3 (1996): 15–22.

Nicome, Anthony, Philip M. Alberti, and Carla S. Alvarado, AAMC, Center for Health Justice, June 25, 2024. www.aamchealthjustice.org/news/polling/down-to-earth.

Ninova-Solovykh, Neda. "Employee Activism: When Employees Speak Out Publicly against Their Employer." In *Advances in Public Relations and Communication Management: (Re)discovering the Human Element in Public Relations and Communication Management in Unpredictable Times*, edited by N. Rodríguez-Salcedo, Á. Moreno, S. Einwiller, and M. Recalde, 139–60. Vol. 6. Leeds: Emerald, 2023.

Nili, Yaron. "Board Gatekeepers." *Emory Law Journal* 72, no. 1 (2022): 91–161.

Nixon, Richard. "Statement on the Merger of the National Alliance of Businessmen and Plans for Progress, June 13, 1969." The American Presidency Project website, www.presidency.ucsb.edu/node/239441.

Odell, Francesca, Victor Hou, and James Langston. "3 Cases Spotlight Shareholder Interest in Public Co. Diversity." Law 360 website, August 4, 2020. www.law360.com/employment-authority/articles/1296071/3-cases-spotlight-shareholder-interest-in-public-co-diversity.

Odell, Francesca, Jennifer Kennedy Park, and Charity E. Lee. "How Boards Should Be Thinking about the Supreme Court's SFFA Affirmative Action Decision." Harvard Law School Forum on Corporate Governance, February 14, 2024. https://corpgov.law.harvard.edu/2024/02/14/how-boards-should-be-thinking-about-the-supreme-courts-sffa-affirmative-action-decision/.

Oranburg, Seth C. "Social Media Activism." In *A History of Financial Technology and Regulation: From American Incorporation to Cryptocurrency and Crowdfunding*, 96–111. Cambridge: Cambridge University Press, 2022.

Parella, Kishanthi. "Reputational Regulation." *Duke Law Journal* 67, no. 5 (2018): 907–80.

Park, James J. "The SEC as an Entrepreneurial Enforcer." *Northwestern Law Review* (2024): 689–746.
Parthiban, David, Matt Bloom, and Amy J. Hillman. "Investor Activism, Managerial Responsiveness, and Corporate Social Performance." *Strategic Management Journal* 28, no. 1 (2006): 91–100.
Patton, Randall L. *Lockheed, Atlanta, and the Struggle for Racial Integration*. Athens: University of Georgia Press, 2019.
Payton, Robert L., and Michael P. Moody. *Understanding Philanthropy: Its Meaning and Mission*. Philanthropy and Nonprofit Studies. Bloomington: Indiana University Press, 2008.
Perry, Andre M., Hannah Stephens, and Manann Donoghoe. "Black Wealth Is Increasing, But So Is the Racial Wealth Gap." Brookings website, January 9, 2024. www.brookings.edu/articles/black-wealth-is-increasing-but-so-is-the-racial-wealth-gap/.
Petrick, Joseph A., Robert F. Scherer, James D. Brodzinski, John F. Quinn, and M. Fall Ainina. "Global Leadership Skills and Reputational Capital: Intangible Resources for Sustainable Competitive Advantage." *Academy of Management Perspectives* 13, no. 1 (1999): 58–69.
Pinilla, Marcela, and Nandini Hampole. "Investors Are Committing to Action on Diversity. Now What?" BSR website, October 7, 2020. www.bsr.org/en/blog/investors-are-committing-to-action-on-diversity-now-what.
Pollman, Elizabeth. "The Origins and Consequences of the ESG Moniker." University of Pennsylvania, Carey Law School, Institute of Law and Economics, Research Paper No. 22–23. May 2022. www.ecgi.global/sites/default/files/Paper:%20Elizabeth%20Pollman.pdf.
Pollman, Elizabeth. "The Making and Meaning of ESG." *Harvard Business Law Review* 14 (2024): 403–53. https://ssrn.com/abstract=4219857.
Porter, Michael E., and Mark R. Kramer. "The Competitive Advantage of Corporate Philanthropy." *Harvard Business Review* 80, no. 12 (2002): 56–9.
President's Committee on Equal Employment Opportunity. *Report to the President by the President's Committee on Equal Employment Opportunity*. Washington, DC, 1963. John F. Kennedy Presidential Library and Museum website. www.jfklibrary.org/asset-viewer/archives/bmpp-034-002#?image_identifier=BMPP-034-002-p0001.
Project 2025 Presidential Transition Project. *Mandate for Leadership the Conservative Promise*. Heritage Foundation (Paul Dans and Steven Groves, eds., 2023).
Rana, Shruti. "Philanthropic Innovation and Creative Capitalism: A Historical and Comparative Perspective on Social Entrepreneurship and Corporate Social Responsibility." *Alabama Law Review* 64 (2013): 1121–74.
Reed, Merl Elwyn. *Seedtime for the Modern Civil Rights Movement: The President's Committee on Fair Employment Practice, 1941–1946*. Baton Rouge: Louisiana State University Press, 1991.
Reed, Susan E. *The Diversity Index: The Alarming Truth about Diversity in Corporate America … and What Can be Done about It*. Seattle: Amazon Publishing, 2011.
Reitz, Megan, and John Higgins. "Leading in an Age of Employee Activism." *MIT Sloan Management Review*, January 19, 2022. https://sloanreview.mit.edu/article/leading-in-an-age-of-employee-activism/.
Reagan, Ronald. "Remarks on Private Sector Initiatives at a White House Luncheon for National Religious Leaders." April 13, 1982. Reagan Library website. www.reaganlibrary.gov/archives/speech/remarks-private-sector-initiatives-white-house-luncheon-national-religious-leaders.
Rutherglen, George. "The Improbable History of Section 1981: Clio Still Bemused and Confused." *Supreme Court Review* 2003 (2003): 303–55. www.jstor.org/stable/3536956.

Saiia, David H., Archie B. Carroll, and Ann K. Buchholtz. "Philanthropy as Strategy When Corporate Charity 'Begins at Home.'" *Business and Society* 42, no. 2 (2003): 169–201.

Sanderson, Laura, and Sarah Galloway. "Activating Sustainability in the Boardroom." Harvard Law School Forum on Corporate Governance, January 4, 2023. https://corpgov.law.harvard.edu/2023/01/04/activating-sustainability-in-the-boardroom/.

Scanlan, Padraic X. *Slave Empire: How Slavery Built Modern Britain*. London: Robinson, 2020.

Schickler, Eric. *Racial Realignment: The Transformation of American Liberalism, 1932–1965*. Princeton: Princeton University Press, 2018.

Schohl, Lisa. "How to Create a Culture of Inclusive Fundraising." *Chronicle of Philanthropy*, March 10, 2021. www.philanthropy.com/article/how-to-create-a-culture-of-inclusive-fundraising.

Scully, Maureen, and Amy Segal. *Passion with an Umbrella: Grassroots Activists in the Workplace*. Vol. 19. Research in the Sociology of Organizations. Stamford, CT: JAI Press, 2002.

Shaeffer, Ruth G. *Nondiscrimination in Employment: Changing Perspectives, 1963–1972*. New York: Conference Board, 1973.

Shanor, Amanda, and Sarah E. Light. "Greenwashing and the First Amendment." *Columbia Law Review* 122 (2022): 2033–118.

Sharfman, Mark. "Changing Institutional Rules: The Evolution of Corporate Philanthropy, 1883–1953." *Business and Society* 33 (1994): 236–69.

Sharma, Amalesh, Aditya Christopher Moses, Sourav Bikash Borah, and Anirban Adhikary. "Investigating the Impact of Workforce Racial Diversity on the Organizational Corporate Social Responsibility Performance: An Institutional Logics Perspective." *Journal of Business Research* 107 (2020): 138–52.

Shiao, Jiannbin Lee. *Identifying Talent, Institutionalizing Diversity: Race and Philanthropy in Post-Civil Rights America*. Durham, NC: Duke University Press, 2005.

Silberman, Charles E. "The Businessman and the Negro." *Management Review* 52 (1963): 17–18.

Smith, Craig. "The New Corporate Philanthropy." *Harvard Business Review* 72, no. 3 (1994): 105–14.

Smith, Hayden W. "Panel One: An Introduction to Corporate Philanthropy: History, Practice, and Regulation: If Not Corporate Philanthropy, Then What." *New York Law School Law Review* 41 (1997): 757–70.

Southern Regional Council. *Special Report, Plans for Progress: Atlanta Survey*. Atlanta: Southern Regional Council, 1963.

Southworth, Ann. *Lawyers of the Right: Professionalizing the Conservative Coalition*. Chicago: University of Chicago Press, 2008.

Sovern, Michael I. *Legal Restraints on Racial Discrimination in Employment*. New York: Twentieth-Century Fund, 1966.

Tesler, Michael. *Post-Racial or Most-Racial?: Race and Politics in the Obama Era*. Chicago: University of Chicago Press, 2016.

The Faculty of the Lilly Family School of Philanthropy. "Inclusive Philanthropy." *Stanford Social Innovation Review*, September 2020. https://ssir.org/articles/entry/inclusive_philanthropy.

"The Skilled Labor Shortage. It's Amazing How Fast You Could Change It." *Business Management* 31, no. 6 (1967).

Thieblot, Armand J. *The Negro in the Banking Industry*. Philadelphia: University of Pennsylvania Press, 1970.

Thomas, David A., and John J. Gabarro. *Breaking Through: The Making of Minority Executives in Corporate America*. Boston, MA: Harvard Business School Press, 1999.

Thompson, Robert B. "The Power of Shareholders in the United States." In *Research Handbook on Shareholder Power*, edited by Jennifer G. Hill and Randall S. Thomas, 441–47. Cheltenham: Edward Elgar, 2015.

Tiwari, Umesh Chandra. "DEI Metrics in Executive Compensation." Harvard Law School Forum on Corporate Governance, June 26, 2024. https://corpgov.law.harvard.edu/2024/06/26/dei-metrics-in-executive-compensation/.

Tomaskovic-Devey, Donald T., Jorge Quesada Velazco, and Kevin L. Young. "We Analysed Racial Justice Statements from the 500 Largest US Companies and Found That DEI Officials Really Did Have an Influence," *The Conversation*, March 28, 2025.

Tomlin, Kasaundra M. "Assessing the Efficacy of Consumer Boycotts of U.S. Target Firms: A Shareholder Wealth Analysis." *Southern Economic Journal* 86, no. 2 (2019): 503–29.

US Equal Employment Opportunity Commission (EEOC). "EEO-1 Component 1 Data Collection Instruction Booklet 2023." EEOC website. https://perma.cc/7HTF-NECB.

US Equal Employment Opportunity Commission (EEOC). "EEO-1 Data Collection." EEOC website. https://perma.cc/Y5Q7-QQRB US Securities and Exchange Commission (SEC), Investor Advisory Committee. "Recommendation of the SEC Investor Advisory Committee's Investor-as-Owner Subcommittee regarding Human Capital Management Disclosure." SEC website, September 21, 2023. www.sec.gov/files/spotlight/iac/20230921-recommendation-regarding-hcm.pdf.

US Securities and Exchange Commission (SEC). Office of Investor Education and Advocacy. "Investor Bulletin: How to Read a 10-K." SEC website, originally published September 2011. www.sec.gov/files/reada10k.pdf.

US Securities and Exchange Commission (SEC). "Search Filings." SEC website. www.sec.gov/edgar/search-and-access.

US Securities and Exchange Commission (SEC). "Statutes and Regulations." SEC website. www.sec.gov/about/about-securities-laws#:~:text=SRO%20proposed%20rules%20are%20subject,they%20can%20go%20into%20effect.

US Securities and Exchange Commission (SEC). "Investor Alerts and Bulletins, Updated Investor Alert: Social Media and Investing – Stock Rumors." SEC website, November 5, 2015. www.sec.gov/oiea/investor-alerts-bulletins/ia-rumors.

US Securities and Exchange Commission (SEC). *The Enhancement and Standardization of Climate-Related Disclosures for Investors*. RIN 3235-AM87, SEC Release Nos. 33-11042, 34-94478. SEC website, March 21, 2022. www.sec.gov/rules-regulations/2024/03/s7-10-22.

US Securities and Exchange Commission (SEC). "SEC Charges Brazilian Mining Company with Misleading Investors about Safety Prior to Deadly Dam Collapse." SEC press release, April 28, 2022. www.sec.gov/news/press-release/2022-72.

US Securities and Exchange Commission (SEC). "SEC Charges BNY Mellon Investment Adviser for Misstatements and Omissions Concerning ESG Considerations." SEC press release, May 23, 2022. www.sec.gov/news/press-release/2022-86.

US Securities and Exchange Commission (SEC). *Enhanced Disclosures by Certain Investment Advisers and Investment Companies about Environmental, Social, and Governance Investment Practices*. RIN: 3235-AM96, SEC Release No. 33-11068. SEC website, May 25, 2022. www.sec.gov/rules-regulations/2022/10/s7-17-22.

US Securities and Exchange Commission (SEC). "SEC Announces Enforcement Results for Fiscal Year 2023." SEC website, November 14, 2023. www.sec.gov/news/press-release/2023-234.

US Securities and Exchange Commission (SEC). Form 19b-4, January 16, 2025. https://listingcenter.nasdaq.com/assets/rulebook/nasdaq/filings/SR-NASDAQ-2025-007.pdf.

Vaidyanathan, Brandon. "Corporate Giving: A Literature Review." Center for the Study of Religion and Society, University of Notre Dame, Working Paper, 2008.

Watkins, Sylvestre C. *Negro Heritage*. Reston, VA: Watkins, 1963.
Webb, Natalie J. "Tax and Government Policy Implications for Corporate Foundation Giving." *Nonprofit and Voluntary Sector Quarterly* 23, no. 1 (1994): 41–67.
Weinreb Group. "The Chief Sustainability Officer 10 Years Later: The rise of ESG in the C-suite." Weinreb Group Report, 2021. https://weinrebgroup.com/wp-content/uploads/2021/05/Weinreb-Group-Sustainability-and-ESG-Recruiting-The-Chief-Sustainability-Officer-10-years-Later-The-Rise-of-ESG-in-the-C-Suite-2021-Report.pdf.
Weiss, Robert S. *Learning from Strangers: The Art and Method of Qualitative Interview Studies*. 1st Free Press paperback ed. New York: Free Press, 1995.
Wells, Harwell. "Shareholder Power in America, 1800–2000: A Short History." In *Research Handbook on Shareholder Power*, edited by Jennifer G. Hill and Randall S. Thomas, 13–30. Cheltenham: Edward Elgar, 2015.
Wilkerson, Isabel. *The Warmth of Other Suns: The Epic Story of America's Great Migration*. 1st ed. New York: Vintage, 2010.
Wilkins, David B., and Mitu G. Gulati. "Why Are There So Few Black Lawyers in Corporate Law Firms – An Institutional Analysis." *California Law Review* 84, no. 3 (1996): 493–626.
Wilks, Stephen. *The Political Power of the Business Corporation*. Cheltenham: Edward Elgar Publishing, 2013.
Williams, Bärí A. "How Companies Use 'Cognitive Diversity' as an Excuse to Keep Hiring White Men, Fast Company." *Fast Company*, May 16, 2024. www.fastcompany.com/90856183/30-ai-tools-you-can-try-for-free.
Williams, Eric Eustace, William A. Darity Jr., and Colin A. Palmer. *Capitalism & Slavery*. 3rd ed. Chapel Hill: University of North Carolina Press, 2021.
Woodson, Kevin. *The Black Ceiling: How Race Still Matters in the Elite Workplace*. Chicago: University of Chicago Press, 2023.
Wright, Gavin. *Sharing the Prize: The Economics of the Civil Rights Revolution in the American South*. Cambridge, MA: Harvard University Press, 2018.
Young, Black & Giving Back Institute. *Grassroots, Black & Giving: How Philanthropy Can Better Support Black-led and Black-Benefiting Nonprofits*. Young, Black & Giving Institute, Research Report, 2023. www.youngblackgivingback.org/research/.
Young, Iris Marion. "Five Faces of Oppression." In *Justice and the Politics of Difference*. Princeton, NJ: Princeton University Press, 2011.
Zettler, Ingo. "A Glimpse into Prosociality at Work." *Current Opinion in Psychology* 44 (2022): 140–45.

ARCHIVAL COLLECTIONS

A. Philip Randolph Papers. Library of Congress.
Harris Wofford Files. John F. Kennedy Presidential Library. Newspaper Clippings Files, 1948–1950. National Archives.
Letters on Final Report, Record Group 220: Records of Temporary Committees, Commissions, and Boards. National Archives.
Randolph, Philip A. Philip A. Randolph to Fiorella H. LaGuardia, the Mayor of New York City, June 5, 1941. Office of Civilian Defense. National Archives, Identifier 7859715.
Roosevelt, Eleanor. Unsigned Letter Eleanor Roosevelt to Philip A. Randolph from Campobello Island. June 26, 1941. Franklin D. Roosevelt Presidential Library & Museum.
Troutman, Robert, Jr. Oral history interview. February 2, 1965. Transcript. JFK Presidential Library.

CASES AND BRIEFS

A. P. Smith Mfg. Co. v. Barlow, 98 A.2d 581 (1953).
Alliance for Fair Board Recruitment v. SEC, 85 F.4th 226 (5th Cir. 2023).
American Alliance for Equal Rights v. Fearless Fund, No. 1:23 CV 3424-TWT (N.D. Ga. 2023).
Amicus Brief of the States of Arizona, et al. in Support of Petitioner National Center for Public Policy Research, Alliance for Fair Board Recruitment v. SEC, 85 F.4th 226 (5th Cir. 2023) (No. 34-92590).
Appeal from the United States District Court for the Northern District of Georgia, American Alliance for Equal Rights v. Fearless Fund, No. 23-13138, (11th Circuit, Sep. 30, 2023).
Bolduc v. Amazon, No. 4:22-cv-00615 (E.D. Tex. July 20, 2022).
Brown v. Board of Education, 347 U.S. 483 (1954).
City of Oakland v. BP p.l.c. et al., No. 3:17-cv-6011, Dkt. 199 ¶ 135 (N.D. Cal. Apr. 3, 2018).
Complaint, American Alliance for Equal Rights v. Fearless Fund (N.D. Ga. Aug. 2, 2023).
Corner Post, Inc. v. Board of Governors of the Federal Reserve System, 144 S. Ct. 2440 (2024).
Crest v. Padilla, No. 19STCV27561, 2022 WL 1565613 (Cal. Super. Ct. May 13, 2022).
Davis v. Old Colony Railroad Company, 131 Mass. 258 (June 28, 1881).
Defendant Starbucks Corporation Motion to Dismiss Complaint, The Starbucks Case, No. 2:22-cv-00267-SAB (E.D. Wash. May 19, 2023), 2023 WL 6962044, at *3.
Do No Harm v. Pfizer, Inc., 646 F. Supp. 3d 490 (S.D.N.Y. 2022).
Exxon Mobil Corporation v. Arjuna Capital, LLC et al Exxon Mobil Corporation v. Arjuna Capital, LLC et al, Docket No. 4:24-cv-00069 (N.D. Tex. Jan. 21, 2024).
Loper Bright Enterprises v. Raimondo, 144 S. Ct. 2244 (2024).
National Center for Public Policy Research. v. Schultz (The Starbucks Case), No. 2:22-cv-00267-SAB, 2023 WL 5945958 (E.D. Wash. Sept. 11, 2023).
Nike, Inc. v. Kasky, 539 U.S. 654 (2003).
SEC v. Jarkesy, 144 S. Ct. 2117 (2024).
State of Delaware v. BP Am. Inc. et al., No. N20C-09-097-AML CCLD, Compl. ¶ 239 (Del. Super. Ct. Sept. 10, 2020).

COMPANY/ORGANIZATION REPORTS

Amazon. *Sustainability Report: Further and Faster, Together.* 2020.
Amazon. *Staying the Course on Our Commitment to Sustainability.* 2020.
Ameren. *Our Sustainability Story: Customers at the Center, Ameren Sustainability Report.* 2020.
Ameren. *Leading the Way to a Sustainable Energy Future Environmental, Social & Governance (ESG).* 2021.
Bank of America Corporation. *2021 Proxy Statement.* 2021.
BNY Mellon. *2020 Enterprise ESG Report.* 2020.
Chevron. *Corporate Sustainability Report.* 2020.
Chevron. *Corporate Sustainability Report.* 2021.
Delaware Division of Corporations. *Annual Report.* 2022.
Devon Energy. *Sustainability Report,* 2020.
Domino's Pizza. *Stewardship Report.* 2021.
Edelman. *Trust Barometer Special Report: Business and Racial Justice.* 2024.

Estée Lauder Companies Incorporated. *Beauty Inspired, Values Driven, Social Impact and Sustainability Report*. 2021.
Etsy. *Annual 10-K Report*. 2021.
Federal Security Agency. *Second Annual Report*. 1941.
Facebook. *Facebook's Civil Rights Audit – Final Report*. 2020.
Gibson Dunn. *Shareholder Proposal Developments During the 2020 Proxy Season*. 2020.
Grainger. *CSR Report*. 2017.
Hartford. *2020 Sustainability Highlight Report*. 2020.
Honeywell. *Corporate Citizenship Report*. 2020.
ITW. *Corporate Social Responsibility Report*. 2020.
Lincoln Financial Group. *CSR Report*. 2020.
Lockheed. *Twenty-Ninth Annual Report*. December 25, 1960.
Lockheed. *Thirtieth Annual Report*. December 31, 1961.
McDonald's Corporation. *2023 Notice of Annual Shareholders' Meeting and Proxy Statement*. 2023.
McDonald's Corporation. *2024 Notice of Annual Shareholders' Meeting and Proxy Statement*. 2024.
McDonald's Corporation. *2025 Notice of Annual Shareholders' Meeting and Proxy Statement*. 2025.
Micron. *Fast Forward, Sustainability Report*. 2021.
Moody's. *Diversity, Equity, and Inclusion Report*. 2020.
Neiman Marcus Group. *Our Journey to Revolutionize Impact, 2021 ESG Report*. 2021.
Nielsen. *Interim Responsibility Update*. 2021.
Pactiv Evergreen Incorporated. *Environmental, Social & Governance Update*. 2021.
P&G. *2020 Citizenship Report*. 2020.
Philip Morris Incorporated. *1968 Annual Report*. 1968.
Prudential Financial Incorporated. *Environmental, Social and Governance Summary Report*. 2021.
Red Ventures. *2020–2021 Annual Diversity, Equity, and Inclusion Progress Report*. 2021.
Robert Half. *Corporate Citizenship Report*. 2019.
Robert Half. *Leading with Integrity, Environmental, Social and Governance Report*. 2021.
Rockwell Automation. *Corporate Responsibility Report*. 2016.
Semler Brossy. *S&P 500, ESG + Incentives Report*. 2022.
Sonos. *Listen Better Report, Environmental, Social and Governance at Sonos*. 2021.
Southwest Airlines. *One Report*. 2020.
Starbucks Corporation. *2020 Global Environmental & Social Impact Report*. 2020.
Starbucks Corporation. *2020 Notice of Annual Meeting of Shareholders and Proxy Statement*. 2020.
State Street. *2020 ESG Report*. 2020.
Sunrun. *Impact Report*. 2020.
Sysco. *2021 Corporate Social Responsibility Report*. 2021.
Target. *2020 Corporate Social Responsibility Report*. 2020.
Time Warner. *CSR Report*. 2017.
Truist. *Corporate Social Responsibility*. 2019.
US Securities and Exchange Commission. *Chevron Corporation Form 8-K*. 2022.
VMware. *Resilience, Global Impact Report*. 2020.
Wells Fargo. *Social Impact and Sustainability Highlights*. 2021.
Western Electric. *1971 Annual Report*. 1971.

Bibliography

EXECUTIVE ORDERS

"Executive Order 8801 of June 24, 1941, Exemption of Archie W. Davis from Compulsory Retirement for Age." *Code of Federal Regulations*, title 3 (1941).

"Executive Order 8802 of June 25, 1941, Reaffirming Policy of Full Participation in the Defense Program by All Persons, Regardless of Race, Creed, Color, or National Origin, and Directing Certain Action in Furtherance of Said Policy." *Code of Federal Regulations*, title 3 (1941).

"Executive Order 9808 of December 5, 1946, Establishing the President's Committee on Civil Rights." National Archives. Harry S. Truman Library Museum.

"Executive Order 9981 of July 6, 1948, Establishing the President's Committee on Equality of Treatment and Opportunity in the Armed Services." *Code of Federal Regulations*, title 32 (1948).

"Executive Order 10925 of March 6, 1961, Establishing the President's Committee on Equal Employment Opportunity." *Code of Federal Regulations*, title 41 (1961).

"Executive Order 12329 of October 14, 1981, President's Task Force on Private Sector Initiatives." *Code of Federal Regulations*, title 5 (1981).

LEGISLATIVE MATERIALS

US Congress, House. *Constitutional Authority Statement*, 118th Cong., 1st sess. Congressional Record 167 (February 18, 2021): H 535.

US Congress, House. Corporate Governance Improvement and Investor Protection Act, HR 1187, 117th Cong. Passed by House. June 16, 2021.

STATUTES & REGULATIONS

California Corporations Code § 301.4(e)(1) (West 2021).
California Corporations Code § 301.3(a)–(b) (West 2021).
Canada Business Corporation Act amendment, R.S.C., 1985, c. C-44 (2020).
Del. Code Ann. tit. 8, § 141(a) (2014).
Del. Code tit. 8 § 122 (2024).
Dodd-Frank Act, Public Law 203, U.S. Statutes at Large 124 (2010).
Economic Opportunity Act, Pub. L. No. 88-452, 78 Stat. 508 (1964).
Fed. R. Civ. P. 23.1(a) (2023).
Model Bus. Corp. Act Ann. § 8.01 annot. (2013).
Notice of Filing of Proposed Rule Change to Adopt Listing Rules Related to Board Diversity, Exchange Act Release No. 90547, 2020 WL 7226158 (December 4, 2020).
NY BSC § 202 (2021).
RCW 23B.08.120 (2020).
Rule 506 of Regulation D, 17 C.F.R. § 230.506 (1933).
Securities Act of 1933, Pub. L. No. 73-22, 48 Stat. 74 (1933).
Securities Exchange Act of 1934, Pub. L. No. 73-291, 48 Stat. 881 (codified as amended at 15 U.S.C. § 77g (1984)).
Senate Bill 261, Chapter 383 (Cal 2023).
Taxpayer Certainty and Disaster Tax Relief Act of 2020, Pub. L. No. 116-260, § 301, 134 Stat. 1182 (2020).
Title VII of the Civil Rights Act, 42 U.S.C. §§ 2000e–2000e17 (1964) (as amended).

U.S. President. Proposed Regulation, "Plans for Progress Program, 1965." *Federal Register* 30, no. 183 (September 22, 1965): Section 4-12.5119-1(a).

42 U.S.C. § 1981 (1866).

15 U.S.C. § 78s(b)(1) (1934).

26 U.S.C. § 170(c) (1954).

15 U.S.C. § 78n(a) (2000).

15 U.S.C. § 77q(a) (2006).

15 U.S.C. § 78j(b) (2006).

17 C.F.R. § 229.407(c)(2)(vi) (2009).

17 C.F.R. § 240.10b-5 (2010).

17 C.F.R. § 240.14a-8 (2012).

17 C.F.R. § 229.101 (2020) [Release Nos. 33-10668; 34-86614, File No. S7-11-19].

41 C.F.R. § 60-1.7(a)(4) (2020).

17 C.F.R. § 275, File No. S7-03-22 (2023).

Index

10-K reports, 56, 57, 71, 73

AAER. *See* American Alliance for Equal Rights (AAER)
AB (Assembly Bill) 979, 142
Administrative Procedure Act, 139
advocacy groups, 149
ALEC. *See* American Legislative Exchange Council (ALEC)
Allen, Ivan, Jr., 25
Alliance for Fair Board Recruitment v. SEC, 115–16
Amazon, 1, 2, 48
   DEI statement, 4, 52–53
   general statements
      in 2019, 4, 52–53
      in 2020, 53
   low-wage Black employees, 2
   majority minority in 2024, 2
   philanthropy in 2021, 53–54
   race-conscious disclosures, 4–5
      in 2025, 5
      after 2020, 53–54
      for excusing from completing racial equity audit, 10–11, 64, 68
   racial equity audit, 2, 10–11, 64, 68–69
      no-action letter for shareholders' allegations for, 10, 11
      risk management and, 69–70
   racial targets in 2021, 54
Ameren Corporation, supplier diversity, 102
American Alliance for Equal Rights (AAER), 157–58
American Bar Association Committee on Business Corporations, 94
American Civil Rights Project, 115
American Legislative Exchange Council (ALEC), 149
American Motors, 43
Atlanta, 18, 39, 87, 88

Bank of New York (BNY), racial targets, 83
Banks, Patricia, 51, 92
Berle, Adolf A., Jr., 145
Berrey, Ellen, 6, 51
Black Codes, 130
Black Lives Matter, 1, 98, 149
Blackrock, 124
Blum, Edward, 157
boycotting, 147
Brown v. Board of Education, 23
buycotting, 147

Canada Business Corporations Act, 138
capitalism, 6, 13, 104–5, 158
Chevron, 67
   CRP, 107
   EEO-1, 53
   philanthropy in 2021, 55
   public statements in 2019, 53
   race-conscious disclosures
      after 2020, 54–55
      for excusing from completing racial equity audit, 64
   racial equity audit, 70
Civil Rights Act of 1866, 130
Civil Rights Act of 1964, 96
   Title II, 41
   Title VII, 34, 37
civil rights audit/assessment. *See* racial equity audits
civil rights movement, 10, 20, 21, 23, 34–35, 39, 96
climate disclosures, mandatory, 138–39
closed-ended racial targets, 83–84
COFEP. *See* Committee on Fair Employment Practice (COFEP)
Color of Change, 149
Comcast Corporation, shareholder proposals of, 62

Committee on Equal Employment Opportunity, 7, 24. *See also* Plans for Progress (PFP) program
  complaints processing for recruitment, 30–32
  exceptional cases, 32
  Executive Order 10925 and, 28
  Lockheed's PFP program, 25–27, 28
  progress report from April 1961 to January 1962, 31, 33
Committee on Equality of Treatment and Opportunity in the Armed Forces. *See* Fahy Committee
Committee on Fair Employment Practice (COFEP). *See* Fair Employment Practice Committee (FEPC)
complete race-conscious retraction, 11, 16, 119, 123–26
  racial progress, constraining, 126
conservative backlash, 2, 55, 86, 102, 114, 127
conservative pushback, 9, 14, 16, 38, 64, 84, 102, 129, 158
consumer regulation, 147
corporate diversity, 3, 6–7, 12, 66, 86, 114
corporate giving, 94, 96
  strategic, 95
corporate governance, 13, 135
Corporate Governance Improvement and Investor Protection Act, 137
corporate governance machine, 135
corporate philanthropy, 92, 93, 104
  Amazon in 2021, 53–54
  charitable giving, 93, 94, 95, 96
  Chevron in 2021, 55
  corporate giving, 94, 96
  HBCUs' corporate funding, 96–97
  by private foundations, 96
  strategic, 93, 95–96
  United States, development in, 93–94
corporate racial philanthropy (CRP), 4, 8, 12, 15, 93, 96–97
  for Black-led nonprofit vs. white-led nonprofit organization, 97
  business transactions, focus on, 101–6
  Chevron, 107
  and constraining racial progress, 106–7
  CRP disclosures, 100
  CSR, 105
  decision-making, 106
  Gates' creative capitalism, 104–5
  internal initiatives, 100, 105
  Micron Technology's loan program for minority-owned business, 101
  nonprofit giving to racial equity causes, 100
  participatory philanthropy, 105, 107

  political donations, 107
  post-2020, 98–100
  pre-2020, 97–98
  prevalence in corporate disclosures of, to minority causes, 98–100
  recommendations for improving, 105–6
  Reiser and Dean on, 101
  Starbucks, 97
  supplier diversity, 102–4
  through third parties, 102
  Visa's Entrepreneurship Program, 102
  Wells Fargo, 102
corporate reputation, 4, 6–8, 14, 49, 126–29
  risk. *See* reputational risks
Corporate Social Responsibility (CSR), 105
Corporate Sustainability Due Diligence Directive (CSDDD/CS3D), 139
Corporate Sustainability Reporting Directive (CSRD), 138–39
Costco, 61
creative capitalism, 104–5
CRP. *See* corporate racial philanthropy (CRP)
CSDDD/CS3D. *See* Corporate Sustainability Due Diligence Directive (CSDDD/CS3D)
CSR. *See* Corporate Social Responsibility (CSR)
CSRD. *See* Corporate Sustainability Reporting Directive (CSRD)
C-Suite members, 88
Cutlip, Scott, 94

Dean, Steven, 95, 101
DEI. *See* diversity, equity, and inclusion (DEI)
Delaware, 98, 102, 143–44, 154
disclosure plus, 138
diversity, equity, and inclusion (DEI), xiv, 67, 84, 85, 89, 105, 117–19, 120, 122, 137
  Amazon, 4, 52–53
diversity disclosures, mandatory, 137–38
diversity fellowships, 103
Dobbin, Frank, 7

earnings calls, 116–17
Economic Opportunity Act (EOA) of 1964, 36
Edelman, Lauren, 6, 40, 51
EEO-1. *See* Employer Information Report (EEO-1)
EEOC. *See* Equal Employment Opportunity Commission (EEOC)
Eisenhower, Dwight D., 23
employee activism, 148
Employer Information Report (EEO-1), 53
employment discrimination (1940s–1950s), 21–23
Enhancement and Standardization of Climate-Related Disclosures for Investors, 138

Index

Environmental, Social and Governance (ESG) Disclosure Simplification Act, 52
environmental, social and governance (ESG) movement, 3, 17, 72, 105
EOA. *See* Economic Opportunity Act (EOA) of 1964
equal employment opportunity. *See* Plans for Progress (PFP) program
Equal Employment Opportunity Act of 1972, 37
Equal Employment Opportunity Commission (EEOC), 34, 37, 53
ESG disclosures, 103, 128
ESG movement. *See* environmental, social and governance (ESG) movement
European Union (EU), mandatory climate disclosure in, 138
   CSDDD/CS3D, 139
   CSRD, 138–39
Executive Order 8802, 22
Executive Order 9981, 23, 39
Executive Order 10925, 7, 24, 28
   provisions of, 28, 35

Facebook, racial equity audit of, 64
Fahy Committee, 23
Fair Employment Practice Committee (FEPC), 22, 23
Fairfax, Lisa, 66
Fearless Fund, 157, 158
federal government information-enforcing role, 139–40, 141
   FTC, 140
   monitoring role, 141
   SEC, 140–41
   setting up accountability mechanisms, 142
   sharing disclosures publicly, 141
   for state governments, 142–44
   tracking role, 141
Federal Trade Commission (FTC), 140
   enforcement action, 140
Federalist Society, 102
FEPC. *See* Fair Employment Practice Committee (FEPC)
First Amendment, 116, 140, 142, 158
Fletcher, Gina-Gail S., 97
Floyd's murder. *See* George Floyd's murder
Fraser, Nancy, 6
FTC. *See* Federal Trade Commission (FTC)

Gabarro, John, 36, 144
Gadinis, Stavros, 63
Gates, Bill, 104
gender diversity, 142–43
General Motors (Kansas), discrimination in, 10, 28

general statements, 4, 52, 89
   Amazon
      in 2019, 4, 52–53
      in 2020, 53
   Chevron in 2019, 53
   in mandatory reports, 56–57
   in voluntary reports, 55, 56
   of private companies, 58, 59
Gensler, Gary, 137
George Floyd's murder, 1, 4, 6, 18, 38, 85, 98, 100, 101, 116, 124, 126, 129, 137, 148
goals, corporate, 78, 79, 80, 84, 85
   publicly traded companies, 80
Goldberg, Authur, 31
Gulati, Mitu, 85

Hamermesh, Lawrence, 143
Hartford Prudential Financial, racial targets, 83
Heldman, Caroline, 147, 155
Holleman, Jerry R., 31
human capital disclosures, 137
hypocrisy, 66

Immergluck, Dan, 87
institutional investors, 60
institutional isomorphism, 6
institutional racism, 3, 53, 54, 66, 104, 124–25
institutional shareholders, 145

Jardina, Ashley, 113
Job Opportunities in Business Sector (JOBS) Program, 36, 37, 38
JOBS. *See* Job Opportunities in Business Sector (JOBS) Program
Johnson, Lyndon B., 25, 27, 35, 79
   Economic Opportunity Act (EOA) of 1964, 36
   Executive Order 11246, 35
   OFCC, 35, 37, 46, 47
   on PFP program progress, 33
   War on Poverty, 36
   NAB-JOBS program, 36
   OEO, 36

Kalmoe, Nathan, 113
Kennedy, John F., 15, 21, 23
   Committee on Equal Employment Opportunity. *See* Committee on Equal Employment Opportunity
   Executive Order 10925, 7, 24, 28
   provisions of, 28, 35
Koehn, Nancy, 96

Lee, Allison Herren, 137
Lewis, John, 158

Light, Sarah, 140
Lin, Tom C. W., 144
litigation risk, 65–66, 89, 128, 129
Lockheed Aircraft Corporation, 21
 C-141 contract, 25
 PFP program, 25–27, 28
 racial segregation in, 24–25
Logan, Nneka, 97
Lovelace, H. Timothy, Jr., 97
Lund, Dorothy, 135

MacLean, Nancy, 31
mandatory disclosures, 3, 55, 136
 in California, 142–43
 climate, 138–39
 diversity, 137–38
 general statements in, 56–57
March on Washington Movement (MOWM), 21–22
Mason, Lilliana, 113
McConnell-Ginet, Sally, 159
McDonald's, 62–63, 85
 incentive structures in, 85–86
 no-action letter request, 91
Means, Gardiner C., 145
Miazad, Amelia, 63
Micron Technology's CRP, 101
military industry, racial discrimination in
 FDR's intervention, 21–23
 Truman's intervention, 23
Minority Depository Institution (MDI), 101
Moody, Michael, 105
MOWM. *See* March on Washington Movement (MOWM)
Muirhead, Russell, 136
Musk, Elon, xiv

NAB. *See* National Alliance of Businessmen (NAB)
Nasdaq board diversity rule, 116, 137, 145
National Alliance of Businessmen (NAB), 36
 PFP program merging with, during Nixon administration, 37
National Center for Public Policy Research v. Schultz, 115
Negro March on Washington Committee, 22
Nike, Inc. v. Kasky, 153
Nixon, Richard, 35
 Business Roundtable, 79
 PFP program and NAB, merging of, 37
no-action letter, 10, 61–62, 91, 127, 163, 167
nondelegation doctrine, 139

Obama, Barack, 113
OEO. *See* Office of Economic Opportunity (OEO)

OFCC. *See* Office of Federal Contract Compliance (OFCC)
Office of Economic Opportunity (OEO), 36
Office of Federal Contract Compliance (OFCC), 35, 37, 46
 diversity programs, 47
open-ended racial targets, 84–85

Pactiv Evergreen, racial targets, 85
partial race-conscious retraction, 11, 16, 39, 119–23, 126
 racial progress, constraining, 126
participatory philanthropy, 105, 107
Patton, Randall, 14, 21
Payton, Robert, 105
PFP program. *See* Plans for Progress (PFP) program
philanthropy, 4, 8, 9, 12, 51, 52, 67, 98, 102, 103. *See also* corporate philanthropy; corporate racial philanthropy (CRP)
Time Warner, 124
Plans for Progress (PFP) program, 7–8, 10, 20, 21, 38, 96, 129, 136
 Certificates of Merit, 29
 civil rights movement and, 34–35
 Committee on Equal Employment Opportunity, 7, 24
 complaints processing for recruitment, 30–32
 exceptional cases, 32
 Executive Order 10925 and, 28
 with Lockheed during Kennedy administration, 25–27, 28
 progress report from April 1961 to January 1962, 31, 33
 companies failed to complying own plans, 35
 diffusion and publicizing of, 28–29
 failure of, 39–47
 and General Motors' refused to disclose information for discrimination, 10, 32–33
 Johnson and Nixon policies effect on, 35–37
 merging with NAB during Nixon administration, 37
 Michigan Bell Telephone Company, 45
 minority employees in PFP companies after Title VII, 34, 37
 plan template and components, 26, 29
 post-2020 image construction vs.
  differences, 39
  similarity, 38–39
 progress
  lacking in, 32–35
  in *Negro Heritage*, 33–34
  President Johnson about, 33
  signing ceremony for, 29, 30

Pollman, Elizabeth, 135
private companies, 5, 26, 49, 52
    racial targets in, 82
    voluntary reports with general statements, 58, 59
private equity industry, 157
Procter & Gamble (P&G), racial targets, 85
Project 2025, 114
proxy season, 75
proxy statements, 10, 60, 61
public companies, 49, 60
    racial targets in, 80, 81
        by racial or ethnic group, 80–81

race-conscious disclosures, 3–4, 5, 14, 48, 102, 106, 114, 118, 124, 125, 127
    after 2020, 53
        Amazon, 53–54
        Chevron, 54–55
    after 2020 vs. before 2020, 51
    before 2020, 52–53
    benefits of, 9
    construction phase, 114
    cycles of, 129
    evolution (before 2020–Present), 126
    partial, 39
    racial targets as, 88–89
    regulation. *See* regulation, disclosure
    retraction. *See* race-conscious retraction
    and risk management, 65–66
    to social and environments litigation, 7
    types of, 52. *See also* general statements; philanthropy; racial targets; statistics on racial composition
    weak regulation by SEC and Congress between 2009 and 2021, 51–52
    without acknowledging past racial inequality, 9
race-conscious image, 48, 114
race-conscious image construction, 12, 49–52, 114, 125, 126, 127, 129, 158
    PFP program vs. post-2020
        differences, 39
        similarity, 38–39
race-conscious retraction, 3, 5, 6, 9, 11–12, 14, 16, 38, 39, 64, 66, 67, 71, 114, 119, 120, 126, 128, 158
    Alliance for Fair Board Recruitment v. SEC, 115–16
    Axios, DEI in earnings calls in, 117, 118
    complete, 11, 16, 119, 123–26
    cycles of, 129
    evolution (before 2020–Present), 126
    legal landscape of, 114–16
    media and, 116–19

National Center for Public Policy Research v. Schultz, 115
    partial, 11, 16, 119–23, 126
    racial progress, constraining, 126
    regulation of *See* regulation, disclosure
    Students for Fair Admissions v. Harvard, 116
    Wall Street Journal (WSJ), use of terms in earning calls in, 116–17
racial discrimination, 4, 7, 8, 11, 15, 20, 21, 38, 48, 67, 68, 127, 147
    in 1950s–1960s, 23–24
    in Amazon, 2
    antidiscrimination laws, 6, 7
    in General Motors (Kansas), 10, 32–33
    interventions. *See also* Plans for Progress (PFP) program
        in 1940s–1950s, 21–23
        Executive Order 8802, 22
        FEPC, 22, 23
        Randolph's MOWM, 21–22
racial diversity, 9, 52, 54, 60, 63, 64–65, 79, 82, 85, 86
racial equity, 6, 8, 9–11, 12, 22, 38, 48, 52, 67, 68, 85, 89, 98, 104, 127, 159
    monetary allocations for racial causes, 92–93
racial equity audits, 2, 63–65, 127, 146
    Amazon, 2, 10–11, 64, 68–70
    Chevron, 70
    Facebook, 64
    institutional investors pressurizing companies for, 64
    Starbucks, 63–64, 69
racial inequality, 2, 3, 4, 5, 7, 9, 10, 11, 12, 13, 15, 16, 20, 22, 36, 38, 39, 40, 48, 49, 50, 51, 52, 53, 54, 55, 57, 60, 61, 63, 64, 65, 66, 67, 68, 69, 79, 89, 93, 107, 114, 116, 119, 120, 123, 124–25, 126, 127, 128, 129, 135, 138, 147, 148, 158
racial injustice, 1, 2, 4, 10, 11, 12, 20, 24, 51, 124
racial justice, 5, 97, 129
racial philanthropy. *See* philanthropy
racial polarization, 113
racial progress, 2, 3, 8, 78, 79, 80, 86, 87, 88, 89, 98, 106, 143, 158, 159
    constraining of, 2, 3, 6, 8–9, 66–68, 93, 119, 129, 138
    complete and partial race-conscious retraction, 126
    CRP in, 106–7
    deploying disclosures to challenge racial equity concerns, 9–11
    past racial inequality, lack of acknowledgement of, 9
    race-conscious retraction, 11–12

racial quotas, 79–80, 84, 114
racial segregation and desegregation, 7, 15, 20, 21, 38
  in 1950s–1960s, 23–24
  Lockheed and PFP program during Kennedy administration, 24–27
  Truman's intervention to, in military, 23
racial targets, 4, 8, 15, 52, 78–79, 102, 114, 115, 124, 130
  after 2020, 80–82
  Amazon in 2021, 54
  Bank of New York (BNY), 83
  benefits and challenges, 85–88
  company categories and, 86–88
  Hartford Prudential Financial, 83
  incentive for executives as, 85–86
  in private companies, 82
  in public companies, 80, 81
    by racial or ethnic group, 80–81
  as race-conscious disclosures, 88–89
  racial quotas vs., 79–80
  Starbucks, 83, 84
  State Street, 84
  Sysco, 84
  Target, 84
  Truist, 84
  Trump's second presidential term, as illegal quotes during, 78
  types of, 83
    closed-ended, 83–84
    open-ended, 84–85
Randolph, A. Philip, 21
Reagan, Ronald, 79
  Task Force on Private Sector Initiatives, 94
Reed, Susan, 14, 21
regulation, disclosure, 16–19, 135–36
  in California, 142–43
  Canada Business Corporations Act, 138
  climate disclosure, mandatory, 138–39
  Corporate Governance Improvement and Investor Protection Act, 137
  diversity disclosure, mandatory, 137–38
  Enhancement and Standardization of Climate-Related Disclosures for Investors, 138
  EU, 138
    CSDDD/CS3D, 139
    CSRD, 138–39
  federal government information-enforcing role, 139–44
  federal government mandating corporate disclosures, 136–39
  multi-institutional approach, 144
    advocacy groups, 149
    boards of directors and managers, 144–45
    consumers, 147

  employees and prospective employees, 148
  media and social media, 149–51
  shareholder activists, 145–47
  stock exchanges, 145
  Nasdaq board diversity rule, 116, 137
  Norway's Companies Act, 138
  Regulation S-K, 137–38
Reiser, Dana Brakman, 95, 101
reputation. See corporate reputation
reputational risks, 65–66, 69, 80, 127, 129
Robert Half's supplier diversity program, 103
Rockwell Automation, supplier diversity, 102–3
Roosevelt, Franklin Delano (FDR), 21
  Executive Order 8802, 22
  Executive Order 9981, 23, 39
  FEPC, 22, 23
  racial discrimination intervention in military, 21–23
Rosenblum, Nancy, 136
Rutherglen, George, 130

Sarbanes-Oxley Act of 2002, 56
Scanlan, Padraic, 20
SEC. See US Securities and Exchange Commission (SEC)
Shanor, Amanda, 140
shareholder activism, 145–47
shareholder proposals, 60–62, 146–47
  Comcast Corporation, 62
  racial diversity/equity concerns, 64–65
  SOC Investment Group to McDonald's, 62–63
Silberman, Charles E., 46
Small Business Act of 1978, 102
SOC Investment Group, shareholder proposals of, 62–63
social media and race-conscious disclosures, 149–51
Sonos' supplier diversity program, 103
Sovern, Michael, 34
Starbucks
  CRP, 97
  racial equity audits of, 63–64, 69
  racial targets, 83, 84
State Street, racial targets, 84
statistics on racial composition, 4, 52, 89
  in voluntary reports, 57–58
  of private companies, 58, 59
stock exchanges, 5, 49, 145
strategic corporate philanthropy, 93, 95–96
Students for Fair Admissions v. Harvard, xiv, 116
supplier diversity, 102–4
Sysco, racial targets, 84

Target, racial targets, 84
Tesler, Michael, 113

Index

Thomas, David, 36, 144
Till, Emmett, murder of, 23–24
Time Warner's racial philanthropy, 124
top projects meeting, 50, 72
transatlantic slave trade, 20
transparency, 50–51, 58–60, 139
Troutman, Robert, 26, 43
Truist, racial targets, 84
Truman, Harry S., 23
    Fahy Committee, 23
Trump, Donald, 11, 39, 40, 55, 69, 102, 107, 113, 118, 123, 128, 137, 138, 142
    illegal DEI, xiv
    Lyndon' executive order, nullification of, xiv, 7
    SEC guidelines for Regulations 13D and 13G in 2025, 74, 155
    second presidential term, xiv, 39, 85, 113, 118, 120, 122, 136, 140, 158
        informal communication, restriction on, 146
        intentionally weakening of federal agencies during, 136
        Project 2025, 114
        racial targets as illegal quotes during, 78

unemployment rate, 21
"ungoverning", state of, 136
United States, corporate philanthropy development in, 93–94
United States Court of Appeals for the Fifth Circuit, 52, 116, 137
US Securities and Exchange Commission (SEC), 4, 10, 11, 49, 60, 73, 137, 140
    enforcement action, 140–41

Enhancement and Standardization of Climate-Related Disclosures for Investors, 138
Nasdaq board diversity rule, 116, 137
Regulation S-K, 137
reports, 163–67
Rule 14a-8, 60, 61

Visa's Entrepreneurship Program, 102
voluntary demographic disclosures, 120–21
voluntary disclosures, 3, 50, 51, 55, 103, 127, 135, 138
    general statements in, 55, 56
    of private companies, 58, 59
    number of racial terms in, 121–22
    with race-conscious disclosures, 120
    statistics on racial composition in, 57–58
    of private companies, 58, 59
voluntary reports, 161–63, 164–67
    sustainability, with race-conscious disclosures, 120

W. W. Grainger, Inc.'s DEI, 124
Walmart, 1, 2
    Center for Racial Equity, 2
War on Poverty, 36
    NAB-JOBS program, 36
    OEO, 36
Wells Fargo's CRP, 102
Wilkins, David, 85
Williams, Eric, 20
Wiriz, W. Willard, 33
Woodson, Kevin, 85
Wright, Gavin, 37

Printed by Integrated Books International,
United States of America